Professional Examinations

Managerial Level

Paper P4

Organisational Management and Information Systems

Exam Kit

KAPLAN

PUBLISHING
FOULKS LYNCH

CIMA

British Library Cataloguing-in-Publication Data

A catalogue record for this book is available from the British Library.

Published by Kaplan Publishing Foulks Lynch
Unit 2
The Business Centre
Molly Millars Lane
Wokingham
Berkshire
RG41 4QZ

ISBN 978-1-84390-918-7

© FTC Kaplan Limited, January 2007

Printed and bound in Great Britain

Acknowledgements

We are grateful to the Chartered Institute of Management Accountants, the Association of
Chartered Certified Accountants and the Institute of Chartered Accountants in England and Wales
for permission to reproduce past examination questions. The answers have been prepared by
Kaplan Publishing Foulks Lynch.

INTRODUCTION

We have worked closely with experienced CIMA tutors and lecturers to ensure that our Kits are exam-focused and user-friendly.

This Exam Kit includes an extensive selection of questions that entirely cover the syllabus – this ensures that your knowledge is tested across all syllabus areas. Wherever possible questions have been grouped by syllabus topics.

All questions are of exam standard and format – this enables you to master the exam techniques. Section 1 contains Section A-type questions you will come across in your exam, Section 2 contains Section B-type questions and Section 3 contains Section C-type questions.

May and November 2006 exams are at the back of the book – try these under timed conditions and this will give you an exact idea of the way you will be tested in your exam.

CONTENTS

Page

Index to questions and answers vi

Syllabus and learning outcomes viii

Revision guidance.. xiii

The exam xiv

Section

1   Section A-type questions... 1

2   Section B-type questions... 29

3   Section C-type questions... 43

4   Answers to Section A-type questions 63

5   Answers to Section B-type questions 93

6   Answers to Section C-type questions 129

7   May 2006 exam questions... 201

8   Answers to May 2006 exam questions 207

9   November 2006 exam questions 213

10   Answers to November 2006 exam questions 219

INDEX TO QUESTIONS AND ANSWERS

Page number

Section A-type questions

	Question	Answer
Information systems (Questions 1 – 43)	1	63
Change management (Questions 44 – 58)	7	70
Operations management (Questions 59 – 95)	10	72
Marketing (Questions 96 – 120)	15	78
Managing human capital (Questions 121 – 176)	19	84

Section B-type questions

		Question	Answer
177	SPEC	29	93
178	New system	30	95
179	Hubbles (Pilot Paper)	30	97
180	Heve Transport	31	100
181	Stand Products	32	102
182	Hilo Consultancy	33	104
183	PMK Manufacturing	34	107
184	Soft Division	35	110
185	Gourmet Company	36	112
186	Marketing-led	37	114
187	V Cosmetics (May 05 Exam)	37	115
188	CFO	38	118
189	Motivation assumptions	39	120
190	Monday Newspapers	40	122
191	Round the Table (Nov 05 Exam)	41	125

Section C-type questions

Information Systems

		Question	Answer
192	Project management	43	129
193	E-mail	43	131
194	Small chain	44	133
195	In-house solution	44	135
196	Database	44	137

		Page number	
		Question	*Answer*

Change Management

197	Zed Bank (Pilot Paper)	45	139
198	Organisational development	45	140
199	K Company	46	142
200	F Steel Company	46	144
201	R & L (May 05 Exam)	47	146
202	T Company	47	148
203	Y	48	150

Operations Management

204	Electric pumps	49	152
205	Production scheduling	49	154
206	Pipe Dream	50	155
207	Urban Dance	50	157
208	Virtual	50	158
209	Process improvement	51	159

Marketing

210	Marketing function: concepts	51	161
211	Segmenting	52	163
212	Green Company	52	164
213	Restful Hotels	52	166
214	Troy Boats	53	167
215	Black Company	53	168
216	H Company	54	170
217	Lo-Sport Ltd	54	171
218	SX Snacks (Nov 05 Exam)	55	173

Managing Human Capital

219	Taxis and tyres (Pilot Paper)	56	174
220	T City Police	57	176
221	Recruitment	57	177
222	Management development	57	179
223	Reward systems	57	180
224	Dismissal, retirement, redundancy	57	181
225	Human resource plan	58	182
226	Appraisal	58	184
227	S Software Company	59	185
228	R Company	59	186
229	CX Beers (May 05 Exam)	59	189
230	Company A and B	60	191
231	Z Company	61	193
232	Jane Smith	61	195
233	NS insurance company (Nov 05 Exam)	62	197
234	NYO.COM	62	199

SYLLABUS AND LEARNING OUTCOMES

Learning aims

This syllabus aims to test the student's ability to:

- describe the various functional areas of an organisation and how they relate to one another,

- apply theories, tools and techniques appropriate to a functional area in support of the organisation's strategy,

- prepare reports and plans for functional areas,

- evaluate the performance of functional areas.

Learning outcomes and syllabus content

A - INFORMATION SYSTEMS - 20%

Learning outcomes

On completion of their studies students should be able to:

- explain the features and operations of commonly used information technology hardware and software;

- explain how commonly used technologies are used in the work place;

- identify opportunities for the use of information technology (IT) in organisations, particularly in the implementation and running of the information system (IS);

- evaluate, from a managerial perspective, new hardware and software and assess how new systems could benefit the organisation;

- recommend strategies to minimise the disruption caused by introducing IS technologies;

- explain how to supervise major IS projects and ensure their smooth implementation;

- evaluate how IS fits into broader management operations.

Syllabus content

- Introduction to hardware and software in common use in organisations.

- Hardware and applications architectures (i.e. centralised, distributed, client server) and the IT required to run them (PCs, servers, networks and peripherals).

- General Systems Theory and its application to IT (i.e. system definition, system components, system behaviour, system classification, entropy, requisite variety, coupling and decoupling).

- Recording and documenting tools used during the analysis and design of systems (i.e. entity-relationship model, logical data structure, entity life history, dataflow diagram, and decision table).

- Databases and database management systems. (Note: Knowledge of database structures will not be required.)

KAPLAN PUBLISHING

- The problems associated with the management of in-house and vendor solutions and how they can be avoided or solved.

- IT-enabled transformation (i.e. the use of information systems to assist in change management).

- System changeover methods (i.e. direct, parallel, pilot and phased).

- IS implementation (i.e. methods of implementation, avoiding problems of non-usage and resistance).

- The benefits of IT systems.

- IS evaluation, including the relationship of sub-systems to each other and testing.

- IS outsourcing.

- Maintenance of systems (i.e. corrective, adaptive, preventative).

B - CHANGE MANAGEMENT - 10%

Learning outcomes

On completion of their studies students should be able to:

- explain the process of organisational development;

- discuss how and why resistance to change develops within organisations;

- evaluate various means of introducing change;

- evaluate change processes within the organisation.

Syllabus content

- External and internal change triggers (e.g. environmental factors, mergers and acquisitions, re-organisation and rationalisation).

- The stages in the change process.

- Approaches to change management (e.g. Beer and Nohria, Kanter, Lewin and Peters, Senge et al).

- The importance of managing critical periods of change through the life cycle of the firm.

C - OPERATIONS MANAGEMENT - 20%

Learning outcomes

On completion of their studies students should be able to:

- evaluate the management of operations;

- analyse problems associated with quality in organisations;

- evaluate contemporary thinking in quality management;

- explain the linkages between functional areas as an important aspect of quality management;

- apply tools and concepts of quality management appropriately in an organisation;

- construct a plan for the implementation of a quality programme;

- recommend ways to negotiate and manage relationships with suppliers;

- evaluate a supply network.

- explain the concept of quality and how the quality of products *and* services can be assessed, measured and improved.

Syllabus content

- An overview of operations strategy and its importance to the firm.

- Design of products/services and processes and how this relates to operations and supply.

- Methods for managing inventory, including continuous inventory systems (e.g. Economic Order Quantity, EOQ), periodic inventory systems and the ABC system (*Note:* ABC is not an acronym. A refers to high value, B to medium and C to low value inventory).

- Strategies for balancing capacity and demand including level capacity, chase and demand management strategies.

- Methods of performance measurement and improvement, particularly the contrast between benchmarking and Business Process Re-engineering (BPR).

- Practices of continuous improvement (e.g. Quality circles, Kaizen, 5S, 6 Sigma).

- The use of benchmarking in quality measurement and improvement.

- Different methods of quality measurement (i.e. operational, financial and customer measures).

- The characteristics of lean production: flexible workforce practices, high commitment human resource policies and commitment to continuous improvement. Criticisms and limitations of lean production.

- Systems used in operations management: Manufacturing Resource Planning (MRP), Optimised Production Technologies (OPT), Just-in-Time (JIT) and Enterprise Resource Planning (ERP).

- Approaches to quality management, including Total Quality Management (TQM), various British Standard (BS) and European Union (EU) systems as well as statistical methods of quality control.

- External quality standards (e.g. the various ISO standards appropriate to products and organisations).

- Use of the Intranet in information management (e.g. meeting customer support needs).

- Contemporary developments in quality management.

- The role of the supply chain and supply networks in gaining competitive advantage, including the use of sourcing strategies (e.g. single, multiple, delegated and parallel).

- Supply chain management as a strategic process (e.g. Reck and Long's strategic positioning tool, Cousins' strategic supply wheel).

- Developing and maintaining relationships with suppliers.

D - MARKETING - 20%

Learning outcomes

On completion of their studies students should be able to:

- explain the marketing concept;

- evaluate the marketing processes of an organisation;

- apply tools within each area of the marketing mix;

- describe the business contexts within which marketing principles can be applied (consumer marketing, business-to-business marketing, services marketing, direct marketing, interactive marketing);

- evaluate the role of technology in modern marketing;

- produce a strategic marketing plan for the organisation.

Syllabus content

- Introduction to the marketing concept as a business philosophy.

- An overview of the marketing environment, including societal, economic, technological, physical and legal factors affecting marketing.

- Understanding consumer behaviour, such as factors affecting buying decisions, types of buying behaviour and stages in the buying process.

- Market research, including data gathering techniques and methods of analysis.

- Marketing Decision Support Systems (MDSS) and their relationship to market research.
- How business to business (B2B) marketing differs from business to consumer (B2C) marketing.
- Segmentation and targeting of markets, and positioning of products within markets.
- The differences and similarities in the marketing of products and services.
- Devising and implementing a pricing strategy.
- Marketing communications (i.e. mass, direct, interactive).
- Distribution channels and methods for marketing campaigns.
- The role of marketing in the strategic plan of the organisation.
- Use of the Internet (e.g. in terms of data collection, marketing activity and providing enhanced value to customers and suppliers) and potential drawbacks (e.g. security issues).
- Market forecasting methods for estimating current (e.g. Total Market Potential, Area Market Potential and Industry Sales and Market Shares) and future (e.g. Survey of Buyers' Intentions, Composite of Sales Force Opinions, Expert Opinion, Past-Sales Analysis and Market-Test Method) demand for products and services.
- Internal marketing as the process of training and motivating employees so as to support the firm's external marketing activities.
- Social responsibility in a marketing context.

E - MANAGING HUMAN CAPITAL - 30%

Learning outcomes

On completion of their studies students should be able to:

- explain the role of the human resource management function and its relationship to other parts of the organisation;
- produce and explain a human resource plan and supporting practices;
- evaluate the recruitment, selection, induction, appraisal, training and career planning activities of an organisation;
- evaluate the role of incentives in staff development as well as individual and organisational performance;
- identify features of a human resource plan that vary depending on organisation type and employment model;
- explain the importance of ethical behaviour in business generally and for the Chartered Management Accountant in particular.

Syllabus content

- The relationship of the employee to other elements of the business plan.
- Determinants and content of a human resource (HR) plan (e.g. organisational growth rate, skills, training, development, strategy, technologies and natural wastage).
- Problems in implementing a HR plan and ways to manage this.
- The process of recruitment and selection of staff using different recruitment channels (i.e. interviews, assessment centres, intelligence tests, aptitude tests, psychometric tests).
- Issues relating to fair and legal employment practices (e.g. recruitment, dismissal, redundancy, and ways of managing these).
- Issues in the design of reward systems (e.g. the role of incentives, the utility of performance-related pay, arrangements for knowledge workers, flexible work arrangements).
- The importance of negotiation during the offer and acceptance of a job.
- The process of induction and its importance.

- Theories of Human Resource Management (e.g. Taylor, Schein, McGregor, Maslow, Herzberg, Handy, Lawrence and Lorsch).

- High performance work arrangements.

- The distinction between development and training and the tools available to develop and train staff.

- The importance of appraisals, their conduct and their relationship to the reward system.

- HR in different organisational forms (e.g. project-based firms, virtual or networked firms).

- Personal business ethics and the CIMA Ethical Guidelines.

REVISION GUIDANCE

Planning your revision

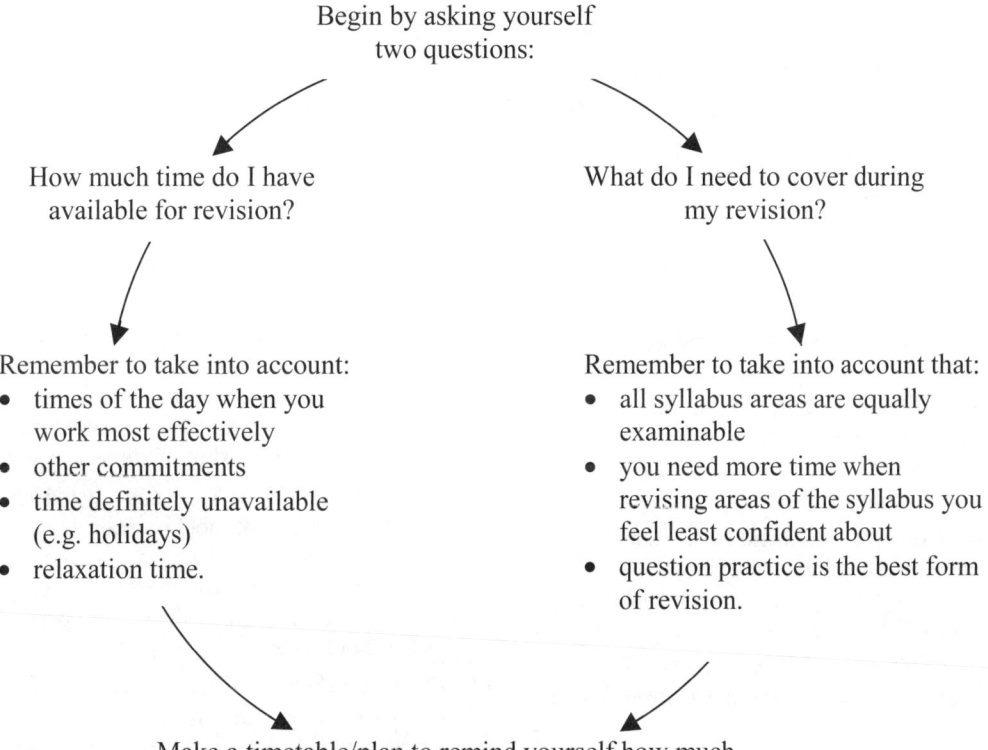

Begin by asking yourself
two questions:

How much time do I have
available for revision?

What do I need to cover during
my revision?

Remember to take into account:
- times of the day when you
  work most effectively
- other commitments
- time definitely unavailable
  (e.g. holidays)
- relaxation time.

Remember to take into account that:
- all syllabus areas are equally
  examinable
- you need more time when
  revising areas of the syllabus you
  feel least confident about
- question practice is the best form
  of revision.

Make a timetable/plan to remind yourself how much
work you have to do and when you are free to do it.
Allow some time for slippage.

Revision techniques

- Go through your notes and textbook **highlighting the important points**

- You might want to produce your own set of **summarised notes**

- **List key words** for each topic to remind you of the essential concepts

- **Practise exam-standard questions**, under timed conditions

- **Rework questions** that you got completely wrong the first time, but only when you think you know the subject better

- If you get stuck on topics, **find someone to explain** them to you (your tutor or a colleague, for example)

- **Read recent articles** on the CIMA website and in *Financial Management*

- **Read** good newspapers and professional journals.

THE EXAM

Format of the exam

There will be a written exam paper of three hours, with the following sections: *Number of marks*

Section A	A variety of compulsory objective test questions, each worth 2 to 4 marks. Mini-scenarios may be given, to which a group of questions relate.	40
Section B	Six compulsory medium answer questions, each worth 5 marks. Short scenarios may be given to which some or all of the questions relate.	30
Section C	One question, from a choice of two, each worth 30 marks.	<u>30</u>
	Total:	100

About the exam

- You are allowed 20 minutes' reading time before the examination begins.

- Where you have a **choice of question**, decide which questions you will do. Unless you know exactly how to answer the question, spend some time **planning** your answer.

- **Divide the time** you spend on questions in proportion to the marks on offer. One suggestion is to allocate 1½ minutes to each mark available, so a 10-mark question should be completed in 15 minutes.

- Stick to the question and **tailor your answer** to what you are asked.

- If you do not understand what a question is asking, **state your assumptions**. Even if you do not answer in precisely the way the examiner hoped, you should be given some credit, if your assumptions are reasonable.

- If you **get completely stuck** with a question, leave space in your answer book and **return to it later.**

- Spend the last **five minutes** reading through your answers and **making any additions or corrections**.

- You should do everything you can to make things easy for the marker. The marker will find it easier to identify the points you have made if your **answers are legible**.

- **Objective test questions** include true/false questions, matching pairs of text and graphic, sequencing and ranking, labelling diagrams and single and multiple numeric entry, but could also involve paragraphs of text which require you to fill in a number of missing

blanks, or for you to write a definition of a word or phrase, or to enter a formula. With multiple-choice questions you have to choose the correct answer (and there is only *one* correct answer) from a list of possible answers.

- **Essay questions**: Your essay should have a clear structure. It should contain a brief introduction, a main section and a conclusion. Be concise. It is better to write a little about a lot of different points than a great deal about one or two points.

- **Computations**: It is essential to include all your workings in your answers. Many computational questions require the use of a standard format: company income statement account, balance sheet and cash flow statement for example. Be sure you know these formats thoroughly before the examination and use the layouts that you see in the answers given in this book and in model answers.

- **Scenario-based questions:** read the scenario carefully, identify the area in which there is a problem, outline the main principles/theories you are going to use to answer the question, and then apply the principles/theories to the scenario.

- **Reports, memos and other documents**: some questions ask you to present your answer in the form of a report or a memo or other document. So use the correct format – there could be easy marks to gain here

SECTION A-TYPE QUESTIONS

All the section A-type multiple-choice questions carry 2 marks unless otherwise stated.

INFORMATION SYSTEMS

1   **Bar code readers, scanners and keyboards are examples of:**

A   hardware input devices

B   software input devices

C   systems processing devices

D   hardware processing devices.

2   **Local area networking is used for:**

A   communication between computers within a limited geographical area

B   structuring an organisation within a division or business unit

C   exchange of information through a trade association or region

D   managing a complex operational issue by global interface with trade associations and professional bodies.

3   **Entropy is a term used to describe:**

A   the tendency of a system to break down into randomness

B   the tendency of a system to develop over time leading to randomness

C   a means of testing candidates in an interview to overcome randomness

D   a means of developing open learning using computers.

4   **Many large organisations have established a computer intranet for the purpose of:**

A   providing quick, effective and improved communication amongst staff using chat rooms

B   providing quick, effective and improved communication to staff

C   providing quick, effective and improved communication to customers

D   providing quick, effective and improved ordering procedures in real time.

5   **The main advantages of a database management system include:**

A   the development of separate data sources.

B   unlimited access and open communication.

C   end user flexibility and a devolution of responsibility.

D   data integrity and elimination of duplication.

6 **An expert system describes:**

A   a database built upon past knowledge and experience

B   a powerful off the shelf software solution

C   an on-line library of operating advice and handy hints

D   an electronic version of working papers assembled by the Research and Development department.

7 **What name is given to system maintenance for an IT system that is concerned with re-writing software for the system to meet new user requirements that emerge after the system has been implemented?**

A   Adaptive maintenance

B   Constructive maintenance

C   Corrective maintenance

D   Perfective maintenance

8 **When an old computer system and a new computer system are both operated throughout an organisation for a period of time, and the outputs from the two systems are compared with each other, the system changeover method is known as:**

A   direct changeover

B   parallel running

C   pilot testing

D   phased changeover.

9 **A system designer has produced the following diagram as part of the documentation for a new system under development.**

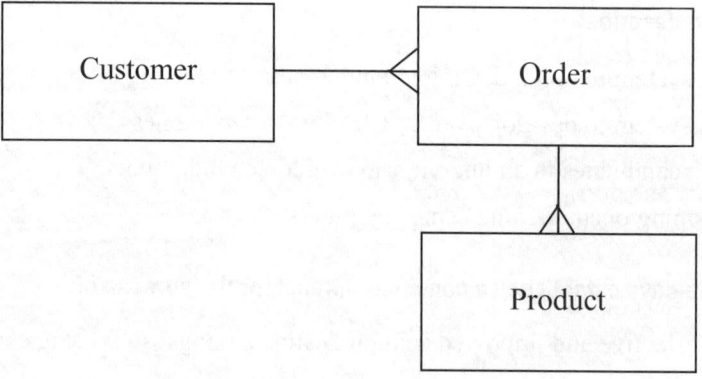

This is an example of:

A   a data flow diagram

B   an entity relationship model

C   structured programming

D   an entity life history diagram.

10 A firm of travel agents has several branches. Each branch has terminals (PCs) linked to a central computer at head office. The central computer has links to the computer systems of all the main airlines and holiday firms. When a customer wishes to book a holiday of a flight with the agent, the branch submits a request for booking to the firm's central computer, which then sends on the request to the appropriate airline or holiday firm. Confirmation of bookings are returned by the same route.

The relationship between a terminal in a branch office and the computer at the firm's head office is known as:

A   a star configuration

B   a WAN

C   client /server

D   distributed data processing.

11 A company uses a computer system for its middle management that can be used to assist with working out possible solutions to management problems. The system includes modelling and forecasting facilities, such as linear regression analysis and statistical analysis.

This type of system is:

A   a management information system (MIS)

B   an expert system

C   an executive information system (EIS)

D   a decision support system (DSS).

12 What is the name given to software that controls the communications between different software applications and files within a database system?

A   Server

B   Database

C   Database management system

D   Database administrator

13 A customer file holding data about customers was used by the sales force to plan direct mailing sales campaigns. However, the information on the file was not kept up-to-date, and the sales force has now stopped using it. This is an example of:

A   decoupling in a system

B   entropy in a system

C   a closed system

D   sub-optimisation in a system.

14 Which of the following describes a dumb terminal in a computer network?

A   A terminal that receives output but cannot be used for input

B   A terminal that can be used for input but cannot be used to receive output

C   A control station for the network

D   A terminal linked to a computer in the network that does not have any processing capabilities of its own

15 **Which of the following is the *least* likely to be a consequence of inadequate staff training in the use of a major new computer system?**

A   Faults in the system design

B   Reluctance to use the new system

C   A higher rate of processing error

D   Slower processing

16 **Which of the following is likely to be the *least effective* method of overcoming the resistance of employees to a new computer system?**

A   Delaying implementation of the system

B   Participation and involvement in system development and testing

C   Education and communication

D   Coercion

17 **An Extranet is:**

A   a system that enables the computer systems of two different organisations to communicate with each other

B   an Intranet system that also provides access to certain selected external users

C   the provision of IT services for a computer network by an external organisation

D   a computer network that uses dedicated communications links for security purposes.

18 **A network server:**

A   routes messages over a network

B   manages files in a network

C   acts as a workstation in a network

D   is the main computer in a network.

19 **The following decision table shows the logic for a program to determine the credit to be offered to customers.**

Conditions					
Sales value $500 or less?	Y	N	N	N	N
Sales value less than $5,000?	-	Y	Y	N	N
New customer?	-	Y	N	Y	N
Action					
No credit	X				
30 days' credit		X			
60 days' credit			X	X	
90 days' credit					X

If a regular customer purchases items costing $4,900, what length of credit will be granted?

A   None

B   30 days

C   60 days

D   90 days

20   An oil company uses a mainframe computer for a major system, and the management believe that it is essential that the continuity of processing must be assured at all times. Which of the following risk control measures is the most appropriate for ensuring that this happens?

A   A secure password protection system

B   A standby mainframe

C   Surplus capacity in the memory of the operational mainframe

D   Fire safety measures

21   A magazine publisher produces its weekly magazine on a computer system, using standard off-the-shelf software for desk-top publishing and word processing. At the end of each week, the most recent copy of the magazine is copied on to a backing storage device, and each magazine (one file) is up to about 600 megabytes.

Which of the following types of storage device is most suitable for the publisher's requirements?

A   Floppy disk

B   CD ROM

C   CD RW

D   DVD

22   A computer system consists of several locally based computers linked in a communications network via a central computer. The local computers can share routine processing tasks. This type of system is best described as:

A   a multi-user system

B   a database system

C   an online real time system

D   a distributed data processing system.

23   A computerised check-out system might use several input devices at each check-out desk (cash desk). These are likely to be:

A   keyboard, mouse, bar code reader

B   bar code reader, mouse, screen

C   keyboard, bar code reader, touch screen

D   touch screen, display screen, scanner.

24   A network in which a number of smaller computers are linked directly to a larger central computer is called:

A   a ring network

B   a tree network

C   a hierarchical network

D   a star network.

25 Stages in the development and implementation of a new bespoke computer system to replace an existing system include the purchase and installation of hardware, software development, system testing, staff training and the production of system documentation. These are followed by:

   A file conversion and data base creation, and changeover

   B file conversion and data base creation, and review

   C changeover and review

   D changeover and maintenance.

26 The most radical form of organisational change includes a cultural shift and is described as:

   A emergent change

   B transformational change

   C step change

   D incremental change.

27 A main aim of electronic data interchange (EDI) is:

   A to improve communication exchanges within an organisation

   B to replace conventional documentation with structured electronically transmitted data

   C to allow employees to work at home

   D to create a shared data resource within an organisation.

28 Explain the purpose of tools such as data flow diagrams, entity life histories, entity-relationship models and decision tables.   (4 marks)

29 Explain why a phased system changeover for a computer development might help employees cope better with technological change.   (4 marks)

30 Describe the main benefits of in-house developed information systems.   (4 marks)

31 Explain the functions that a file server might perform within a computer system.   (4 marks)

32 De-coupling is a term used in general system theory. A DBMS is an example of de-coupling within a computer system.

   (a) Explain briefly what is meant by de-coupling.

   (b) Explain why a DBMS is an example of de-coupling.   (4 marks)

33 Explain the nature of system software, and describe the three main types of system software.

                                                                                 (4 marks)

34 The operating system:

   A forms part of a system's software

   B forms part of a system's hardware

   C is another term for a system's hardware

   D is a standalone end-user (operator) system solution.

35   The five elements of a computer system are:

A   data, communication, flexibility, hardware and data integrity

B   installation, hardware, maintenance, audit and compliance

C   hardware, software, procedures, data and people

D   input, processing, monitoring, control and reporting.

36   Describe the main advantages of an organisation developing and using an 'Extranet'.

(4 marks)

37   Explain the relationship between open systems and adaptive maintenance.   **(4 marks)**

38   Parallel running and pilot schemes are methods of systems changeover. Explain the reasons why an organisation might instead choose a direct approach to a system changeover.

(4 marks)

39   Explain the reasons why a department of an organisation might be continuing to use manual records rather than using a new, recently installed and fully operational computer system.

(4 marks)

40   Explain the difference between a scanner and a digital camera, and how each device might be used in a computer system.   **(4 marks)**

41   Describe the four elements used in a data flow diagram.   **(4 marks)**

42   Explain the relationship between 'data independence' and a database approach to flexible data management.   **(4 marks)**

43   Briefly explain the main factors management should take into account when choosing computer hardware.   **(4 marks)**

CHANGE MANAGEMENT

44   Which of the following would be an internal trigger for change in an organisation?

A   A major acquisition

B   A major development in IT technology

C   New legislation for protection of the environment

D   Trade union demands for a shorter working week for all employees

45   Kurt Lewin's force field theory of change in organisation identifies driving forces and restraining forces that influence change. When there is strong resistance to change, Lewin recommended that the most effective way for management to achieve the desired change would be to:

A   increase the strength of the driving forces

B   reduce the strength of the driving forces

C   increase the strength of the restraining forces

D   reduce the strength of the restraining forces.

46 Senge argued that learning organisations adapt best because they have mastered five disciplines or 'component technologies'. Which of the following is one of these component technologies?

A Effective control systems

B Participation by everyone in decision-making

C Building a shared vision

D Overcoming resistance to change

47 Kanter argued that change-adept organisations, which are organisations that manage change successfully, share three key attributes. These are:

A imagination to innovate, openness to collaborate, professionalism to perform

B openness to collaborate, professionalism to perform, resilience to survive

C professionalism to perform, imagination to innovate, resilience to survive

D resilience to survive, openness to collaborate, imagination to innovate.

48 Beer and Nohria identified two approaches to transformational change within an organisation, the Theory E and Theory O approaches. Theory E is a 'hard' approach based on maximising economic value and Theory O is a 'soft' approach based on organisational capability.

According to Beer and Nohria, when the management of an organisation wish to implement transformational change, the most effective approach is to use:

A the Theory O approach only

B the Theory E approach first, followed by the Theory O approach

C the Theory O approach first, followed by the Theory E approach

D the Theory E and Theory O approaches simultaneously.

49 Which of the following is an example of incremental change within an organisation?

A Downsizing

B Introducing a new IT system

C Restructuring

D Changing the corporate culture

50 The management of a hospital are trying to persuade its doctors and qualified medical staff that due to a chronic shortage of trained medical staff throughout the country, the problems that the hospital faces in dealing with patients will be eased if unqualified staff are given training to carry out certain types of medical treatment on patients.

According to Lewin's three-step model of change, which stage in the process is gaining acceptance by qualified staff of the need to allow unqualified staff to treat patients?

A Unfreezing

B Movement

C Re-freezing

D None of these

51   At what stage in Kurt Lewin's model of organisational change does the process of unfreezing take place?

A   The termination stage

B   The diagnostic stage

C   The intervention stage

D   The evaluation stage

52   Planned organisational change is most commonly triggered by the need to respond to new threats or opportunities presented by:

A   the organisation's culture

B   developments in the external environment

C   the internal environment

D   action by the organisation's management.

53   Which *one* of the following factors is most likely to lead to successful organisational change?

A   Imposed by external consultants

B   Maintaining existing policies and procedures

C   Autocratic leadership

D   Initiated and supported by top management

54   An approach that focuses on the adaptation of organisations to change is commonly associated with the use of management consultants as agents of change, who apply diagnostic and problem-solving skills to an organisation's problems. This type of change management is known as:

A   Total Quality Management

B   Business Process Re-engineering

C   Continuous improvement

D   Organisational development.

55   Establishing a staff help line when attempting to cope with resistance to change is an example of:

A   facilitation

B   manipulation

C   coercion

D   co-optation.

56   Third party consultants, therapy groups and confrontation are normally all associated with:

A   industrial disputes over terms and conditions

B   the process of job evaluation

C   a firm experiencing severe trading difficulties

D   organisational development (OD).

57   In defining a learning organisation, Senge distinguished between adaptive and generative learning organisations. Explain the difference between these types of learning and their relevance to organisational change.

(4 marks)

58   Change occurs when there is organisational growth through takeover. Certain basic 'rules' for takeovers to succeed have been suggested which need to be considered before the takeover occurs. Identify what these rules are for an organisation considering a takeover.

(4 marks)

OPERATIONS MANAGEMENT

59   Quality management thinker J.M. Juran once suggested that 85% of an organisation's quality problems are:

A   a result of ineffective control by supervisors and managers

B   a result of ineffective systems

C   a result of ineffective workers

D   a result of ineffective incentive bonus schemes.

60   The five S (5S) practice is a technique aimed at achieving:

A   effective investment of resources in training and recruitment

B   standardised procedures to improve the physical and thinking organisational environments

C   excellence in strategy, style, skills, staff and structure

D   diversity of activity and independence of thought in order to achieve closeness to the customer.

61   A system of production planning that focuses on bottlenecks in the production system and schedules production accordingly is known as:

A   MRPII

B   ERP

C   OPT

D   JIT

62   W.E. Deming promoted concepts of quality management, and his work is most closely associated with:

A   the quality planning road map

B   continuous improvement

C   the concept of zero defects

D   statistical quality control.

63 The 5S practice is an approach to achieving high quality in the working environment. One of its concepts is that things should be arranged properly and placed where they can easily be found and reached when needed. This is the 5S concept of:

A sort

B straighten

C shine

D sustain.

64 Which of the following is an objective of performance benchmarking?

A To identify the competitive advantage the company has over its rivals

B To identify improvements in products features and design

C To search for new ideas and practices to adopt

D To establish what the key performance variables should be

65 Which of the following statements about MRPI is correct?

A MRPI is a computer system that uses a database to integrate the systems for all functions within the organisation, such as operations management, engineering, sales and marketing and accounting.

B MRPI ensures that inventory levels are maintained at sufficiently high levels to avoid the risk of 'stock-outs'.

C MRPI is a computerised system for scheduling production based on economic batch quantities.

D MRPI converts a master production schedule into production schedules for sub-assembles and parts and purchasing schedules for parts and raw materials.

66 Which of the following statements about TQM is correct?

A TQM relies on motivating employees to improve quality rather than on quality standards and statistical control methods.

B The level of defects must remain below a minimum acceptable level.

C All individuals within the organisation must be involved in quality improvements.

D The aim should be to eliminate all costs relating to quality.

67 The greatest cost to an organisation arising from external failures is probably:

A the cost of replacing defective items

B the cost of handling customer complaints

C the cost of rejects and re-working defective items in production

D the cost to reputation.

68 The Toyota Production System, from which the concept of lean manufacturing was derived, identified seven types of waste in manufacturing. These included:

A making defective products; motion; over-production

B motion; overspending; inventory and work-in-progress

C over-production; waste in processing; system defects

D waiting; human error; transportation.

69 **A characteristic of lean manufacturing or a lean process is:**

A   production initiated by 'supply push' rather than 'demand pull'

B   large batch production

C   small work cells

D   workers with specific skills.

70 **Kanban is a system of:**

A   continuous improvement

B   signalling work flow requirements using signalling devices

C   forming small groups to discuss quality issues

D   production in small work cells.

71 **Which of the following is a concept in Just in Time production?**

A   The aim at all times should be to achieve maximum capacity utilisation of production resources.

B   It is better to have one large and complex machine than several small and simpler machines.

C   Set-up times should be increased.

D   The layout of a shop floor and the design of work flow can reduce production times.

72 **Which type of sourcing strategy for purchases uses a single but different source of supply at each of its plants or factories?**

A   Single sourcing

B   Multiple sourcing

C   Parallel sourcing

D   Network sourcing

73 **Which strategy for balancing capacity and demand has the objective of trying to balance available capacity with sales demand?**

A   Level capacity planning

B   Chase demand planning

C   Demand management planning

D   Yield management planning

74 **Which of the following approaches to operations management is inconsistent with the concept of continuous improvement?**

A   BPR

B   6 Sigma

C   Quality circles

D   5S

75 International standard ISO 14001 *Environmental Management Systems* encourages processes for controlling and improving an organisation's:

    A   performance on 'green' issues

    B   performance on quality issues as they relate to the competitive environment

    C   performance on scanning an industry environment

    D   performance on its internal investment in people.

76 Explain the relationship between a (Just-in-Time) JIT system and cash flow management.

(4 marks)

77 Explain how computer software can assist in achieving quality in a manufacturing organisation.

(4 marks)

78 Distinguish quality control from quality circles.   **(4 marks)**

79 Describe the underlying concept of the Six Sigma approach to quality management.

(4 marks)

80 Explain the reasons why a company might seek to obtain a certificate for meeting ISO 9000 quality management standards.   **(4 marks)**

81 Explain briefly the difference between MRP II and ERP.   **(4 marks)**

82 Core features of world-class manufacturing involve:

    A   competitor benchmarking and an investment in training and development

    B   an investment in IT and technical skills

    C   global sourcing networks and an awareness of competitor strategies

    D   a strong customer focus and flexibility to meet customer requirements.

83 An ABC system refers to:

    A   a Japanese style problem solving device that is particularly helpful in inventory management

    B   an inventory management method that concentrates effort on the most important items

    C   accuracy, brevity and clarity in the quality of system reporting

    D   a mainframe solution to managing inventory.

84 Corrective work, the cost of scrap and materials lost are:

    A   examples of internal failure costs

    B   examples of external failure costs

    C   examples of appraisal costs

    D   examples of preventative costs.

85   **Economies of scope refers to:**

A   the economic viability of making alterations to systems

B   an organisation becoming economically viable through a process of 'rightsizing'

C   mass production assembly lines achieving economies through volume of output

D   economically producing small batches of a variety of products with the same machines.

86   **Reck and Long's strategic positioning tool identifies an organisation's:**

A   purchasing approach

B   sales approach

C   manufacturing approach

D   warehousing approach.

87   **Inbound logistics is:**

A   a secondary activity that refers to price negotiation of incoming raw materials

B   a secondary activity that refers to receipt, storage and inward distribution of raw materials

C   a primary activity that refers to inbound enquiries and customer complaints

D   a primary activity that refers to receipt, storage and inward distribution of raw materials.

88   **Supply chain partnerships grow out of:**

A   quality accreditation

B   recognising the supply chain and linkages in a value system

C   an expansion of trade

D   adopting a marketing philosophy.

89   **A company has arranged to compare the performance of its distribution operations with those of another company in a different industry, in order to identify weaknesses in its operations and areas where improvements might be made. This type of comparison might be known as:**

A   external benchmarking

B   operations benchmarking

C   internal benchmarking

D   competitive benchmarking.

90   **Which practice or activity is defined as 'the process of identifying, understanding and adapting outstanding practices and processes from organisations anywhere in the world to help your organisation improve its performance'?**

A   Total Quality Management

B   Continuous improvement

C   Business Process Re-engineering

D   Benchmarking

91 Describe the ways in which Total Productive Maintenance might contribute towards a manufacturing organisation's quality programme. **(4 marks)**

92 State the main principles of Total Quality Management. **(4 marks)**

93 Explain the meaning of a 'quality chain' within an organisation and suggest how service level agreements can be used to strengthen the quality chain. **(4 marks)**

94 ISO 9001 : *2000 Quality Management Systems: Requirements* requires that, to meet the required quality management standards, an organisation should document key processes and activities.

Explain why documentation is necessary and what processes or activities should be documented. **(4 marks)**

95 Distinguish quality assurance (QA) systems from quality control systems.

(4 marks)

MARKETING

96 A company is deciding to sell its designer jewellery products over the internet for the first time, using its web site to display its product range and accept orders and payments. This represents a change in which of the following elements of the marketing mix?

- A Product
- B Price
- C Place
- D Promotion

97 Which *one* of the following statements explains 'concentrated marketing'?

- A The entity produces one product for a number of different market segments.
- B The entity introduces several versions of the product aimed at several market segments.
- C The entity produces one product for a mass market.
- D The entity produces one product for a single segment of the market.

98 For a retailer, what are the two most important marketing considerations when deciding which products to display on the shelves in its stores?

- A Sales promotion and price
- B Product assortment and sales promotion
- C Product sizes and price
- D Product assortment and price

99 Differentiated marketing is a marketing strategy based on:

- A offering a range of different products to one segment of the market
- B offering one product only to one segment of the market
- C offering the same range of products to all segments of the market
- D offering a number of different products, each to a different segment of the market.

100 Market research into the size of the market that might exist for a new product or service is market research into the:

A   market potential

B   market penetration

C   sales potential

D   sales demand.

101 The following sales report has been prepared for the manager responsible for sales of Product X and Product Y.

	Product X		Product Y	
	This year	*Last year*	*This year*	*Last year*
	£ million	£ million	£ million	£ million
	9.7	8.4	10.2	10.1
Estimated total market sales for similar products	160	140	225	210

Which of the following statements is correct?

A   The market potential for Product X has risen by 14% since last year.

B   The sales potential for Product Y has risen by 3.9% since last year.

C   The market share for Product X has fallen since last year.

D   The market share for Product Y has fallen since last year.

102 The primary aim of the marketing strategy for a commercial organisation should be to:

A   sell its products or services to customers

B   meet the overall business objectives by satisfying customer needs

C   promote a marketing culture amongst all its employees

D   maximise sales efficiency.

103 Which of the following is an example of interactive marketing?

A   Television advertising

B   Direct mail

C   Telemarketing

D   Advertising on a web site

104 An exercise to assess the attitudes of customers or potential customers towards a particular consumer product is classified as:

A   market research

B   marketing research

C   a survey of buyers' intentions

D   test marketing.

105 **A marketing decision support system (MDSS) might be used to:**

A   provide a list of customers to target with a direct mail shot

B   provide a forecast of future sales from an analysis of past sales

C   provide sales reports comparing actual with budgeted sales

D   hold a record of the buying history of each customer.

106 **Differential pricing means:**

A   charging different prices for the same product in different parts of the market

B   charging prices that are different from those of competitors' products in the same market

C   charging different prices for the same product at different times of the day

D   offering price discounts for purchasing in large quantities.

107 **Which of the following is marketing or selling with a 'pull' effect?**

A   Placing products in display baskets or 'gondolas' in a supermarket, to encourage impulse buying

B   Offering a low price to a distributor to persuade him to stock the product

C   Direct selling by members of the sales team

D   Television advertising for a product

108 **A comprehensive, systematic, independent and periodic examination of a company's marketing environment, objectives, strategies and objectives is called :**

A   a marketing audit

B   market research

C   marketing research

D   strategic marketing.

109 **Which of the following market research data-gathering techniques is most likely to be effective in estimating how many people buy a consumer product, in what quantities and how often?**

A   Sample surveys

B   Observation

C   Analysis of past sales

D   Group interviewing

110 **Which of the following is the most suitable definition of internal marketing?**

A   Marketing the organisation's products to its own employees

B   Training employees who deal with customers to provide customer satisfaction in the work they do

C   Marketing activities carried on from the organisation's own premises, such as direct mail activities and telemarketing

D   Training employees in the features of the products and services sold by the organisation

111   'Market shakeout' involves the weakest producers exiting a particular market and occurs in a period between:

   A   growth through creativity and growth through direction

   B   introduction and market growth

   C   market growth and market maturity

   D   market maturity and decline.

112   The choice to buy a fast-moving consumer good (FMCG) is normally:

   A   a personal choice involving relatively low financial outlays

   B   a personal choice involving relatively high financial outlays

   C   a choice made on behalf of an organisation involving moderate outlays

   D   a personal choice influenced by new features, fashions and old product wearout.

113   Analysing a market into sub-groups of potential customers with common needs and behaviours in order to target them through marketing techniques is called:

   A   market research

   B   market development

   C   segmentation

   D   product adaptation.

114   Separate people or groups such as initiators, influencers, buyers and users are all involved in a buying decision in the context of:

   A   fast-moving consumer goods marketing

   B   business-to-business marketing

   C   business-to-consumer marketing

   D   services marketing.

115   When planning the activities of a sales force, management must decide to which selling activities the sales staff should give priority. A distinction can be made between the following sales force activities:

   (a)   'hunting' versus 'farming'

   (b)   'selling' versus 'servicing'.

   Explain the differences between these types of activities.   **(4 marks)**

116   Describe the features of e-commerce and explain:

   •   the advantages of e-commerce for marketing, and

   •   why the marketing of services with e-commerce might be easier than marketing products.   **(4 marks)**

117 Explain how price can be used as part of the marketing mix for consumer goods, giving examples of how 'price' is used in marketing. **(4 marks)**

118 In what ways does B2B marketing differ from B2C marketing? **(4 marks)**

119 Describe the stages in a product life cycle, and explain how the concept of the product life cycle might be relevant to marketing. **(4 marks)**

120 Compare and contrast product-orientated organisations and production-orientated organisations. **(4 marks)**

MANAGING HUMAN CAPITAL

121 When someone commences a new job, the process of familiarisation is known as:

A   probationary period

B   recruitment

C   appraisal

D   induction.

122 An effective appraisal system involves:

A   assessing the personality of the appraisee

B   a process initiated by the manager who needs an update from the appraisee

C   advising on the faults of the appraisee

D   a participative, problem-solving process between the manager and appraisee.

123 The motivating potential score, developed by Hackman and Oldham, is calculated to assess:

A   the knowledge of an individual

B   the satisfaction with work

C   the content of the job

D   the quality of work performed.

124 Job rotation involves:

A   a redesign of a person's post based upon job analysis

B   the movement of an individual to another post in order to gain experience

C   the expansion and enrichment of a person's job content

D   the relocation of a post holder in order to benefit from the experience of a number of potential mentors.

125 A grievance procedure is established by an organisation in order that:

A   there is a standing process to deal with the arbitration of disputes

B   the organisation can fairly discipline members of the workforce for wrongdoing

C   the workforce might formally raise issues where ill treatment has occurred

D   collective bargaining between the employer's side and the workforce might proceed smoothly.

126 An 'assessment centre' approach is used:

A   as part of an appraisal process

B   as part of a process of training and development

C   as part of a selection process

D   as part of an exit interview process.

127 Selection tests that fail to produce similar results over time when taken by the same candidate are:

A   contradictory

B   unreliable

C   too general

D   unstable.

128 According to F.W. Taylor, which one of the following is a characteristic of scientific management?

A   Work specialisation

B   Group working

C   Socio-technical system

D   The informal organisation

129 Why is succession planning desirable in a large organisation?

A   To ensure that promotion opportunities exist

B   To ensure business continuity

C   To ensure competence in key functions

D   To prevent natural wastage of staff

130 When it wishes to appoint full-time office staff, a company might use the services of an employment agency for:

A   recruitment and selection only

B   recruitment and screening only

C   screening and selection only

D   screening only.

131 When a performance appraisal scheme is ineffective, this may be due to:

A   a lack of objective criteria for the appraisal of personality

B   under-performing employees

C   excluding discussions about pay

D   a lack of objective criteria for the appraisal of performance.

132 In which of the following situations is it most likely that an unfair dismissal has occurred?

   A   An employee leaves his job claiming that the employer was in breach of contract by demoting him

   B   The employer terminates a fixed term contract with a sub-contractor without notice

   C   The employer dismisses a lorry driver who has been banned from driving by the court

   D   The employer dismisses an employee because of redundancy

133 Which of the following would be classified as personal development rather than training?

   I   Job rotation

   II   Time off work to study for accountancy examinations

   III   A course in leadership skills

   IV   Self-teaching of word-processing skills using an online software package

   A   I, II and III only

   B   I and IV only

   C   I, II and IV only

   D   III and IV only

134 What is the major difficulty in establishing a basic pay structure for knowledge work?

   A   Job evaluation

   B   Benchmarking

   C   Scarcity of individuals with knowledge skills

   D   Performance evaluation

135 A document recording the current development objectives of an individual, the time scales for achieving them and the means by which they should be achieved, is known as:

   A   a competence statement

   B   a performance review

   C   an appraisal report

   D   a development action plan.

136 One example of a flexible work arrangement is a compressed work week. A compressed work week involves:

   A   working for longer-than-usual hours on some days in exchange for a day off work

   B   working for some days at home instead of in the office

   C   allowing employees to choose their hours of attendance each day, provided that they work a full day

   D   allowing employees to work less than the standard number of hours each week.

137 **What is the main practical reason for asking an applicant for a reference from a former employer, as part of the selection process for a vacant job?**

A   To gain another person's opinion about the suitability of the candidate for the job

B   To find out whether the candidate has any personal faults or weaknesses

C   To assess what the candidate's future performance in the job might be

D   To establish whether the candidate has been telling the truth about his previous employment history

138 **A test used in the selection of individuals for jobs might ask questions about their likes and dislikes, attitudes, and what they would do in certain non-work situations. This type of selection test is:**

A   an intelligence test

B   an aptitude test

C   a personality test

D   a situational test.

139 **The purpose of job evaluation is to:**

A   assess the personal qualities required to do the job

B   assess what the responsibilities of the job should be

C   assess the performance of the job holder

D   assess a fair rate of pay for the job.

140 **Which of the following factors can be both a hygiene factor and a motivator for employees?**

A   Pay

B   The quality of management

C   Working conditions

D   The level of responsibility the individual is given

141 **Which of the following is *not* a relevant factor in forecasting the future availability of human resources to meet the expected employment requirements of a company over the next two to three years?**

A   Skills of existing staff

B   Holiday entitlements

C   Staff turnover rates

D   Numbers of existing staff

142 An employer has decided to offer a job to a candidate following a selection process, but still has some doubts about whether the individual will be well-suited to the job. Which of the following options would be the most effective way of dealing with these concerns about the individual's aptitude for the job?

A Making the employee redundant if he/she fails to perform well

B Offering the job initially for a probationary period

C Offering the candidate a low rate of pay until he/she has demonstrated the ability to do the job well

D Dismissing the individual for incompetence if he/she does the job badly

143 Lawrence and Lorsch argued that specialisation within an organisation and greater decentralisation are most needed in organisations:

A with a stable and predictable environment

B where there is a low level of change in its environment and technology

C where there is a high level of predictable change in its environment and technology

D where there is a high level of unpredictable change in its environment and technology.

144 What are the three ingredients in Handy's motivation calculus?

A Needs, motivation, satisfaction

B Needs, effectiveness, results

C Participation, pay, recognition

D Motivation, effort, rewards

145 One of the major consequences of changing an organisation towards a virtual structure will be:

A less trust of employees

B fewer meetings

C a reduction in outsourcing

D less motivation to perform.

146 The following assumptions underlie a well-known theory of motivation.

(1) The expenditure of physical and mental effort at work is as natural as play or rest.

(2) If a job is satisfying, then the result will be commitment to the organisation.

These assumptions apply to:

A Maslow's hierarchy of needs

B McGregor's Theory X

C McGregor's Theory Y

D Ouchi's Theory Z.

147   According to Likert, which of the following is not a feature of effective management?

A   The motivation to work must be supplemented by a system of rewards.

B   Employees should be seen as individuals with needs, whose self-worth should be developed.

C   An organisation should be developed as a closely-knit structure of effective work groups, all committed to achieving the organisation's objectives.

D   Supportive relationships must exist within each work group, characterised by mutual respect not actual support.

148   According to Herzberg, one of the motivator factors in employment is:

A   advancement

B   status

C   interpersonal relations

D   the employer's policies and administration.

149   Performance-related pay involves:

A   rewarding employees with a proportion of total profits

B   rewarding employees with a proportion of total profits in excess of a target minimum level

C   rewarding employees on the basis of the amount of work they have done

D   rewarding employees for achieving agreed personal targets.

150   Rensis Likert argued that the most effective style of management:

A   is benevolent authoritarian

B   is participative

C   is consultative

D   depends on the circumstances and the situation.

151   Recent developments towards greater employee involvement, flexible working and flatter organisational structures have placed greater emphasis on which one of the following styles of management?

A   Exploitative authoritative

B   Autocratic

C   Participative

D   Benevolent authoritative

152   Any claim that unethical behaviour is in an organisation's best interests is an attempt to:

A   follow the principle of procedural justice

B   do the right thing for society

C   rationalise the unethical conduct

D   look after the interests of oneself.

153 **Which one of the following is a part of the recruitment rather than the selection process?**

A   Job analysis

B   Interviewing

C   Testing

D   Assessment centres

154 **According to M.A. Devanna, which one of the following describes the components of the HR cycle?**

A   Job design, selection, involvement, appraisal, rewards

B   Selection, performance appraisal, rewards, development

C   Performance, job design, appraisal, involvement, development

D   Appraisal, development, job design, involvement, rewards

155 **According to F.W. Taylor, which one of the following is a characteristic of scientific management?**

A   Work specialisation

B   Group working

C   Socio-technical system

D   The informal organisation

156 **Which of the following HR activities should be the most difficult to outsource to an external organisation?**

A   Staff development

B   Re-location

C   Training

D   Recruitment

157 **In staff recruitment, an appraisal method based on identifying the skills required for a job and assessing which applicant has those required skills is known as:**

A   psychometric testing

B   work sample tests

C   a competence-based approach

D   an assessment centre.

158 **An assessment centre:**

A   helps selection by assessing job candidates by using a comprehensive and interrelated series of techniques

B   is the training headquarters where job interviews take place

C   is a desk-based process of reviewing job application forms for suitability

D   is a place where job applicants are subjected to psychological testing.

159   Training workers in methods of statistical process control and work analysis:

A   overcomes a crisis of control in an organisation's life cycle

B   is part of a succession planning approach to Human Resources

C   is part of a quality management approach

D   is part of a scientific management approach.

160   The use of standard questions in job interviews helps ensure:

A   fairness

B   validity

C   reliability

D   completeness.

161   The so-called 'psychological contract' is a notion that is based on:

A   segmenting then accessing a market

B   the buyer/supplier relationship

C   a distinctive style of testing used in selection procedures

D   the expectations the organisation and employee have of one another.

162   According to Douglas McGregor:

A   'Theory X' people dislike work, need direction and avoid responsibility

B   'Theory Y' people dislike work, need direction and avoid responsibility

C   self-actualising people dislike work, need direction and avoid responsibility

D   hygiene factors determine whether people like work, need direction or take responsibility.

163   The purpose of a person specification is to provide details of:

A   organisational size and diversity of activity

B   the types of responsibilities and duties to be undertaken by the post holder

C   personal characteristics, experience and qualifications expected of a candidate

D   individual terms of engagement and period of contract.

164   The processes of job analysis and individual performance appraisal are related in the sense that:

A   they are different terms for the same process

B   performance appraisal is based on job analysis

C   both form part of the selection process

D   job analysis is based on performance appraisal.

165 **Content theories of motivation tend to focus mainly on:**

A   the needs of the group

B   feelings of complacency or dissatisfaction

C   the needs of individuals

D   the use of 'carrots' and 'sticks' as devices.

166 **It is the role of 'outplacement consultants' to:**

A   provide help to redundant employees including training and finding jobs

B   provide help to employees wishing to gain experience in other roles

C   arrange for placing products in an untested market place

D   arrange for placing under-used assets at the disposal of start-up businesses.

167 **F.W. Taylor's thinking on motivation in the workplace involved a belief that:**

A   social groups and individuals as part of a culture should be key considerations

B   reward for effort and workplace efficiency should be key considerations

C   managers had two different sets of assumptions about their subordinates

D   'motivators' and 'hygiene factors' should be key considerations.

168 **In terms of employment CIMA's Ethical Guidelines require members to:**

A   act responsibly in the way that all other professionals do

B   act responsibly but in a way that satisfies organisational demands and pressures

C   act responsibly but in a way that satisfies the individual's own ethical code

D   act responsibly, honour any legal contract of employment and conform to employment legislation.

169 **360 degree feedback is part of a system that encourages:**

A   organisational appraisal based on feedback from customers and suppliers

B   organisational appraisal based on relative industry and competitor performance

C   personal appraisal based on feedback from peers, subordinates, line managers and even external parties

D   personal appraisal based on line manager feedback and self-appraisal documentation.

170 **Explain the difference between:**

(a)   job enlargement

(b)   job rotation

(c)   job enrichment.   **(4 marks)**

171 **Describe how a company might use the Internet to carry out tests on potential recruits.**

(4 marks)

172 **Describe the difference between 'hard' and 'soft' human resources management.**

(4 marks)

173   Handy suggested that as an organisation grows, it needs to plan its HR requirements. He suggested that the human resources used by an organisation should be a combination of three types, giving rise to his concept of a 'shamrock' organisation (with three 'leaves'). One type of employee is the long-term, full-time employee. Describe the other two types.   (4 marks)

174   Explain the nature of a psychological contract between an individual and an organisation, and describe the three types of psychological contract identified by Handy.   (4 marks)

175   Employers might identify certain key skills that make employers more employable, and that are portable from one job to the next. Explain why employers might want all workers to possess key skills and suggest what these key skills might be.   (4 marks)

176   Elton Mayo was a founder of the 'human relations school' of management thinking, and his ideas originated from the so-called 'Hawthorne experiments' in the 1950s. Explain briefly the views of Mayo about the behaviour of individuals in their work.   (4 marks)

Section 2

SECTION B-TYPE QUESTIONS

177   SPEC

SPEC manufactures spectacles and sunglasses, which it sells through retail organisations and specialist opticians. It is planning to introduce a major new computer system for marketing. The new system will be developed in-house. In the past, the company has neglected both IT and marketing activities, and the managing director has been calling for major changes in the way that marketing staff think and operate. He has accused the marketing management of being too sales-oriented and not sufficiently marketing-oriented. He sees the new computer system as an opportunity to introduce big changes.

At a recent project development meeting, the IT director and senior systems analyst presented ideas for the design of the new system. These were presented largely in the form of diagrams and tables: data flow diagrams, entity-relationship models, entity life histories and decision tables. Several points were raised at the meeting.

(1)   The managing director is very concerned about the problems of implementing what he regards as major changes into the organisation, particularly marketing activities. He believes that the change must be managed carefully.

(2)   The marketing director is looking forward to having the new system, which will provide a marketing decision support system and a customer database. He believes that the database will be useful for direct marketing.

(3)   The managing director added that he has been advised to check whether the new system will raise any legal issues that the company will have to consider.

Required:

(a)   Explain the potential benefits of a new IT system to an organisation.   **(5 marks)**

(b)   Explain the purpose in systems development of:

   (i)   data flow diagrams

   (ii)   entity-relationship models

   (iii)   entity life histories

   (iv)   decision tables.   **(5 marks)**

(c)   Suggest an approach to the management of change within the organisation, based on the views of Beer and Nohria.   **(5 marks)**

(d)   Explain the difference between mass marketing, direct marketing and interactive marketing, giving examples of each.   **(5 marks)**

(e)   Explain how market research can be used to support a marketing decision support system.   **(5 marks)**

(f)   Describe three legal issues that might affect the marketing of spectacles and sunglasses.   **(5 marks)**

(Total: 30 marks)

178 NEW SYSTEM

A company is planning a major new IT system for order processing, inventory control and order despatch operations. Senior management would prefer to develop a bespoke system, although an off-the-shelf software package is available that could be used instead. The IT manager recognises the need for the new system to be introduced quickly, and has suggested that the systems development, if done in-house, would make use of prototyping.

One of the main reasons for introducing the new system is that customers for the company's products demand reliable delivery dates for the items they order, and several rival companies have been gaining market share because they have been able to develop better order delivery systems. All the customers of the company are businesses. The company's new system will be used for taking customer orders and informing customers about the availability of the items, and will provide the customer with a 'guaranteed' delivery date.

Another feature of the new system is that it will speed up order processing, and it is expected that about 100 staff will be made redundant. The staff who are kept on will need training in the use of the new system.

Required:

(a) Explain the main disadvantages of buying off-the-shelf software rather than developing a bespoke information system.   **(5 marks)**

(b) Explain how prototyping would speed up system implementation and improve the quality of the final system.   **(5 marks)**

(c) The new computer system is intended to improve operating processes within the company. Explain the importance of operations strategy for the company.   **(5 marks)**

(d) Suggest how the new IT system might be seen as an element of the marketing mix by the company's marketing management.   **(5 marks)**

(e) Suggest how staff should be trained in operating the new system.   **(5 marks)**

(f) Suggest the procedures the company should follow if it has to make some staff redundant.   **(5 marks)**

(Total: 30 marks)

179 HUBBLES (PILOT PAPER)

Hubbles, a national high-street clothing retailer has recently appointed a new Chief Executive. The company is well established and relatively financially secure. It has a reputation for stability and traditional, quality clothing at an affordable price. Lately, however, it has suffered from intense competition leading to a loss of market share and an erosion of customer loyalty.

Hubbles has all the major business functions provided by 'in house' departments, including finance, human resources, purchasing, strategy and marketing. The Strategy and Marketing Department has identified a need for a comprehensive review of the company's effectiveness. In response, the new Chief Executive has commissioned a review by management consultants.

Their initial findings include the following:

*   Hubbles has never moved from being sales-oriented to being marketing-oriented and this is why it has lost touch with its customers;

*   Hubbles now needs to get closer to its customers and operate a more effective marketing mix;

*   Additional investment in its purchasing department can add significantly to improving Hubbles' competitive position.

The Chief Executive feels that a presentation of interim findings to senior managers would be helpful at this point. You are a member of the management consultancy team and have been asked to draft a slide presentation of some of the key points. The Chief Executive has identified six such points.

Required:

Prepare a slide outline, and brief accompanying notes of two to three sentences, for each of the Chief Executive's key points identified below. (Your responses should be contained on no more than six pages in total.)

(a) Describe the difference between a company that concentrates on 'selling' its products and one that has adopted a marketing approach. **(5 marks)**

(b) Explain how Hubbles might develop itself into an organisation that is driven by customer needs. **(5 marks)**

(c) Explain what is meant by the 'marketing mix'. **(5 marks)**

(d) Identify examples of ways in which the management of Hubbles could make use of the marketing mix to help regain its competitive position. **(5 marks)**

(e) Describe the main areas in which Hubbles' Human Resources Department might reasonably contribute to assist the Purchasing Department. **(5 marks)**

(f) Explain how an efficient Purchasing Department might contribute to effective organisational performance. **(5 marks)**

(Total: 30 marks)

180 HEVE TRANSPORT

Heve Transport is a large transportation company whose directors have decided to invest in a new computer system for planning and controlling operations, and for management decision-making support. The new system is seen as an essential requirement for the company if it is to maintain a competitive advantage in its business.

There has been a considerable amount of discussion about whether the company should buy available off-the-shelf software packages, or whether to develop a bespoke system. The balance of opinion is in favour of a bespoke solution, but the directors do not want the development work on the new system to take too long and are hoping to have a new system in operation within 12 months, which is reliable and free of any major error or design fault.

The head of IT operations has been asked to prepare a plan for an in-house system development, specifying the stages of system development that will be required and the nature of the testing on the new system that will be made.

The head of human relations management believes that the new system will be much more user-friendly than the current system and should help the company to promote policies that he favours for more flexible employment by the company and for flexible working for full-time employees.

Required:

(a) Explain the advantages of using off-the-shelf software instead of developing bespoke software for a new computer system. **(5 marks)**

(b) Prototyping is a method of introducing a new in-house or 'bespoke' computer system. Describe the features of prototyping and explain the main advantages of prototyping for designing and implementing a major new computer system. **(5 marks)**

(c) Describe the main stages in the in-house design and development of a large new computer system. **(5 marks)**

(d) Explain the purpose during system development of:

    (i) program testing, and

    (ii) system testing. **(5 marks)**

(e) Explain the nature of flexible employment, and the problems that flexible employment might create for HR management. **(5 marks)**

(f) Explain the nature of flexible working and indicate what factors should be considered when first designing a flexible work policy. **(5 marks)**

(Total: 30 marks)

181 STAND PRODUCTS

Stand Products is a manufacturing organisation that has been established for many years, producing electrical and electronic products. It is currently facing tough market conditions. The management of the company believe that the market as a whole is currently expanding quite rapidly, but the annual sales turnover of Stand Products is growing much more slowly and the company is losing market share.

At a recent meeting of the senior management to discuss the difficulties facing the company, there was general agreement that the company had suffered badly from a general lack of innovation and new thinking, and that change was urgently needed.

The marketing director believes that the need for change was being driven by a variety of factors outside the company, which he calls 'triggers for change'. The managing director disagrees: his view is that too much authority has been delegated to the profit centre managers within the company and that head office was now losing control of its operations and marketing strategies. He thinks the time has come, given the continuing growth of the company's business, to make organisational changes and bring back more power and influence to head office.

The managing director has also stated the view that even if changes are introduced, the company will have to make some staff redundant in order to cut costs.

The operations director stated his view that many of the difficulties of the company were caused by difficulties that the company was having with suppliers, and with poor performance in some of the company's manufacturing centres. Referring to the concept of the supply wheel, he would like to carry out a strategic review of the entire supply chain and consider outsourcing many of the company's current manufacturing operations. He has also argued that if manufacturing continues to be carried on in-house rather than outsourced, he will carry out a major review of performance objectives and performance measurements in manufacturing operations. He thinks that there is currently too much emphasis on cost control and not enough on other elements of performance.

Required:

(a) Kanter, in *The Change Masters: Corporate Entrepreneurs at Work*, argued for the need for organisations to be creative and encourage change, and criticised the widespread management indifference in the US to innovations suggested by employees.

Describe the ways in which she suggested that creativity should be encouraged within organisations. **(5 marks)**

(b) Describe the nature of external triggers for change that affect organisations.

(5 marks)

(c) The views of the managing director are compatible with Greiner's growth model. Describe the five stages in Greiner's growth model, and suggest which stage the company might have reached, if the managing director's views are correct.

(5 marks)

(d) When an employer needs to make some employees redundant, it may use measures that reduce the need for compulsory redundancies.

Define 'compulsory redundancies' and suggest measures that might be taken to reduce or avoid the amount of compulsory redundancies. **(5 marks)**

(e) Describe the concept of the supply wheel and the elements within it. **(5 marks)**

(f) Explain what types of performance objectives and performance measurement criteria can be applied to operations. **(5 marks)**

(Total: 30 marks)

182 HILO CONSULTANCY

Hilo Consultancy specialises in providing IT solutions to business clients. The company has been growing successfully, and is a project-based organisation. A project team is created whenever a client commissions new work, and is disbanded when the work is completed. The company assembles the teams from a pool of its own full-time staff, and also employs temporary staff as required to meet the particular skills requirements for each project. Much of the company's work is involved with developing complex databases for clients, such as marketing databases.

The company's organisation structure and reward systems are based on high-performance arrangements, although there have been some problems recently with members of staff who are dissatisfied with their salaries and career prospects.

The HR manager attributes much of the success of the company to the excellent leadership qualities of the managing director, who has great skills in dealing with the highly-skilled and intelligent work force. The HR manager has described the work force as a mixture of 'self-actualising man' and 'complex man'.

The managing director recognises that as the company grows and develops, changes will be needed. He is particularly interested in the need to reinforce the company's policies for high-quality working, and he is an advocate of quality management. Some clients have already asked whether Hilo Consultancy has any certification of its quality standards. The managing director believes that in several years' time, a significant number of potential clients might insist on certification of quality management standards from its suppliers, and he intends that Hilo Consultancy should apply for certification under the ISO 9000 series.

Required:

(a)   Describe the nature and purpose of a customer database for marketing, and explain how might a database be used.   **(5 marks)**

(b)   Explain the meaning of 'high performance work arrangements'.   **(5 marks)**

(c)   Describe the main features of a project-based organisation and explain the particular problems for HR management in this type of organisation.   **(5 marks)**

(d)   The views of the HR manager about the leadership skills of the managing director relate to the views of Schein on motivation. Describe the four types of employee behaviour identified by Schein, and explain their relevance to management.

(5 marks)

(e)   The ISO 9000 series of quality management standards is based on certain quality principles. Explain the purpose of the ISO 9000 quality standards and describe the quality principles on which they are based.   **(5 marks)**

(f)   Explain the framework for an exercise to establish quality management systems in conformity with ISO 9001: *2000 guidelines*.   **(5 marks)**

(Total: 30 marks)

183   PMK MANUFACTURING

PMK Manufacturing, a division of a global manufacturing company, has been experiencing difficulties with its operations in manufacturing and purchasing and supply. A new managing director for the division has been appointed, with the task of improving the division's performance.

He has found several features of the management and organisation that he does not like. The previous managing director had concentrated on improving efficiency through work organisation and work standards. The new managing director considers this approach to be rather old-fashioned, and too much like scientific management; worse still, it has not been successful.

He has also found that the management information systems are poor. Reports are often produced late, and do not provide the feedback that operations managers need to control work quality and work flow adequately. Feedback reporting systems will need to be improved.

In his previous job in another division of the company, the managing director had worked with his management team and employees to develop a continuous improvement programme, which had been very successful. However, he is not convinced that a continuous improvement programme would be appropriate for the PMK division, in view of the culture change required, and he suspects that an overhaul of operational and purchasing systems based on a business process re-engineering approach might be more appropriate. He considers that a reorganisation of production on a Just-In-Time basis might be appropriate, and that there will have to be a major improvement in purchasing and supply.

He supports the views of Reck and Long, that purchasing should be used as a strategic weapon to promote competitiveness, but the division has so far failed to engage in any long-term relationships with its suppliers.

(a)   F.W. Taylor is regarded as the founder of scientific management. Describe the objectives of management as suggested by Taylor.   **(5 marks)**

(b)   Feedback systems provide negative and positive feedback for control purposes. Explain the difference between positive and negative feedback in a management information system, and give an example of a management system in which feedback is used.   **(5 marks)**

(c)   Describe the features of continuous improvement or kaizen.   **(5 marks)**

(d)   Describe the nature of Business Process Re-engineering (BPR) and explain the principles on which it is based.   **(5 marks)**

(e)   Describe the operational requirements for a system of JIT production.   **(5 marks)**

(f)   Explain the approach of Reck and Long to supply strategy, and describe their four stages in the development of purchasing to becoming a competitive weapon in a company's strategic planning and battle for markets.   **(5 marks)**

(Total: 30 marks)

184   SOFT DIVISION

The Soft Division of TTFN International has had a poor reputation for human relations management, and a new management team has been installed to introduce change and improvements. The new team has found that the previous management used a very authoritarian style of leadership, and had discouraged innovative ideas and suggestions for improvements from their employees.

Although the new team expect to use a different style of leadership, they have discovered several other problems that demand their attention. A major cause of concern is the lack of adequate HR planning by the division. The division is undergoing a period of great change, with new technology and increasing environmental regulations affecting both product design and production systems. New skills will be needed from employees and some of the existing skills of the work force will no longer be required after the next one or two years.

A second problem is that for some jobs in the division, the wrong type of person has been employed and recruitment methods ought to be introduced. The new management favour the use of testing of job applicants, such as psychometric testing. In addition, they believe that there ought to be a formal system of job appraisal. The senior management of TTFN International have indicated that the Soft Division would be permitted to introduce a performance-related pay scheme, if this would improve the efficiency and performance of the division.

A third issue is that employees need to be alerted to the growing significance of social and environmental issues, particularly in view of the increasing environmental regulations, and the new management intend to pursue a corporate social responsibility policy.

Required:

(a)   In the 1980s, Kanter criticised the lack of innovation in many US companies, and accused senior management of discouraging new ideas and change. Describe six ways in which senior management might discourage innovation.   **(5 marks)**

(b)   Describe the methods that might be used by the HR department to forecast the organisation's demand for employees over the next five years.   **(5 marks)**

(c)   A company might identify from its HR plan that it will need fewer of a particular group of employees in about two years' time, and some employees might have to be made redundant.

Suggest measures that the company might take now, based on the HR plan, to reduce the amount of redundancies in the future.   **(5 marks)**

(d)   Explain the nature of psychometric testing, and the advantages and disadvantages of using this form of testing for recruitment purposes.   **(5 marks)**

(e)   (i)   Explain the purpose of an appraisal system.

(ii)   Explain the problems that a organisation might have to deal with in operating a performance-related pay scheme for its employees.   **(5 marks)**

(f)   Explain the concept of corporate social responsibility (CSR) and suggest how CSR might be relevant for the marketing of an organisation's products or services.

(5 marks)

(Total: 30 marks)

185   GOURMET COMPANY

Gourmet Company is a private European company. Its founder and main shareholder began in business by manufacturing food processing equipment. This remains an important part of the company's operations, but it has diversified into the manufacture of Gee-May branded food products and also into operating a chain of Gee-May food stores and a chain of Gee-May restaurants. Gourmet Company is now a large and successful international company, with over ten different divisions operating as investment centres.

Each division is structured and organised in a different way from the other divisions, according to the circumstances in which the division operates. Central management do not impose a particular management or organisation structure on its divisions, even though some divisions need to work together in close co-operation.

However, divisional managers are continually being urged by head office to improve their operational performance. There have been several innovations recently in efforts to improve systems and operations.

(i)   The division that manufactures food processing equipment has recently introduced an MRPI system to improve production and inventory planning and control.

(ii)   The food stores division is trying to introduce a Just-In-Time philosophy into the operation of its food stores, with the aim of improving customer service.

(iii)   The food stores division has also introduced a new user-friendly computer system, that enables customers in its shops and stores to check out and pay for their own purchases, without having to queue for service at a cash desk.

(iv)   The company is continually producing new products to maintain competitive advantage, and the marketing departments in the various divisions collaborate with operational management in product screening and in developing new products of a very high quality, in keeping with the Gee-May brand name.

Required:

(a)   The organisation structure of Gourmet Company is consistent with the contingency theory of organisation. Explain the basic proposition in contingency theory, and explain how the requirements for differentiation and integration affect the efficiency of an organisation structure. (Your answer should refer if possible to the work of Lawrence and Lorsch.)   **(5 marks)**

(b)   (i)   Explain the difference between continuous inventory management, periodic inventory systems and ABC inventory management.

(ii)   Explain, giving your reason, which type of inventory management system is appropriate for an MRPI system of production scheduling.   **(5 marks)**

(c)   Explain how the JIT philosophy might be applied to the provision of services to customers.   **(5 marks)**

(d)   Explain the meaning of a 'user-friendly' computer system, and suggest what the user-friendly features of the check-out system in the food stores might be.   **(5 marks)**

(e)   Explain the nature of concept screening in the product design process.   **(5 marks)**

(f)   Explain the purpose of branding consumer products.   **(5 marks)**

(Total: 30 marks)

186   MARKETING-LED

Cleves Corporation is a marketing-led business that sells a range of entertainment and leisure products and services. The 'Big C' brand name used by the corporation is very well-known, and the corporation promotes all its various services through this brand name. The success of the company has been on built on a marketing-led approach.

For each business activity of the company, the market is segmented and products and services are developed for different segments of the market. The corporation aims to be the market leader in each market segment that it targets.

Its management are also very marketing-conscious, and develop a marketing mix for their services based on an appropriate mix of the '7 Ps'.

Required:

(a)   Describe the nature of market segmentation for consumer products, explaining why an organisation might segment a market giving examples of how it might be segmented.

(5 marks)

(b)   Explain how a market for a consumer product or service might be segmented according to life style, and give an example of a product or service for which the segmenting of the market according to lifestyle could be useful for marketing purposes.   **(5 marks)**

(c)   Originally, the marketing mix was defined as a combination of 'the 4 Ps' – product, place, price and promotion. It is now often defined as 'the 7 Ps', with people, processes and physical evidence added to the original 4Ps.

Suggest an example of a product or service where people, processes and physical evidence might be important elements in the marketing mix, giving reasons for your choice of example.   **(5 marks)**

(Total: 15 marks)

187   V COSMETICS (MAY 05 EXAM)

V is an innovative company run according to the principles of its entrepreneurial owner. V operates a package distribution service, a train service, and sells holidays, bridal outfits, clothing, mobile telephones, and soft drinks. V is well known for challenging the norm and 'giving customers quality products and services at affordable prices and doing it all with a sense of fun'. V spends little on advertising but has great brand awareness thanks to the 'visibility' of its inspirational owner.

V has just announced the launch of 'V-cosmetics' to exploit a gap in the market. The cosmetic range will be competitively priced against high street brands and have the distinctive V logo.

You work for a market analyst who is about to appear on a radio discussion of V's business interests. You have been asked to provide a clear, short briefing for the market analyst on the thinking behind V-cosmetics. Your research of the V-cosmetics range identifies innovative marketing proposals. V-cosmetics will not be on sale in shops, instead it will use two approaches to promotion and selling, namely:

- The use of 'cosmetic associates'. Individuals may apply to become an associate and, if accepted, will be required to buy a basic stock of every V-cosmetic product. The associate will then use these products as samples and "testers". After initial training associates organise parties in the homes of friends and their friends where they take orders for products at a listed price. Associates receive commission based on sales.

- The internet and mobile telephone technology will also be heavily used to offer Vcosmetic products to the public.

Required:

Prepare brief notes containing bullet points and no more than two to three sentences for each of the key points identified below. (Your notes should be contained on no more than six pages in total.)

(a) Explain how the proposed approach can be understood within the context of the marketing mix. **(5 marks)**

(b) Explain the human resource implications of using 'cosmetic associates'. **(5 marks)**

(c) Explain the concept of direct marketing. **(5 marks)**

(d) Explain the advantages of the internet as a marketing channel. **(5 marks)**

(e) Describe how V might use internet and mobile phone technology as part of its marketing approach. **(5 marks)**

(f) Identify the main ethical issues associated with the proposal to market V cosmetics. **(5 marks)**

(Total: 30 marks)

188 CFO

CFO Ltd is an organisation based in the United Kingdom. It offers a range of financial services, including home, life and car insurance products, personal and business loans and home loans (known as 'mortgages').

The structure of CFO is shown below:

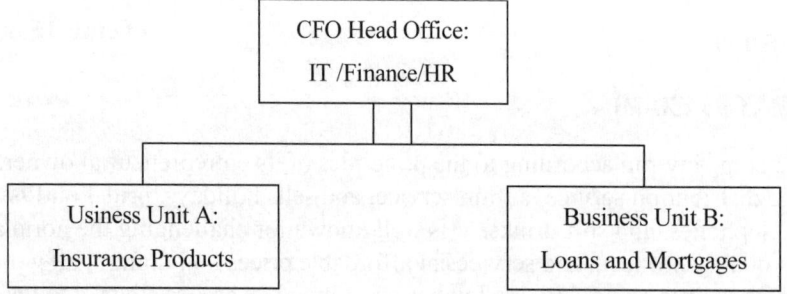

Business Unit A

Business Unit A operates five call centres located throughout the country, selling home, life and car insurance products. In recent years, Business Unit A has lost market share to rivals, largely due to its slowness in introducing information technology to deliver its products to customers.

Business Unit B

Business Unit B is smaller and less technologically innovative, operating from two call centres. CFO loan and mortgage customers are less likely to require on-line website facilities than insurance product customers, instead being more interested in high quality customer care and on-going customer service.

Market environment

The financial services industry has become increasingly regulated in recent years, and a number of job losses have occurred in CFO as a result of increased competition and falling profits. This has resulted in low morale. For the last two years, CFO has been a member of a benchmarking group called 'The Forum for Quality in Lending', the aim of which is to improve the quality of customer service and standards of excellence in the mortgage industry.

IT infrastructure upgrade

At the start of May, the CFO board of directors committed to a new operating system and the redesign of the organisation's website and intranet. The updated website will improve the firm's marketing as it will allow customers to review all products on offer, to obtain quotes, to compare quotes with rival companies, to send email queries and to instantly sign up for insurance products and make payments electronically. A basic website is already in existence showing all current products on offer, the ability to make comparisons with rivals, and the ability to get on-line quotes.

Required:

(a) Explain the term 'operating system', and describe three main features of commonly used operating systems such as Microsoft Windows **(5 marks)**

(b) Explain the benefits of these features to CFO. **(5 marks)**

(c) Explain the importance to CFO of an updated website. **(5 marks)**

(d) Explain what is meant by benchmarking and outline the four types of benchmarking.

(5 marks)

(e) Explain the advantages to CFO of benchmarking. **(5 marks)**

(f) Identify and explain four reasons why improvements in staff training in CFO (both in the use of the technology and in the products sold), could improve quality of customer service. **(5 marks)**

(Total: 30 marks)

189 MOTIVATION ASSUMPTIONS

R Company employs about 50 sales people, each of whom covers his or her own territory . They are between 25 and 63 years old, have served for varying lengths of time, and include both married and single people. They have a basic salary and can earn a similar amount again in commission. The company now feels that this method of payment has become inequitable because of variable conditions in each region. Some of the sales people have also commented that the company's reliance on the state pension arrangements compares unfavourably with alternative employers.

It has now been decided to abandon the commission system and to compensate the sales people by:

- consolidating part of their commission into a higher salary

- establishing a non-contributory pension scheme

- providing more prestigious cars for them

- increasing their holiday entitlement by 25%.

Required:

(a)   Describe briefly the assumptions underlying the following theories of human motivation:

    (i)   Maslow's need-based theory   **(5 marks)**

    (ii)   Herzberg's motivation-hygiene theory   **(5 marks)**

    (iii)   McGregor – Theory X and Theory Y.   **(5 marks)**

(b)   Explain what effect the following changes may have on the sales people at R Company and on other staff:

    (i)   consolidating part of their commission into a higher salary   **(5 marks)**

    (ii)   establishing a non-contributory pension scheme   **(5 marks)**

    (iii)   changing the car and holiday entitlements.   **(5 marks)**

(Total: 30 marks)

190   MONDAY NEWSPAPERS

Monday Newspapers is a national newspaper publisher with two national titles. Each title is positioned differently in the market. The company operates in a highly competitive market, where marketing is crucial to success. The two main sources of revenue are sales of newspapers and advertising income. The marketing objective is to improve profitability by increasing circulation. The newspapers operate in a rapidly changing technological environment, and in recent years there have been major changes in production and printing methods.

Newspapers are produced on six days each week, in two editions each day, an early and a late edition. The editorial copy is produced by reporters and editors, using DTP software, and the copies are printed on large printing presses at two printing works, one in the north and one in the south of the country. The printed newspapers are then delivered from the printing works to distributors around the country. The sales demand for newspapers varies according to the day of the week, with low sales on Mondays and Saturdays, and the highest sales on Wednesdays and Thursdays. Unsold copies are returned by distributors for pulping.

Required:

(a)   Explain the nature of market positioning and suggest how newspapers might position themselves in their market.   **(5 marks)**

(b)   Suggest how a newspaper publisher might use different elements of the marketing mix to market its titles to consumers.   **(5 marks)**

(c)   Information about the total size of the market for newspapers and the circulation figures for each newspaper title is extremely important for the industry, and independent verification of circulation figures is necessary. Explain why circulation figures might be highly important, and suggest how independently verified circulation figures might be obtained.   **(5 marks)**

(d)   Suggest how newspaper publishers might make use of the Internet and e-mail in producing newspapers and delivering other services to customers.   **(5 marks)**

(e)   Suggest how production might be scheduled at the printing works, and explain, with reasons, whether Monday Newspapers would benefit from the introduction of an MRPI system for production scheduling or a JIT system of production.   **(5 marks)**

(f)   Monday Newspapers produces colour supplements for one of its newspaper titles. Supplements are each published monthly on Saturdays. Three supplements are published each month, one on sport, one on living and one on cooking. From a marketing perspective, suggest what the purpose of publishing supplements might be, and what benefits Monday Newspapers might expect to obtain.   **(5 marks)**

(Total: 30 marks)

191   ROUND THE TABLE (NOV 05 EXAM)

You are a researcher employed by a topical business discussion television show 'Round The Table'. Next week's discussion is about managing supply to achieve quality and customer satisfaction. Invited guests will be a leading academic, public and private sector senior managers and the chief executive of a car producer. You have been asked to prepare an outline briefing that will give some background information to the show's presenter.

Your research shows that the automobile industry is highly competitive and globally suffers from 'overcapacity'. In certain countries however, there is unfulfilled demand for specialist makes and models, implying some under capacity 'hot spots'. You understand that, for any organisation, whether producing goods or services, effective capacity management is vital. It ensures that customers' needs are more fully met and that there are fewer unfulfilled delivery date promises. There are several ways of dealing with variations in demand and matching production capacity including:

- concentrating on inventory levels (a 'level capacity' strategy)

- concentrating on demand (a 'demand' strategy)

- adjusting levels of activity (a 'chase' strategy).

As part of your investigation you note that distinctive issues exist for service organisations (such as those found in the public sector) compared with manufacturing organisations (such as car producers).

Required:

As the show's researcher you are required to produce guidance notes to support the show's presenter which:

(a)   discuss why a level capacity strategy might be difficult for a firm wishing to adopt a just-in-time (JIT) philosophy   **(5 marks)**

(b)   discuss the impact of demand strategies on an organisation's marketing practices

(5 marks)

(c)   discuss the relationship between chase strategies and the flexible organisation

(5 marks)

(d)   identify the ways that service organisations differ from manufacturing organisations when considering capacity management   **(5 marks)**

(e)   describe the types of software applications a manufacturing firm might introduce to improve its inbound logistics   **(5 marks)**

(f)   describe the types of computerised assistance that could be used by those involved in selling cars and wanting to improve demand.   **(5 marks)**

Notes: (a) to (d) should have particular regard to quality, capacity and other organisational issues.   **(Total: 30 marks)**

Section 3

SECTION C-TYPE QUESTIONS

Note: With effect from the May 2007 diet, section C of this paper will comprise one 30-mark question from a choice of two. Previously, the questions in this section were worth 20 marks each.

INFORMATION SYSTEMS

192 PROJECT MANAGEMENT

Developing and implementing large-scale administrative computer systems requires a formalised and disciplined approach to project management and control.

Required:

(a) Outline an approach to project management suitable for controlling the development of such a system. **(15 marks)**

(b) How can computers be used to help in the administrative support and technical development of a project? **(5 marks)**

(c) Discuss the advantages and disadvantages of writing the software associated with a new project in-house rather than using a third party supplier. **(10 marks)**

(Total: 30 marks)

193 E-MAIL

E-mail is becoming one of the most common forms of communication, both for sending messages within organisations and across the Internet.

Required:

(a) Discuss the impact of communication by e-mail on work practices. **(12 marks)**

(b) Discuss situations where e-mail would NOT be an appropriate communication medium. **(10 marks)**

(c) Explain why many organisations forbid the use of email for personal purposes.

(8 marks)

(Total: 30 marks)

194 SMALL CHAIN

A small chain of four department stores is located in and around a major metropolitan area. It is about to implement, in all stores, a point of sale system with linkages to a central computer. The stores all currently use conventional cash registers. You have been asked to assist in the conversion to the new system.

You are required to produce:

(a) an evaluation of the various approaches to the system changeover **(10 marks)**

(b) a checklist, in sequence, of the activities likely to be carried out during implementation **(6 marks)**

(c) suggestions as to how the new system might be evaluated after three months of operational running. **(8 marks)**

(d) a list of the personnel problems that might be created by the introduction of this system. **(6 marks)**

(Total: 30 marks)

195 IN-HOUSE SOLUTION

MTK is a large construction company that operates internationally in highly-competitive markets. The board of directors of the company have decided that a major new computer system is required for planning and controlling projects. It has also decided that in order to give the company a competitive advantage over its rivals, the system must be designed and developed in-house.

The directors recognise, however, that there are significant problems with developing a major new computer system in-house, and that measures should be taken to ensure that any such problems are either avoided or resolved.

Required:

Explain the risks or problems that are commonly encountered with a major new in-house system development, and suggest how they might be managed. **(30 marks)**

196 DATABASE

TUN currently has different computer application systems for production scheduling, inventory control, accounting, purchasing, product design and engineering, marketing and human relations. A decision has been taken to develop a new database for the company's operations.

An IT consultant advising management has commented that a database with a database management system (DBMS) achieves de-coupling of applications from data, and that a DBMS can bring substantial benefits to the company.

Required:

(a) Explain the difference between a database and a DBMS, and why there is decoupling of data from applications. **(4 marks)**

(b) Describe the advantages of a database and DBMS over having a different computer system for each major application. **(16 marks)**

(c) Explain how a database and DBMS might be used in conjunction with an executive information system (EIS). **(10 marks)**

(Total: 30 marks)

CHANGE MANAGEMENT

197 ZED BANK (PILOT PAPER)

Required:

(a)   Using prescriptive, planned change theory, as outlined by Lewin and others, describe how any major new organisational initiative can be successfully implemented.

(10 marks)

(b)   Zed Bank operates in a fiercely competitive market and has decided to implement a number of important initiatives, including:

- enhancing its current services to customers by providing them with on-line internet and telephone banking services, and

- reducing costs by closing many of its rural and smaller branches (outlets).

In an attempt to pacify the employee representatives (the Banking Trade Union) and to reduce expected protests by the communities affected by branch closure, a senior Bank spokesperson has announced that the changes will be 'incremental' in nature.

In particular, she has stressed that:

- the change will be implemented over a lengthy time period

- there will be no compulsory redundancies

- banking staff ready to take on new roles and opportunities in the online operations will be retrained and offered generous relocation expenses.

For customers, the Bank has promised that automatic cash dispensing machines will be available in all the localities where branches (outlets) close. Customers will also be provided with the software needed for Internet banking and other assistance necessary to give them quick and easy access to banking services.

The leader of the Banking Trade Union is 'appalled' at the initiatives announced. He has argued that the so-called 'incremental' change is in fact the start of a 'transformational' change that will have serious repercussions, not only for the Union's members but also for many of the Bank's customers.

Required:

(i)   Distinguish incremental change from transformational change. Explain why the Bank spokesperson and the trade union leader disagree over their description of the change.   **(10 marks)**

(ii)   Explain whether Zed Bank might benefit from allowing employees to participate in the management of the change process.   **(10 marks)**

(Total: 30 marks)

198 ORGANISATIONAL DEVELOPMENT

The B Company, a long-established food company with about 200 employees, is experiencing a number of problems including the need to implement new hygiene regulations, changes in consumer tastes, rising cost of materials, increasing competition and a demand for higher pay from its employees. But, rather than rising to the challenges as was the case in the past, the current staff seem unable to respond effectively. Morale is generally at a low level, departments are not co-operating and there have even been instances of conflict between quality control and operations. There also seems to be a lack of confidence in the management in general and a feeling that the company has lost direction.

A consultant called in to assist the B Company has recommended the use of techniques drawn from the field of organisational development as one means of tackling B's problems.

Required:

(a) Describe the overall approach of organisational development. **(8 marks)**

(b) Explain how you would use methods and techniques of organisational development to deal with the problems in the B Company. **(14 marks)**

(c) Explain how you would go about selecting a suitable consultant to facilitate the organisational development process. **(8 marks)**

(Total: 30 marks)

199 K COMPANY

K Company is experiencing rapid change. Increasing competition necessitates continual up-dating of its product offerings, its technology and its methods of working. Like other companies today, K Company has to be responsive to frequently changing customer requirements, the challenges posed by fast-moving competitors and the many other threats from a changing world.

One of the ways in which K Company might seek to cope with the challenges of the rapidly-changing environment is to become a 'learning organisation'.

Required:

(a) Advise K Company what would be involved in building a learning organisation.

(10 marks)

(b) The changing environment has implications for K Company's selection process and, given the limitations of interviews and selection tests that constitute the traditional methods of selection, the company has decided to make use of an assessment centre to improve its chances of obtaining people who fit the needs of the company.

Describe the key features of an assessment centre and explain why it is considered to be more effective than traditional methods of selection. **(10 marks)**

(c) K Company's chief executive has suggested that a new corporate vision statement might focus the attention of every member of staff and management and create a much tighter sense of cohesion.

Describe the problems that can be created by the adoption of corporate vision statements. **(10 marks)**

(Total: 30 marks)

200 F STEEL COMPANY

The recently appointed Chief Executive Officer (CEO) of the F Steel Company is intent on making the organisation more competitive. He has made it clear that costs are too high and productivity too low. The trade union that represents the steel workers in the F Steel Company is well-organised and has promised the workers that it will defend their wage levels and working conditions.

The exchange rate of the local currency has been rising in value over the last year, and the company has to compete internationally with subsidised state steel companies. Though domestic demand for steel is weak, the market for steel in the Pacific Rim economies is still growing.

The company is suffering from a number of problems at the operational level. Deliveries have been late on a number of occasions and some customers have complained that the steel they have received does not match the agreed specification. Despite these problems, some of the F Steel Company's long-serving managers are complacent. They have seen the company come through many a business cycle and simply interpret the present situation as the trough of just another such cycle, which will pass. As a result, they see no need for any radical change.

Required:

(a) Analyse the forces for change and causes of resistance in the F Steel Company. Classify these according to whether they can be considered as deriving from internal or external sources. **(10 marks)**

(b) Recommend how the newly-appointed Chief Executive Officer in the F Steel Company might go about managing the process of change. **(10 marks)**

(c) Explain how Peters' idea of 'thriving on chaos' might have reduced the problems faced by the F Steel Company. **(10 marks)**

(Total: 30 marks)

201 R & L (MAY 05 EXAM)

R & L is a large manufacturing firm that is well known as a 'good employer'. Over the past few years, R & L has experienced difficult times with reducing sales and mounting losses. In desperation it employed management consultants to analyse its situation. The consultants have concluded that the downturn in sales is permanent and that R & L needs to reduce its workforce by 50% over the next year in order to survive. Reluctantly, R & L's board of directors has accepted these findings, including the need to reduce the number of staff. The directors have also agreed to act as honestly and as fairly as possible, but realise that any changes they propose will be unpopular and may meet with resistance.

Required:

(a) Discuss what initiatives R & L can take to achieve the job reductions needed given the company's reputation for being a good employer. (Your answer should include reference to appropriate support for any individuals affected.) **(10 marks)**

(b) Discuss the potential strategies available in order to overcome resistance to change, and identify those strategies that would be most suitable for R & L. **(10 marks)**

(Total: 20 marks)

202 T COMPANY

T Company was, until recently, a national telephone company that enjoyed monopoly status, but a decision to deregulate by the government means that it is now exposed to aggressive competition from new entrants. T Company's competitive position has also been undermined by developments in wireless technology. As customers increasingly choose to use mobile phones, T Company's vast investment in fixed line technology is becoming increasingly uneconomic. This change in technology and the associated shift in consumer tastes have left T Company with no option but to invest in mobile technology itself.

T Company also suffers from its history as a monopoly provider; its bureaucratic culture and structure means that it tends to be slower to respond to market changes than the new entrants. The high proportion of telephone engineers who belong to the telecoms trade union does not help this situation. When earlier this year, T Company announced job cuts, the trade union members voted for industrial action that lasted for several weeks and cost the Company millions in lost revenue.

The development of broadband digital technology, however, allows high speed access to the Internet. This has meant a new lease of life for fixed line operators like T Company because existing fixed line systems can be adapted for broadband use. This opportunity has been seized by T Company's senior management. The Company has been successful in attracting

50,000 subscribers to the new broadband service in its first year of operation. The Company has also introduced a service that allows people on the move to access the Internet at selected public venues using a wireless enabled laptop.

This installation of broadband does, however, require training in new skills and the engineers required to undertake this training have threatened strike action in support of a large pay increase to compensate them for using the new skills required for the job.

Required:

(a) Identify the internal and external triggers for change in the strategy and operations of T Company. Discuss the difficulties that the Company is likely to experience in introducing the change programme. **(8 marks)**

(b) Evaluate the success of T Company in managing the change process to date. By application of any model of change management, explain how T Company might go about managing change in the future. **(12 marks)**

(c) Assuming that the need to transform T Company was identified and championed by senior management, describe some of the political mechanisms that they might have used to deal with any reluctance of middle managers to resist change. **(10 marks)**

(Total: 30 marks)

203 Y

Y is one of the five main high street banks in the country. Since banking deregulation in the late 1980s, Y, like other banks, has been facing increasing competition, first from other existing financial institutions but more recently from new entrants who have started to offer deposit accounts and a number of other financial services.

In seeking to respond to these competitive threats, the bank's senior management has started to implement a number of changes. These involve a significant restructuring of the organisation with the removal of a number of layers of management, and a consequent reduction in staffing levels in most divisions. The closure of a number of high-street branches is also planned. The telephone-banking arm is being substantially enlarged, and a major investment in IT is being undertaken. The effect on staff will be considerable. A programme of voluntary redundancy and redeployment is planned and, given the demand for new skills, a considerable amount of training will need to be carried out. Despite clear evidence of the threat to the future of the bank, the plans set forth by management are meeting resistance from the workforce. The banking unions in particular seem determined to obstruct the changes wherever possible.

Required:

With reference to the above scenario:

(a) explain why the implementation of organisational change often proves to be so difficult **(15 marks)**

(b) advise Y's management about the ways in which change can be facilitated. **(15 marks)**

(Total: 30 marks)

OPERATIONS MANAGEMENT

204 ELECTRIC PUMPS

The O Company, founded in the early 1970s, manufactures electric pumps. Despite developments in globalisation, technology, methods of production, techniques of quality management and global sourcing of supplies, the O Company has retained its original approach to operations.

Unfortunately, this reluctance to adapt to the new operations environment has resulted in a decline in competitiveness, a consequent fall in market share, and an overall threat to the future viability of the O Company.

Required:

(a) Describe the key activities in the operations function of an organisation such as the O Company. **(8 marks)**

(b) Explain how the O Company could take advantage of the opportunities offered by developments in technology, production methods, quality management and global sourcing to improve its competitiveness. **(12 marks)**

(c) Distinguish strategic decisions from tactical in the context of operations management.

(10 marks)
(Total: 30 marks)

205 PRODUCTION SCHEDULING

VB Production has a large production plant where it makes three products, A, B and C. Items are produced in batches, and the production planning and control department uses the economic batch quantity model to decide the batch sizes for each product.

Recently, there have been some production scheduling difficulties, and for short periods there has been a stock-out of one of the products. At a meeting of the production management team, it has been suggested that it might be appropriate to introduce a levelled scheduling system for the three products.

Estimates of sales demand in the next four weeks have been provided for the meeting, as follows.

Product	A	B	C
	Units	Units	Units
Week 1 demand	5,000	8,000	5,000
Week 2 demand	6,000	11,000	5,000
Week 3 demand	3,500	12,000	8,000
Week 4 demand	4,500	7,000	6,000

Another suggestion that has been put to the meeting is that the company should switch to Just in Time production methods.

Required:

(a) Explain how a levelled scheduling system would differ from batch production based on economic batch quantities, and suggest the problems that would have to be addressed if the company were to move to a levelled scheduling production system.

(15 marks)

(b) Explain how a levelled scheduling system differs from a Just-In-Time production system, and suggest the problems that would have to be addressed if the company were to move to a JIT production system. **(15 marks)**

(Total: 30 marks)

206 PIPE DREAM

Pipe Dream manufactures a wide range of pipes and tubes. The company has recently appointed a new chief executive who has announced his intention to convert Pipe Dream into a world class company. After several months in the job, he has succeeded in converting his management team to his point of view. He has argued that although the company's operations appear to be fairly efficient, there are many areas in which improvements need to be made.

A major planning meeting has been called, to discuss the steps that might be needed to introduce Total Quality Management (TQM) concepts into the company.

Required:

Prepare a discussion paper for the meeting in which you:

(a) describe the main features of TQM **(12 marks)**

(b) recommend an approach for introducing TQM into the company, and the problems you would expect to encounter **(12 marks)**

(c) justify the use of TQM for a company whose products do not need to be manufactured to the very highest level of precision. **(6 marks)**

(Total: 30 marks)

207 URBAN DANCE

Urban Dance is a small company operating a number of dance schools. The owner of the company, who also acts as managing director, spent many years working in schools for the arts, such as dance schools, music schools and art schools, in both the public and private sector of the economy, and he is well-known and well-respected in the profession.

Urban Dance was established eight years ago, and the company has performed reasonably well during that time. Students come from many parts of the country, and many are referred from state-owned schools and private schools. The ages of students range from 14 to 18, and students are given a normal academic education as well as specialising in dance.

The owner/managing director would like to open more schools, but he believes that before he can do this, he needs to improve various aspects of the current schools and make them better-managed. He is interested in the idea of benchmarking.

Required:

(a) Suggest methods of benchmarking that might be used to assess the performance of the schools explaining how benchmarking might be used to help the company improve performance. **(12 marks)**

(b) Recommend the initial steps that management should take to establish a benchmarking programme. **(8 marks)**

(c) Identify some potential problems and shortcomings associated with benchmarking.

(10 marks)

(Total: 30 marks)

208 VIRTUAL

At a recent conference of purchasing and supply managers, a guest speaker discussed the view that within a few years, many international companies might be able to operate almost as virtual companies. He argued that outsourcing, supply chain management and global sourcing were all that was necessary to create a company that could sell its products successfully in markets around the world.

Required:

Suggest how a virtual company might use outsourcing, supply chain management and global sourcing to make consumer durable products and deliver them to markets around the world.

(30 marks)

209   PROCESS IMPROVEMENT

At a recent board meeting at GGE, there was a lengthy discussion about the problems the company has been experiencing. In the past 12 months, competitors have introduced some new products into the market, which are technically superior to GGE's products, and competitors appear to be capturing a much bigger share of the market.

The quality of service to customers has been a problem. Sales orders seem to take a long time to process, and there have been problems with production scheduling. The despatch department and the production department do not liaise as closely as they should, in spite of long and frequent meetings between the departments to discuss production and despatching difficulties.

The finance director has suggested that the company should consider introducing a continuous improvement programme. The production director believes that the company's problems are serious, and a continuous improvement programme would be of little value. He is in favour of hiring a firm of management consultants with a view to designing a business process re-engineering project.

The managing director recognises the competitive threat from rival companies, and he is concerned that GGE has not responded to technological change as fast as it should.

Required:

(a)   Describe the main features of business process re-engineering (BPR).   **(5 marks)**

(b)   Compare a continuous improvement or kaizen approach to process improvement with a BPR approach, and suggest the circumstances in which a BPR approach might be more appropriate.   **(10 marks)**

(c)   Describe the approach that is taken in a BPR model for change.   **(15 marks)**

(Total: 30 marks)

MARKETING

210   MARKETING FUNCTION: CONCEPTS

Marketing mix has been defined as 'the set of controllable variables and their levels that the firm use to influence the target market'. There are a great number of marketing mix variables, the most popular classification being the four Ps.

(a)   Outline the characteristics of each of the four Ps.   **(12 marks)**

(b)   Discuss how you would expect a manager to apply many, but not necessarily all, of the principles of the four Ps to the marketing of a well-established tourist attraction, for example a theme park, whose popularity is beginning to fall slightly.   **(18 marks)**

(Total: 30 marks)

211   SEGMENTING

In the last few decades, companies have moved increasingly towards the targeting of particular customer segments rather than seeking to sell a single product range to all customers.

Required:

(a)   Explain the advantages that a company might hope to gain by targeting particular segments of the market.   **(10 marks)**

(b)   Describe three variables you think would be useful as a basis for segmenting the market for clothing sold by a large retail chain, and two variables for segmenting the market in paint sold to other businesses by a paint manufacturer.

Explain your reasons for the choice of all five variables.   **(10 marks)**

(c)   Explain how the growth of the internet and online shopping has created a variety of opportunities for reaching small, previously unprofitable segments.   **(10 marks)**

(Total: 30 marks)

212   GREEN COMPANY

Green Company produces gardening equipment which it sells mainly through garden centres and retail outlets in domestic markets, although there are a few sales to distributors in other countries. Its products are well-established, and its Greengrowers brand name for gardening equipment is well-known. The market is very competitive, and the company is continually designing and developing new products and new models. However, the sales management have expressed some concern that changes in the age structure of the population and changes in life style preferences could have a damaging effect on gardening equipment sales.

At a recent meeting, the company's new sales director raised two issues. First, he expressed some concern that the company did not seem to have reliable information about the position of the company's products in its market, how large the markets might be and what the company's share of its markets is. Secondly, he said that he would like to obtain reasonable forecasts of expected sales of a new range of gardening products that the company has designed and plans to launch on the market early next year.

Required:

(a)   Suggest why a company might want to obtain estimates of the total market size, and suggest the methods the Green Company might use to establish the current size of the market and its own market share.   **(15 marks)**

(b)   Suggest the methods that might be used to forecast sales demand for the new range of products.   **(15 marks)**

(Total: 30 marks)

213   RESTFUL HOTELS

Restful Hotels operates a chain of four-star hotels in several countries. Some of the hotels are situated in city centres, but others are in holiday resort centres and on holiday islands. The company's management has been very successful in controlling its operating costs, and the company is profitable. The company is opening new hotels currently at the rate of about three each year.

However, the management are concerned that total sales revenue is growing slowly, and sales income at the new hotels is particularly disappointing. The room occupancy rate is below budget, and there are vacant rooms in most hotels at most times of the year. The quality of service to guests does not appear to have deteriorated, and customers appear to be satisfied with the service they receive.

Two suggestions have been made to increase the rate of revenue growth. One is to use pricing as a marketing tool to attract more customers. The other is to try to attract more customers by focusing on an additional segment of the market.

Required:

(a) Suggest how the company might use pricing as an element in its marketing mix, as a means of increasing total sales revenue. **(14 marks)**

(b) Suggest how market segmentation, and focusing on new segments of the market, might possibly help to increase total sales. **(6 marks)**

(c) Suggest why the company has to be careful in using pricing as an element of its marketing strategy. **(10 marks)**

(Total: 30 marks)

214 TROY BOATS

Troy Boats manufactures and sells a range of boats, from small sailing boats up to medium-sized motor cruisers. Sales demand for boats of all kinds is growing at a very fast rate, and the management of the company are very excited about future prospects. Sales growth is expected to continue, as an increasing proportion of the population take to sailing as a leisure activity.

The company's sales director believes that now might be the right time to use brand awareness as a method of establishing Troy Boats as a major producer in the market. Branding is currently not much used, but as the market expands, the sales director believes that branding will be a major feature of the market. He has proposed that Troy Boats should develop a new brand, Argo 0, as a way of positioning itself in this growing market.

He recognises that establishing a brand in a market can be a difficult task, and if Troy Boats is to succeed with a branding initiative, it will need to go through four stages of brand positioning in the market. If the company can do this successfully, it could become extremely successful.

Required:

(a) Explain the stages of brand positioning for a new branded range of products.

(12 marks)

(b) Suggest how the company might develop the Argo 0 brand in each of these stages.

(12 marks)

(c) Suggest why it might be difficult to build a brand for this type of product. **(6 marks)**

(Total: 30 marks)

215 BLACK COMPANY

Black Company sells a range of confectionery (sweets and chocolates) under a very popular brand name. Some of its products are made in its own factories, but others are purchased from suppliers in Central Europe. The company has several product ranges, each sold under a different brand name. It spends heavily on advertising.

One of its most successful products is a range of children's sweets, sold in plastic containers that the children can use for a while as toys when the sweets have been eaten.

The newly appointed managing director has stated his intention of making the company more socially and environmentally aware. He has introduced a business ethics policy, and has discussed with all his directors the need to consider Corporate Social Responsibility (CSR) in all its operations and activities. The marketing director has been asked to consider how the company might implement CSR initiatives in marketing.

Required:

(a) Describe the factors that the company should consider when developing its CSR policies. **(10 marks)**

(b) Suggest ways in which CSR policies might be applied within the area of marketing.

(10 marks)

(c) Suggest reasons for Black Company to have a commercial interest in focusing on its CSR policies. **(10 marks)**

(Total: 30 marks)

216 H COMPANY

H Company, a high-street clothing retailer, designs and sells clothing. Until recently, the company name was well-known for quality clothing at an affordable price, but the situation has changed dramatically as new entrants to the market have rapidly taken market share away from H Company.

One marketing analyst has commented that the problem for H Company is that it has never moved from being sales orientated to being marketing orientated and that this is why it has lost touch with its customers.

Required:

(a) Describe the difference between a company that concentrates on 'selling' its products and one that has adopted a marketing approach. Advise H Company on how to develop itself into an organisation that is driven by customer needs. **(10 marks)**

(b) Explain how the management in H Company could make use of the marketing mix to help regain its competitive position in the clothing market. **(10 marks)**

(c) The fashion editor of a national newspaper has offered to feature H Company's clothes regularly in a new 'makeover' article that will appear in weekend editions. In return, H Company will have to agree to running a full-page advert in the newspaper at least once per week.

Explain whether this offer is worth considering. **(10 marks)**

(Total: 30 marks)

217 LO-SPORT LTD

Lo-Sport Ltd (LS) is a manufacturer of sports equipment. It was set up in the south of England in 1988 by two famous, retired professional tennis players Rodney Connors and James Laver, who are the directors and sole shareholders. The company currently produces two types of product – sports rackets and sports shoes.

It manufactures specialist rackets for squash, tennis and badminton, using the latest technology, making them suitable for professional and advanced players. The rackets sell for approximately ten times the average price of rackets available in the high street.

LS also manufactures sports shoes for the mass market. The company's sales of these shoes have, however, been declining for some years, largely due to severe competition from much larger international manufacturers. There has also been a decline in industry sales in recent years. Sports shoes are nevertheless still seen as a fashion item and the large companies support their products with significant advertising.

A friend of the LS directors, Barry Borg, who is a retired research scientist, is employed by LS. Last year he developed a new rubber product, Katex, which he incorporated into a redesigned sports shoe. Early tests of the 'Katex shoe' proved extremely successful, demonstrating enhanced comfort, durability and performance. The product was patented by LS but sales have not yet commenced. However, a major marketing boost was given to the product recently when a prototype shoe was used by an athlete to achieve a world record time for running 400 metres.

Requirements:

(a) Describe the main features of the product lifecycle ('PLC'). **(8 marks)**

(b) Identify and explain the strategic position of each of LS's products within the PLC. Assess the implications of this positioning in determining the extent to which LS should invest in each of its products. **(12 marks)**

(c) Describe the advantages and disadvantages of penetration pricing over price skimming for the new product Katex. **(10 marks)**

(Total: 30 marks)

218 SX SNACKS (NOV 05 EXAM)

SX is a growing company that has successfully used local radio advertising for the past few years to raise awareness of its products. It supplies fresh 'quality' sandwiches, home-baked snacks, the finest coffee and freshly squeezed fruit juices for sale at premium prices in petrol filling stations. Products are produced by traditional methods from very early morning by a team of employees at a central depot and are delivered throughout the day by a few casual workers in a fleet of vehicles.

SX has for the first time undertaken a full strategic marketing planning process. One weakness identified was that the number of deliveries required was increasing, while some of the drivers were becoming increasingly unreliable. The owner is worried that this may create an unfavourable image with customers and lead to delays in delivery.

In terms of opportunities, the owner of SX is now aware that, by using technology to a greater degree and identifying customer needs more fully, the firm can grow at an even greater rate. To this end it is proposed that time-saving food preparation and packaging equipment be purchased. This will mean considerably fewer people involved in food preparation but the owner feels that some employees could be redeployed as drivers on a permanent basis. The role of driver would be redefined and, in addition to making deliveries, he or she would be expected to:

- get direct feedback from customers

- persuade petrol stations to take new product lines

- provide intelligence on competitor's products and likely future demand

- hopefully persuade other petrol stations and outlets (such as railway stations and newspaper shops) to stock SX products.

The owner is keen to progress change, consequently:

- The head of delivery and customer relationships has been tasked with developing new job and person details for the driver posts. These will then be discussed with existing food preparation staff.

- A marketing action plan will soon be prepared based on the strategic marketing plan, which will contain immediate marketing issues and actions required. Some detail is already available on people and price so the main areas to consider are product, place and promotion.

Required:

(a) Based on your understanding of the changes proposed by SX, identify the main issues that will be included in the marketing action plan and discuss the implications of these. Your response should consider issues of product, place and promotion only.

(10 marks)

(b) Based upon the information given to you concerning SX, and your own study and experience, produce a draft job description for the redefined post of driver. **(10 marks)**

(Total: 20 marks)

MANAGING HUMAN CAPITAL

219 TAXIS AND TYRES (PILOT PAPER)

A year ago, the owner-manager of a taxi service also moved into a new business area of fitting tyres. This came about as a result of the experience of using unbranded tyres on the fleet of ten taxis. Based on several years of use, the owner-manager found that the unbranded tyres lasted almost as long as the branded tyres, but had the advantage of being obtainable at half the price. The set-up costs of the tyre-fitting business were relatively modest and the owner-manager initially fitted the tyres himself. Demand picked up quickly, however, and he was forced to employ an experienced fitter. A few months later, demand accelerated again and he has just advertised for another fitter but, unfortunately, without success.

The tyre-fitting business has produced additional challenges and the owner-manager is finding it increasingly difficult to manage both the taxi service and the new business where he seems to be spending more and more of his time. He already employs one receptionist/taxi controller, but has realised that he now needs another.

As if this were not enough, he is in the middle of extending his operations still further. Customers who buy tyres frequently request that he check the wheel alignment on their car following the fitting of new tyres. He has started to provide this service, but when done manually it is a slow process, so he has invested heavily in a new piece of electronic equipment. This new technology will speed the alignment operation considerably, but neither he nor his tyre-fitter can operate the equipment. The owner feels that tyre fitters should be able to operate the equipment, and an additional member of staff is not required just to operate it.

To add to all these problems, two of his taxi drivers have resigned unexpectedly. Past patterns suggest that of the ten drivers, normally one or two leave each year, generally in the summer months, though now it is winter.

Given all these staffing difficulties, the owner-manager has made use of a relative who happens to have some HR expertise. She has advised the owner-manager on recruitment and selection, training and development. The relative also suggests that the business needs a well thought out human resource plan.

Required:

(a) Prepare an outline human resource plan for the business and explain each aspect of your plan.
(12 marks)

(b) Discuss the important human resource activities to which attention should be paid in order to obtain the maximum contribution from the workforce.

Note: For requirement (b), exclude those areas upon which the relative has already provided advice to the owner-manager (recruitment and selection, training and development).
(8 marks)

(Total: 20 marks)

220   T CITY POLICE

The T City Police Force has been subjected to considerable criticism in recent years. The first criticism is from some of the citizens of T City who claim racial harassment and slow response to emergency calls. The second is from a government audit which found that T City Police Force had a poorer record on crime prevention and convictions for crime than any of the other nine city police forces in the country.

As well as a number of other measures the T City Chief of Police has accepted a recommendation from the head of human resources to implement a performance appraisal system linked to a Performance-Related Pay (PRP) system. A spokesman for the Association of Police Officers has objected to the proposed appraisal and PRP systems on the grounds that limited government funding and the poor socio-economic conditions of T City district will make the system unworkable.

Required:

(a)   Explain the purpose of performance appraisal. Discuss how the T City Police Force could use the information from the performance appraisal system to improve the performance of its police officers.   **(12 marks)**

(b)   In the light of comments made by the spokesman for the Association of Police Officers, discuss the potential problems associated with the introduction of the proposed performance appraisal system and the performance-related pay system.

(18 marks)

(Total: 30 marks)

221   RECRUITMENT

Required:

(a)   Describe the process of recruitment.   **(10 marks)**

(b)   Discuss some of the major problems and issues for firms in selecting the right candidate.   **(10 marks)**

(c)   Describe the importance of job analysis in the context of recruitment.   **(10 marks)**

(Total: 30 marks)

222   MANAGEMENT DEVELOPMENT

You are required to:

(a)   define 'management development'   **(4 marks)**

(b)   describe the steps that an organisation should take to implement a formal management development system.   **(16 marks)**

(c)   describe the proces of succession planning.   **(10 marks)**

(Total: 30 marks)

223   REWARD SYSTEMS

Describe and discuss the main features to be included in a reward system.   **(30 marks)**

224   DISMISSAL, RETIREMENT, REDUNDANCY

Describe the various processes which lead to employees leaving an organisation, whether planned or unplanned.   **(30 marks)**

225 HUMAN RESOURCE PLAN

Like many other companies, X has to respond to a variety of pressures for change. Increasing competition has forced company X to reduce costs by downsizing its personnel numbers and reducing the size of the head office. Further measures have included a greater concentration on its core business and processes. To date, these pressures have had a limited effect on the finance department, but the finance director is now under pressure to reduce the number of personnel employed in her department by 30 per cent over the next two years, and by a total of 50 per cent within a five-year period.

In the initial review of the task facing her, the finance director appreciates that she has to take into account a number of changes that are affecting the finance function. These include the ever-increasing application of IT, the increasing financial pressure to outsource transactions and other routine operations to large service centres, and the expectation by the chief executive that finance personnel will play a fuller part in the management of the business.

The department currently employs 24 people divided almost equally between three areas: financial accounting, management accounting and the treasury function.

The age/experience profile is a mix of older, experienced specialist staff, a young to middle-aged group of qualified accountants (many of whom also possess MBA degrees), and a group of trainees with limited experience who have yet to qualify.

Three of the older staff are within five years of the statutory retirement age; two more will move into this category within the time period set by senior management. One or two of the younger qualified staff have been looking for other jobs and one of the trainees has applied for maternity leave.

The finance director has arranged a meeting with the human resources director to discuss the development of a human-resource plan for future staffing, training and development of personnel in the finance department.

Required:

(a)   Describe the main stages of the human resource planning process and briefly explain how manpower planning fits into this process.   **(12 marks)**

(b)   Taking the role of the finance director, prepare a paper by way of preparation for your forthcoming meeting. Explain the key considerations that you will need to take into account in the development of a human resource plan for your department.

(18 marks)
(Total: 30 marks)

226 APPRAISAL

The performance appraisal process is now well established in large organisations.

Required:

(a)   Describe briefly the most common objectives of a performance appraisal system.

(6 marks)

(b)   Explain why appraisal systems are often less effective in practice than they might be, and advise what management can do to try to ensure their effectiveness.   **(14 marks)**

(c)   Describe the role of the appraisal interview in determining the success or failure of the appraisal system.   **(10 marks)**

(Total: 30 marks)

227 S SOFTWARE COMPANY

Discussion of the human resource development plan in the S Software Company has revealed considerable disagreement between members of the management team. Janet, the managing director, and Jean, the human resource manager, have ambitious long-term plans for the training and development of staff. By contrast, Andy, the production manager, is concerned with how production will be staffed when these people 'go on a company-paid training course at a luxury hotel'. Colin, the marketing manager, is afraid that other firms will 'recruit our newly-trained workers'. Maurice, the management accountant, wonders whether the costs of training and development will ever show a return.

Required:

(a) Explain why Andy, Colin and Maurice have some concerns about training and development, and discuss the likely reasons for those concerns. **(8 marks)**

(b) Taking the role of Jean, describe to your management colleagues the key factors that you would have considered in drawing up the S Software Company's human resource development plan. Explain how the implementation of the plan could contribute to the overall performance of the company. **(12 marks)**

(c) Taking Colin's position to its logical conclusion, explain why it might be undesirable to rely on recruiting suitably trained and experienced staff from competing software companies as an alternative to training existing staff. **(10 marks)**

(Total: 30 marks)

228 R COMPANY

The finance department of R Company, a large hotel group, has experienced a range of human resource problems following the recruitment of a large number of professional members of staff. Several people have left within the first year and others have not performed as well as might have been expected.

The R Company's human resource management department has suggested that one possible reason might be the Company's lack of a systematic induction programme for new staff.

Required:

(a) Produce a plan detailing the key activities that need to be covered in a systematic induction programme for the R Company. **(15 marks)**

(b) Explain how an induction programme can help to overcome the problems experienced by the finance department of R Company as described in the scenario above.

(15 marks)

(Total: 30 marks)

229 CX BEERS (MAY 05 EXAM)

The country Mythland contains several areas of high unemployment, one such area is where CX Beers were produced until recently. CX was an old, family-owned brewery that supplied licensed outlets, including local restaurants, with its beer. CX represented one of the last local brewers of any size, despite retaining many working practices that evolved at least a century ago. Situated on a (now) underused dockside site, the company had, over the years, invested little in plant and machinery and someone jokingly once suggested that much of the brewing equipment should rightfully be in a museum! The company was forced to cease trading last month, despite having an enthusiastic, long-serving, highly skilled workforce and a national reputation for the beer 'CX Winter Warmer' (thanks to winning several national awards). The workforce, many of whom have only ever worked for CX Beers are now facing up to the difficulty of finding alternative employment.

In a press statement the owners said that the brewery's closure was sad for the area, the local workforce and traditionally brewed beer in general. The owners blamed the situation on inefficient and expensive brewing methods, fierce competition from large rival brewers and limited geographical sales. They also mentioned a dependence on seasonal sales that made cash flow difficult (35% over the Christmas period). They concluded that they would like the CX tradition to continue by selling the company as a going concern, however unlikely this was.

It is speculated that property developers may be interested in the site as the dockland area is showing signs of regeneration as a leisure and tourism attraction (thanks to the efforts of the Mythland government). However, two of CX's managers would like to save the business and are drawing up a business plan for a management buy-out. They have three main initiatives that they feel could, in combination, save the enterprise:

- use the site as a basis for a 'living' museum of traditionally brewed beer (with out of date brewing equipment and methods of working as an attraction)

- produce bottled beer for sales in supermarkets

- employ a more flexible but suitably experienced workforce.

One of the managers (your former boss) has asked for your help in advising him how to draft a detailed human resource (HR) plan to inform the business plan.

Required:

(a)   Describe the main issues and stages involved in developing a human resource (HR) plan for the CX buy-out idea.   **(12 marks)**

(b)   Discuss how the buy-out team can achieve workforce flexibility.   **(8 marks)**

(Total: 20 marks)

230   COMPANY A AND B

Company A has acquired Company B. As part of a wide ranging effort to integrate Company B into its operations, systems and procedures, the management of Company A has decided to combine the two existing finance departments. A new finance department will be formed in the headquarters building of Company A. The move by Company B Finance staff to Company A headquarters will mean, for most, a daily road journey of some 20 miles each way.

Required:

(a)   Discuss the concerns that Company B finance staff will have as they consider their move to Company A headquarters. Explain why an induction programme is necessary for Company B staff.   **(12 marks)**

(b)   Produce an induction programme that will help support Company B finance staff in their move to Company A, and which will enable them to contribute productively to the enlarged Company.   **(12 marks)**

(c)   Explain how Company A should organise its grievance procedures with respect to the integration of former Company B staff.   **(6 marks)**

(Total: 30 marks)

231 Z COMPANY

On appointment to her new post as Head of Finance in the Z Company, H discovers that the training and development of the finance staff has been badly neglected. This lack is all the more surprising to H when she reflects on the many changes that have affected the work of accounting and finance professionals in the last decade.

The Company does not have a specialist human resource management function so departmental heads have to organise training and development for the staff within their departments.

Required:

(a) Describe the potential problems associated with the neglect of staff training and development in a time of rapid change for:

(i) Z Company's finance staff

(ii) the Z Company. **(15 marks)**

(b) Discuss the activities that must be undertaken in order to provide a set of effective training and development programmes for Z Company's finance staff. **(15 marks)**

(Total: 30 marks)

232 JANE SMITH

Jane Smith has very recently been made a partner in a medium-sized accounting practice with the requirement that she take charge of the practice's Casterbridge office. The office comprises about ten secretarial, technician and part-qualified audit staff. Jane has never worked at the Casterbridge office and, as part of a first attempt to familiarise herself with the office, she has examined the staff files and associated correspondence. She has been surprised to find that staff turnover and sickness are far higher than in the other practice offices and that there appears to have been a succession of quality problems related to poor client care and operational mistakes.

She has also asked the senior partner if he can explain the reasons for the apparent staff related problems to which he replied 'Well we may have had a number of unavoidable changes in partners responsible for Casterbridge over the last few years but remember, Jane, that we do pay staff above market wage rates and provide good working conditions. What we undoubtedly are looking at here is a case of far too slack management control and supervision'.

Required:

(a) In the light of relevant theories of motivation and the statement made by the senior partner comment on the apparent staff problems in the Casterbridge office. **(15 marks)**

(b) Acting in the role of Jane explain how you would proceed in seeking to improve the apparent staff problems in the Casterbridge office. **(15 marks)**

(Total: 30 marks)

233 NS INSURANCE COMPANY (NOV 05 EXAM)

NS is a large insurance company. The company is structured into four divisions and supported by a small headquarters that includes the personnel function (recently renamed the Human Resources (HR) Division). The post of Head of HR is vacant following the retirement of the long-serving post holder, and the HR strategy is in urgent need of review and revision.

NS has recently announced a new corporate initiative of continuous improvement through the empowerment of its workforce. The Chief Executive explained: "We value our people as our most prized asset. We will encourage them to think, challenge and innovate. Only through empowering them in this way can we achieve continuous improvement. Staff will no longer be expected just to obey orders; from now on they will make and implement decisions to bring about continuous improvement. We want to develop clear performance objectives and be more customer focused." Your line manager is one of the four Divisional Directors and will soon form part of a panel that will interview candidates for the vacant role of HR Director. She is particularly keen to ensure that the successful candidate would be able to shape the HR Division to the needs of the organisation. She is aware of your CIMA studies and has asked for your help in preparing for the interview.

Required:

Produce outline notes for your Divisional Director which discuss the main points you would expect candidates to highlight in response to the following two areas she intends to explore with candidates at the interview, specifically:

(a) the likely role that the HR Division will perform in the light of the changing nature of the organisation; and **(10 marks)**

(b) the aspects of the HR strategy that will change significantly, given the nature of recent developments within NS. **(10 marks)**

(Total: 20 marks)

234 NYO.COM

NYO.com was established in February 20X3. Since then, the company, which provides on-line financial advice, has experienced rapid growth and the management has not really had the time to get all management systems and procedures into place.

The company has asked you to look at the way in which the company deals with its disciplinary problems and procedures. The chief executive officer has asked you to do two things.

Required:

(a) Recommend guidelines for drawing up a disciplinary procedure. **(12 marks)**

(b) Explain why NYO.com should have a formal disciplinary procedure. **(8 marks)**

(c) Describe the circumstances under which NYO.com would be within its rights to dismiss an employee. **(10 marks)**

(Total: 30 marks)

Section 4

ANSWERS TO SECTION A-TYPE QUESTIONS

INFORMATION SYSTEMS

1   A

These are examples of hardware (equipment) and all are used for the input of data (and so are input devices rather than processing devices).

2   A

A local area networks (LAN) is a linked network of computers, terminals and other devices (such as printers) within a limited geographical area. The small geographical area means that the communications links can be provided by cables without the need for modems (unlike wide area networks (WANs), which are linked through an external communications network).

3   A

In General System Theory, entropy is a measure of disorder in a system. Left on its own, an open system will tend to break down into randomness and disorder.

4   B

An intranet is an internal network within an organisation that makes use of the internet. It can be used for communications to employees and also between employees. However, e-mail is used for communications between employees within an intranet, not chat rooms.

5   D

With a database, there is a single set of data files, rather than several different systems, each system with its own separate set of files. A major advantage of a database is avoiding the duplication of data. Data integrity means avoiding inconsistencies between the data used by different computer applications. Having one set of files and avoiding duplication of data (where the duplicated data might not be consistent with each other) therefore helps to achieve data integrity.

Note that databases do not provide unlimited access. Access to some or all of a database can be restricted by the use of passwords. Answer B is therefore incorrect.

6   A

An expert system such as a system for law or taxation might be purchased 'off the shelf', but it does not provide a 'powerful software solution' (whatever this means!). Answer C describes a help facility. Answer A is the most appropriate answer: an expert system is a database that contains data obtained from expert knowledge (e.g. in the law or medicine) and experience.

7   A

Re-writing software for an existing system to meet new user requirements is called adaptive maintenance. The re-written software enables the system to *adapt* to meet the changing requirements.

8   B

The old and new systems are run in parallel for a time, until the new system is seen to be operating efficiently and as intended. This is parallel running when the entire organisation switches to operating both systems simultaneously. With a pilot test, one part of the organisation (such as one branch or one region) switches from the old to the new system first, as a test. With phased changeover, the entire organisation switches from the old to the new system one part or phase at a time, until the entire new system is introduced.

9   B

A diagram that illustrates the relationships between 'entities' in a system is an entity relationship model. The relationships are 'one-to-one', 'one-to-many' or 'many-to-many', as indicated by the ends of the lines joining the related entities (which are a single line indicating one or a 'crow's foot' indicating many).

10   C

The PCs in the branches are 'clients' linked to a central server, and the relationship is therefore 'client/server'.

11   D

Decision support systems are used to assist managers in developing forecasts or solutions to problems. They are generally used at middle management level, whereas executive information systems are used by senior managers to obtain information from both internal and external sources. A MIS is a system providing information for management, in the form of reports or file interrogation facilities, but do not offer any decision-making support (such as forecasting model software).

12   C

The controlling software is the database management system (DBMS). A database administrator is an individual who looks after the operation of the database system.

13   B

Entropy represents the disorder or chaos in a system. It occurs when an 'open system', such as a sales system, does not receive new inputs continually from its environment so that it can continue to adapt. Here, the system does not receive new information about customers. When entropy occurs, a system moves into a state of disorder: here, the sales system that made use of the customer file no longer functions.

14   D

A dumb terminal is usually a terminal with keyboard, mouse and screen, which has no processing capabilities of its own, but which is used for input to and output from a central computer. In large computer systems, there may be dumb terminals and/or intelligent terminals. Intelligent terminals are usually PCs, which have processing capabilities for 'local' data processing.

15   A

Faults in the system design are the responsibility of the system designer (systems analyst) or a weakness in the user specification for the system: they have nothing to do with the consequence of inadequate training for employees. A lack of training will make employees more suspicious of a new system (as a threat to their job security, perhaps) and will be reluctant to use something they know little about and mistrust. In addition, since they are unfamiliar with the system, employees are likely to make a high number of errors, and will be slow in carrying out their processing tasks (for example, slow in preparing input of transaction data to the computer).

16   A

Delaying the implementation of the system will simply delay the problems with employees, and at the same time it will delay the benefits to the organisation from using the new system. It should be apparent that participation and involvement, and education and communication are effective methods of overcoming employee suspicions and resistance. Another way of overcoming resistance might be to negotiate an agreement with employee's trade union or staff association representatives.

Coercion might also be an effective way of overcoming resistance. Employees might be told to use the system efficiently, or face the consequences. However, the use of coercion tactics would probably be considered unethical by most organisations.

17   B

An Extranet is similar to an Intranet, with the exception that access to the system is provided to some external users as well as to employees of the organisation. Answer A describes electronic data interchange (EDI) and answer C describes outsourcing.

18   D

A network server is a computer (usually high-end, i.e. 'faster', 'bigger') that allows computers in a network to have a shared resource. Most servers in the district are used to share files, to run programs, or to share printers.

19   C

If the sales value is below $5,000 but the customer is not new, the credit granted should be 60 days.

20   B

A standby mainframe (in a different location) can ensure continuity of processing, provided that backup files of the system are continually produced (and also stored in a different location).

21   B

Floppy disks do not have the capacity to hold a file, and DVDs have too much capacity if files are only up to 600 Mb in size. CD is the most appropriate medium. In this case, it would appear that the back-up files are copies of magazines already published, which means that there will not be any requirement to alter the files at any later time. CD ROM is therefore more suitable than read/write CDs.

22 D

In a distributed data processing system, processing tasks can be distributed to computers throughout the network and shared by those computers. Distributed data processing is an alternative to having all transactions processed centrally.

23 C

A mouse is not a practical input device for busy check-out desks. A display screen is an output device, not an input device. A check-out desk will use mainly a bar code reader or scanner device. A touch screen is used for pricing 'loose items' such as fresh vegetables and fruit. A keyboard is used for input when a bar code cannot be read properly, and to input some basic commands.

24 D

A star network has a central computer and all other computers in the network are linked to it directly. In a tree network, also called a hierarchical network, the computers are in three or more layers or tiers. A central computer is linked to a number of second tier computers, and each second tier computer is linked to a number of third tier computers, and so on. Computers in the third tier are not linked directly to the central computer, only to their second tier computer.

25 A

New files need to be created for the new system. When an old system is being replaced, this involves a conversion of files in the 'old' format to files in the format required for the new system. This is followed by implementation of the system, by whatever changeover method is preferred (pilot testing, etc). Review and maintenance are stages in the system life cycle after implementation, but are not a part of the development and implementation process.

26 B

By definition the answer is B.

27 B

EDI usually involves the transfer of information between different companies and is used for buying and selling.

28 These tools are used by systems analysts to help in designing a new system, and also with the documenting of a new system, for the benefit of:

- themselves, to ensure that they understand the logic of the system

- programmers

- future systems adaptations and maintenance.

The tools enable a systems analyst to draw the logic or features of the system in a form that is more easy to read and understand than a long narrative explanation.

29 The advantages of phased changeover might be as follows:

- It provides better opportunities for testing each part of the new system and resolving any difficulties, before introducing the next part of the new system.

- It gives employees more time to adapt to the new system. This might reduce 'hostility' to the new system.

- It gives more time for re-training and re-deployment of staff whose jobs are taken away by the new system.

30 In-house development of a new system is an alternative to a purchase of an 'off the shelf' software package.

- An in-house developed IS should be designed more closely to meet the specific information requirements of the organisation.

- An in-house developed IS should be designed by means of collaboration between the system designers and the system users. Because the system is designed and tested in-house, users are more likely to accept it quickly and make good use of it.

31 A server is a computer within a computer network. It may be used for:

- holding shared data files for users of the network

- holding shared programs for users of the network

- acting as a 'host computer' for the organisation's intranet system

- operating the organisation's internal e-mail system.

32 (a) De-coupling means reducing the interdependence between two sub-systems within a system, so that each sub-system can operate independently of the other. Changes in one sub-system do not therefore have an immediate effect on the other sub-system. De-coupling can therefore be useful for controlling sub-systems and for introducing changes into sub-systems.

(b) A DBMS and a database provide de-coupling within an information system because the data held on file (the database) is de-coupled from the uses to which the data is put (the applications software). Changes can be made to the data on file without affecting the user software. Application software can be altered without affecting the data on file.

33 System software is software that enables a computer system to carry out basic operational functions so that the computer 'works'. Systems software can be distinguished from application software, which is software that enables a computer user to process data and access information.

The three main categories of system software are:

- An operating system. This directs and controls the basic functions of the computer and its peripheral equipment and the transfer of data within the computer and between the computer and its peripheral equipment.

- Utility programs. These are programs that carry out certain 'housekeeping' routines or functions, such as copying files, sorting data on a file and checking for viruses.

- Communications software. This is used in computer network systems to control the communication links between computers, terminals and other equipment (for example coding, transmitting and receiving data over communications links).

Tutorial note

You might not have identified these three categories of system software, and other solutions – *if correct* in identifying different types of system software – would be acceptable.

34 **A**

For example, Windows XP.

35 **C**

A computer system must include both hardware and software – answer C is the only one to include both of these.

36 An extranet is an intranet that has been extended to include business partners. The advantages are:

- quicker information flow to/from partners
- makes e-procurement easier as a supplier can check whether or not you need more stock
- quicker transactions if partners are customers or suppliers
- strengthens relationship with partners due to implied trust.

37 An open system has a high level of interaction with its external environment. Adaptive maintenance is amending the system to adjust to changes in its environment. In a dynamic business environment an open IS system will require regular adaptive maintenance or it will quickly become out of date and irrelevant.

38 A direct changeover from an old to a new system without pilot schemes or parallel running would be used if:

- the managers have complete trust in the new system (for example, an off-the-shelf package that has been used elsewhere)

- the problems for the computer user will be tolerable, even if the system fails to function properly

- none of the other changeover methods are practicable

- as a symbolic gesture – for example, as part of a larger change process.

39 Some firms may prefer to use manual systems for the following reasons:

- lack of confidence in the computer system, due to problems with other IT systems before

- lack of training in the new system

- group resistance to change

- fears of job losses

- staff feel that the manual system is very efficient

- lack of effective leadership.

40   Both are used as input devices to some computer systems.

A scanner is used to read a document, and capture its image digitally for input to the computer. The scanned image can be a document, including text, diagrams and pictures, and the layout of the scanned document is also retained. Scanners are used in an office environment, typically for the input of images into a program that produces documents, such as a desktop publishing system.

A digital camera is used to take photographs in digital form, and can be used in any location or environment. The captured images can be fed from the camera into a computer and filed. The images can also be manipulated if required. The stored images can be used to produce photographs, or for input to other computer systems (such as desk-top publishing systems).

41   A data flow diagram (DFD) is a method of documenting how data is transferred, processed and stored within a system. There are four elements in a DFD:

(1)   Data sources. A data source is the source from which data comes or the destination to which data is sent. Typically, a data source is an organisation, department or individual.

(2)   Data processes. A data process is a process or activity within the system. A box depicting a data process in a DFD will indicate both what the process is and who carries out the process.

(3)   Data flows. A data flow is the movement of data from one element in the system to another, for example from a data source or a data store to a data process, or from a data process to a data process or a data store.

(4)   Data stores. A data store is a data file.

42   Data independence is the separation of data from the programs that use the data. The whole concept of a database management system (DBMS) supports the notion of data independence since it represents a system for managing data separately from the programs that use the data. The data can be used by different users for different applications and in different ways.

Flexible data management is thus enabled in the following ways:

-   **Less duplication** – data is input once only to update the data on file.

-   Less processing – by minimising data redundancy, storage space in the system files is reduced, and **storage space is used more efficiently**.

-   Updating is much easier, and data is equally up-to-date for all applications.

-   There is **data consistency** (or **data integrity**). All users access the same data and therefore inconsistencies between data in different application systems do not exist.

-   **Improving access to data**. Database systems are designed to allow many different users access to the shared files.

43   Management should consider the following factors when choosing computer hardware:

-   Windows PC or Macintosh?

-   Configuration – do you need DVD drives, wireless capability, etc?

-   Power/speed – do you really need the latest top of the range model for word processing?

-   Upgradeability – how future-proof is the system?

-   Portability – do you need laptops or permanent desk workstations?

-   Cost?

-   Reliability – what reputation does the supplier have?

-   Guarantees / after sales service – e.g. help lines, on-site maintenance?

CHANGE MANAGEMENT

44   A

An internal trigger for change is an event or development within the organisation itself, rather than a change that is started by external developments. IT technological change, environmental legislation and demands for a shorter working week are all examples of external triggers for change, caused by technological, political or social change.

45   D

Driving forces are the forces for change, and restraining forces are the factors resistant to change. To achieve desired change, management should recognise what the key driving and restraining forces are. In principle, change can be achieved either by making the driving forces stronger or the restraining forces weaker. Lewin argued that in practice, it is more effective to reduce the strength of the main restraining forces.

46   C

The five component technologies are:

(a)   systems thinking

(b)   personal mastery

(c)   mental models

(d)   building shared vision

(e)   team learning.

47   A

Kanter suggested that change-adept organisations share the following attributes:

(a)   effective leaders who encourage the development of new concepts – imagination to innovate

(b)   leaders who provide competence both personally and in the organisation as a whole – professionalism to perform

(c)   leaders who make connections with and collaborate with 'partners' outside the organisation – openness to collaborate.

48   D

Beer and Nohria argued in favour of a 'balanced approach', combining concern for economic value (such as reducing the size of the workforce, restructuring or incentive schemes) and concern for human capabilities and the learning process. Using one approach followed by the other will be much less effective in introducing change successfully.

49   B

The other changes are all major 'transformational' changes, that affect the organisation's culture and way of operating.

50   A

Unfreezing is the process of both getting employees to recognise that the current situation is unsatisfactory, and also identifying a better way of doing things. Getting qualified staff to accept that some of their work can be done by trained but unqualified people would be a part of the unfreezing process.

51   B

'Diagnostic' refers to identifying the nature of a problem, and the word is perhaps best understood in the context of carrying out a medical diagnosis to identify the cause of a disease. The 'unfreezing' part of the change process involves identifying the existence of an unsatisfactory situation, and gaining acceptance for an improved situation towards which the organisation should move. The 'intervention' stage is presumably the 'change' or movement' phase in Lewin's model. The change process ends with 're-freezing' which is presumably the 'termination' stage.

52   B

Change in most organisations is triggered by changes in their external environment rather than internal developments. The external changes might affect the organisation's culture and will eventually prompt management action (answers A and D). The trigger for change, however, comes from the external environment.

53   D

Perhaps this is the obvious solution. Answer B implies no change at all. Attempts to impose change are likely to end in failure, and answers A and C are both incorrect. A change culture within an organisation has to start with top management, who must give their full support and encouragement to change programmes.

54   D

An OD programme begins with recognising a problem, which is then analysed and diagnosed. A change agent (typically a firm of management consultants) discusses the problem with the organisation's management and agree a programme for change. This is then planned and implemented. After implementation, the changes are reviewed and evaluated. OD is often associated with the work of Warren Bennis.

55   A

The help-line is to assist staff, not to coerce or manipulate them, and has little to do with appointments (co-optation).

56   D

OD is partly concerned with resolving problems limiting effectiveness and as such could involve each of the three techniques listed.

57 Senge described a learning organisation in which people are continually learning and being creative and adaptive. In a fast-changing environment, learning organisations will excel because they will respond to the changes in the most effective ways. Senge argued that in a learning organisation, there must be two types of learning:

(a) adaptive learning, which is learning how to change the organisation in response to changes in the environment, in order to survive

(b) generative learning, which is learning that improves the ability of individuals to generate new ideas and be creative.

58 Drucker suggested the following as key issues for success in takeovers:

- The purchaser must be convinced that value be added to the target.

- There must be a common core of unity between the two businesses.

- Management must understand the business being acquired.

- The purchaser must be able to put in a quality management team quickly.

- The purchaser must be able to hold onto the best management of both companies.

OPERATIONS MANAGEMENT

59 B

Juran argued that most quality problems are the result of ineffective systems, but poor management is also largely to blame. Although there is some merit in answer A, answer B is more appropriate.

60 B

The '5S' practice aims at achieving and maintaining a high quality work environment. Answer B therefore gives the most appropriate answer. The 5Ss are Sort, Straighten, Shine (or Sweep), Standardise and Sustain. Do not be fooled by the five words beginning with the letter S in answer C.

61 C

Optimised Production Technology (OPT) is a computer-based production scheduling system based on Goldblatt's Theory of Constraints, which states that the capacity to produce is restricted at any time by one bottleneck (key limitation or constraint) in one part of the system. Production scheduling is optimised by recognising this key constraint, and planning production so as to optimise output within the limits imposed by the constraint.

62 D

The main contribution of Deming to quality management was the use and development of statistical control methods. The quality planning road map was devised by Juran; continuous improvement (kaizen) originated in Japan, and the concept of 'zero defects' as promoted by Crosby.

63   B

'Sort' means eliminating unnecessary things in the work place: keeping what is needed and discarding what is not needed. 'Shine' refers to keeping the work place clean. 'Sustain' refers to the need to sustain all improvements, and not slip back into 'bad habits'. The correct answer is 'Straighten'.

64   C

Performance benchmarking is used to compare the organisation's levels of performance in certain key areas (identified before the benchmarking exercise begins, so answer D is wrong). These might be quality, speed of delivery, reliability, flexibility and cost. By making comparisons, the organisation can identify ways in which the benchmark comparison is better, and devise ways of making improvements (so answer B is correct).

Performance benchmarking is not concerned with product design, nor with confirming competitive advantage.

65   D

A Materials Requirements Planning or MRPI system creates a production schedule for end-products from existing and forecast customer demand quantities. It then uses the master production schedule, a bill of materials file, the inventory file and data about production times to produce a detailed schedule for the in-house manufacture of parts and sub-assemblies. It can also produce a purchase requirements schedule for raw materials and components.

An MRPI system is not linked to the computer systems of other functions in the organisation, and answer A refers to MRPII. MRPI schedules production to meet actual and anticipated demand (so answer B is not correct), and is an alternative to scheduling production in economic batch quantities (so answer C is not correct).

66   C

A principle of TQM is that commitment to total quality calls for a TQM culture within the organisation, and all employees should be committed to quality improvement (answer A). The ideal level of defects is zero and there should not be any minimum acceptable level of defects (answer B is incorrect). Statistical quality control is used to monitor defects and provide control reports to management: TQM relies both on employee commitment and statistical quality control – so answer A is not correct. The aim should be to eliminate failure costs, such as costs arising from handling customer complaints, warranties and guarantees, damage to reputation and re-working rejected items. However, some costs relating to quality – prevention costs in particular – have to be incurred – so answer D is incorrect.

67   D

An external failure cost is a cost arising from a quality failure after the product (or service) has been delivered to the customer. Costs arising from defective work before it leaves the organisation's premises (such as the cost of rejects and re-working) are *internal* failure costs.

External failure costs include the cost of meeting claims under warranties or guarantees, (such as replacing defective products) and handling customer complaints. However, although it is very difficult to quantify, it is generally considered that the biggest cost to an organisation from high external failure costs is the cost to the organisation's reputation and future sales orders. For example, dissatisfied customers will not buy its products again.

68   A

The seven types of waste are:

- over-production

- inventory and work-in-progress

- transportation

- waste in processing

- motion

- waiting

- making defective products.

69   C

Lean manufacturing is closely associated with JIT production. In lean manufacturing, production is initiated by customer demand (demand-pull) and products are made to order. Production should either be a continuous work flow, if there is continuous demand, or in small batch sizes. The ideal batch size is 1 – the customer's order. Large batches are not produced, because these create unwanted inventory. There should be small work cells, with all the equipment needed to make the product and all the necessary labour skills: work cells in a small area that do all the work on a product eliminate waste from motion, transportation and waiting. Workers need to be multi-skilled, so that they can switch from one task to another as the situation requires.

70   B

Kanban is a system that originated in Japan, that uses cards or other signalling devices to indicate when work is required at the next stage of the production process. Production occurs only when the appropriate signals are given. This system helps to improve production flow and prevents the over-production of unwanted items.

Answer A refers to kaizen and answer C to quality circles.

71   D

Work flow design, with work organised in small work cells within a small area of the factory floor, can seed up production times and prevent inventory building up. Work flow can be arranged so as to reduce the physical movement of materials and people.

Production should be scheduled to meet customer demand; if necessary, there will be unused capacity. It is better to have several small machines than one large complex machine, because production will be more flexible. The aim should be to reduce set-up times between batches or jobs, because waiting is wasteful.

72   C

With parallel sourcing, Plant A might obtain its key supplies from Supplier 1, whereas Plant B will obtain all its supplies of the same item from Supplier 2 and Plant C from Supplier 3, and so on.

73   B

To meet the objective of adjusting capacity to meet demand, it will be necessary to vary employee numbers or working hours and times, and to hire more or less equipment, to meet changes in demand. Chase demand planning could be appropriate for operations where there are no inventories (or small inventories) and where operations are not capital-intensive.

74   A

BPR seeks radical/transformational change in process (and the processes should be 're-engineered'). In contrast, 5S, 6 Sigma and quality circles are all based on the concept of continuous and incremental improvements.

75   A

'Environment' here relates to green issues.

76   A Just-in-Time system involves purchasing items from suppliers and the production of items only when they are needed to meet demand. A consequence of JIT should be a reduction in inventories of raw materials and components, and finished goods. Expenditure will therefore be incurred later than in a traditional operating environment and the 'cash cycle' should be shorter. This is the time between paying for expenses and receiving payments from customers. As a result, working capital should be lower and cash flows should improve.

77   Quality in manufacturing arises both from the features of a product and also from the elimination of waste and bad workmanship in production. Computer software can assist with the design of new products (computer-aided design) and also with the control of production (computer-aided manufacture). The use of robotics in manufacturing, which helps to achieve error-free production, requires software to control the equipment.

78   Quality control, as the name suggests, is control over the quality of an activity, operation or product. Quality control might involve the inspection of output or the use of statistical techniques by management (quality control charts).

Quality circles are groups of employees from different parts of an organisation, brought together to share ideas and devise ways of improving aspects of quality at work, no matter how small the quality improvements might be.

79   The Six Sigma approach is based on the view that a product (or service) is the end result of a series of processes or operations. If the acceptable rate of error in each process is, say, 1%, the likelihood of error for each unit of end product will be much higher than 1%. In order to control the overall quality of products or services, it is therefore essential to control the quality at each stage in the overall operation to very high standards of rigour.

The overall aim of Six Sigma, conceptually, is to reduce the probability level of defects to the sixth standard deviation (six sigmas) from the norm. If this aim is achieved, total defects will be just 3.4 in one million – close to perfection.

Six Sigma is therefore associated with rigorous risk management and quality control.

80   A company might seek ISO 9000 certification for the following reasons:

- Customers might require a major supplier to have ISO 9000 certification as a pre-condition of doing business with it. Government departments, for example, might be required as a matter of policy only to use ISO 9000 – certificated suppliers.

- ISO 9000 certification provides independent evidence that the company achieves minimum quality standards for its processes. This can enhance the status of the company in comparison with competitors, and make customers more likely to buy from them rather than another supplier.

- Obtaining certification imposes a considerable amount of self-discipline on a company and provides a framework for the company's management to improve its quality standards.

- In some cases, obtaining an appropriate ISO9000 certification might be the 'norm' for the particular industry, which all major manufacturers or suppliers are expected to have.

81   MRP II is a computer system for the integrated planning of a company's equipment, materials and people in order to meet the business plan, requiring the same information (sales forecasts, actual orders, bill of materials and so on) to be used throughout the company.

An ERP system can be described as an MRP II system with the addition of resources planning for non-manufacturing activities and functions, such as plant maintenance and human resources planning.

82   **D**

This is a difficult question as all four aspects are likely to feature in a company with WCM. Answer D is correct as it is the strong customer focus within WCM that drives all other aspects of the business.

83   **B**

ABC can refer to activity based costing (not mentioned here) or a system of stock control where more important lines of stock are given more time and sophisticated sytems to manage them.

84   **A**

The need for correction shows that a failure has occurred, so the answer is A or B. If the corrective work is because a customer has sent the goods back, then it would be an external failure cost. The fact that there is scrap and materials have been lost would indicate that the problem was picked up before goods left the factory, making them internal failure costs.

85   **D**

By definition. Do not confuse with economies of scale, which would be answer C.

86   **A**

Reck and Long's strategic positioning tool looks at the extent to which supply chain management is a strategic issue, so answer A is the closest.

87   D

By definition, according to Porter's value chain.

88   B

You could argue that all four answers could be involved in why a firm decides to consider its supply chain in more etail. However, only answer B gives a direct cause of supply chain partnerships being established.

89   A

It is external benchmarking because the comparison of performance is with an external organisation that is not a rival or competitor. Competitive benchmarking involves making comparisons with a competitor, but this is unlikely to be a co-operative arrangement. (A well-known example of competitive benchmarking was performed in 1979 by Rank Xerox, the US manufacturer of photocopiers, because it had lost significant amounts of market share to new and cheaper Japanese products.)

External benchmarking might also be called 'non-competitive benchmarking' or by the more general term 'performance benchmarking'.

90   D

This definition of benchmarking comes from the American Productivity and Quality Centre.

91   TPM reduces the number of machine breakdowns and makes repairs quicker and easier. It can contribute towards a quality programme by:

- ensuring consistent production
- reducing mistakes and the associated quality failure costs
- motivating staff
- enabling more accurate forecasting and budgeting.

92   • Aiming to meet the needs and expectations of customers.

- Application of TQM to all aspects of the organisation's activities.
- TQM should involve everyone in the organisation.
- Seeking continuous improvement (or getting things right first time).
- Developing systems and procedures to support quality and quality improvement.

93   The concept of a quality chain within an organisation is that the operations within the organisation to make a product or provide a service can be seen as a chain of inter-related activities. For each activity or 'micro-operation', there is an internal supplier who does work for an internal customer, who is then an internal supplier to the next internal customer in the chain. The quality of the end-product or service depends on the quality at each link in the chain, and the overall quality is only as good as the weakest link in the chain.

Internal service level agreements (SLAs) can be used in an organisation to ensure the strength of each link in the quality chain. Each internal supplier and internal customer agrees on quality standards and service standards that the internal supplier undertakes to meet. The internal customer is then able to demand that the internal supplier meets the agreed standards.

94 Documentation is required as evidence that the organisation is actually meeting the necessary quality management standards. Without this evidence, there would be insufficient information for external quality auditors to make a fair assessment.

ISO 9001: 2000 specifies that, as a minimum, there should be documentation relating to:

- the control of documents
- the control of records
- the control of non-conformance with standards
- internal auditing of standards
- corrective action taken
- preventive actions taken.

95 Quality control is concerned with the management of quality and ensuring that actual quality standards, as measured, meet the target or benchmark standards that have been set. There are usually procedures to check quality of bought-in materials, work-in-progress and finished goods.

Quality assurance is the term used where a supplier guarantees the quality of goods supplied and allows the customer access while the goods are being manufactured.

The main differences are as follows:

- Quality control seeks to stop faulty goods reaching the customer ('corrective'), while quality assurance seeks to prevent faulty goods happening in the first place ('preventative').
- Quality control is more concerned with the product, quality assurance with the process.
- Quality assurance looks at building in quality, quality control on detecting quality.

MARKETING

96 C

Selling through the company's website and the internet is a new channel of distribution. Channels of distribution are an element of 'place' within the marketing mix.

97 D

Concentrated marketing means selling a single product to one segment of the market. This is often a suitable marketing strategy for a small business.

98 D

For a retail organisation, the most important considerations are what range and assortment of each product it should stock on its shelves, and what range of different products it should offer and the prices at which they should be (or will be) sold. The task is to find the optimum mix of product assortment and price to maximise sales turnover and/or gross profit margin.

99   D

Differentiated marketing involves offering a product in different forms to different segments of the market, and the product offered to each segment is different from the products offered to the other segments. For example, a car manufacturer makes different models of car, and targets each model at a different segment of the market.

100   A

Market potential is the size of a market that might exist for a product. Sales potential is the possible volume of sales that an organisation might achieve for its own product. In a competitive market, the sales potential for a product is less than the total market potential for the products of all competitors.

101   D

The market share of Product Y last year was 4.8% (10.1/210) and this year it has fallen to 4.5% (10.2/225). Although total sales of Product Y have risen since last year, the total market sales has risen faster. The sales manager might be concerned about this loss of market share.

102   B

Answer B provides the most appropriate definition of marketing and what the aim of marketing strategy should be. Marketing strategy should support the overall business strategy, both long term and short term, with a marketing orientation in its approach. Promoting a marketing culture (answer C) is an aspect of marketing strategy, but not its primary aim.

Focusing on sales (a sales-oriented strategy) is more short-term in outlook. With a sales-oriented approach, there is no particular concern whether or not the organisation's products actually meet customer needs. Taking a marketing-oriented view, meeting customer needs is essential for long-term success as well as short-term profit.

103   C

Interactive marketing involves interaction between the seller and the potential buyer. This happens with telemarketing, where the sales person calling a target customer by telephone speaks to the customer. A direct mail shot and a TV advertising campaign are not interactive forms of marketing. Advertising on a web site is also not interactive, although it would presumably be possible to devise some form of interactive advertisement for putting on the seller's web site.

104   A

Market research is research into a market to establish the potential size of the market, the sales potential for an entity's product or service, or to obtain information about customer needs, or customer satisfaction or dissatisfaction with existing products in the market.

Marketing research is research into marketing activities and methods (for example, research into the effectiveness of billboard advertising). Test marketing is the testing of a new product or service in a small, selected market area. A survey of buyers' intentions is carried out to estimate future sales for industrial goods, and the buyers are commercial organisations, not consumers.

105 B

A marketing decision support system is a DSS for use by marketing management. A DSS is used to assist management planning and decision-making, for example by providing sales forecasts. A DSS includes forecasting models, which can produce forecasts from data about past sales.

Answers A and D relate to a customer database and answer C relates to a management information system.

106 A

Answer A gives a definition of differential pricing. Answer C is an *example* of differential pricing (for example, charging different prices for a rail ticket at different times of the day). Differential pricing can also be applied to place (for example, charging different prices for seats in different parts of a theatre), and to market segment (for example, offering lower prices to students or pensioners).

107 D

'Pull' marketing is aimed at persuading end-consumers to demand a product from distributors (such as retailers), which in turn will result in the distributor wanting to stock and sell the item. TV advertising is an example of a promotion that could be intended to have this 'pull' effect.

108 A

A marketing audit looks at the marketing environment, marketing strategy and objectives and marketing activities (the marketing mix), in order to assess the effectiveness of current marketing strategy and the marketing mix, and to recommend future action.

109 A

An analysis of past sales (answer C) will provide information about total sales, but not about how many customers buy the product, nor in what quantities or how frequently. Observation is useful for looking a customers' buying habits, but does not provide information about the numbers of customers for a product or the frequency of buying. Group interviews can be useful for obtaining information about customer attitudes/consumer attitudes, but the group size is fairly small and so cannot provide reliable estimates of sales measurements.

Sample surveys in different geographical areas – based on interviews with questionnaires – is likely to provide reasonably reliable information about numbers of customers, buying quantities and buying frequency.

110 B

Internal marketing is an activity aimed at getting employees who come into contact with customers (after-sales service staff, counter staff and floor staff in shops, customer service call centre staff etcetera) to recognise the need to meet customer requirements – and training them how to do this.

111 C

The 'classic' life cycle for a product has four phases:

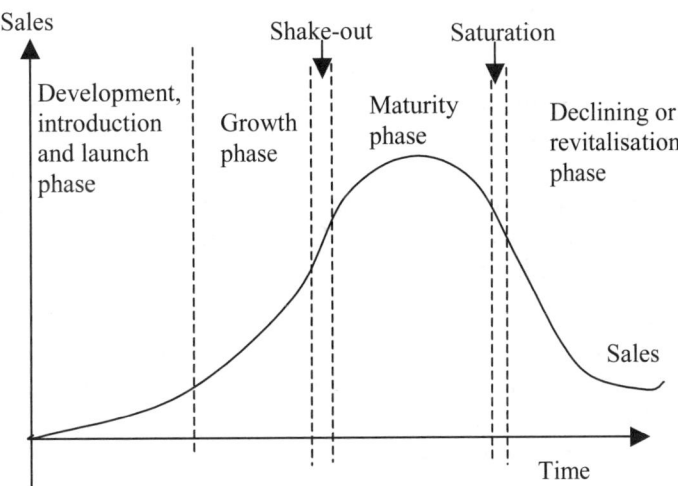

112 A

Consider buying the classic FMCG – a tin of baked beans.

113 C

By definition the answer is C.

114 C

An initiator starts the buying process, usually by identifying a need. The influencer will affect which product is bought, perhaps based on their expertise. The buyer buys it and the user uses it. As such, this terminology could be applied to B2C or B2B marketing:

Example: **Purchasing a child's bike (B2C)**

Member	Role
Initiator	Child pesters parents for new bike
Influencers	Older siblings have an opinion on the choice of bike, once parent recognises child has grown out of present one
Buyer	Parent pays the bill
User	The child

Example: **Purchasing new machinery (B2B)**

Member	Role
Initiator	Machine breaks down, the operator reports it, thus initiating the process
Influencers	User may influence, may also involve supervisor, R&D staff, accountant, sales reps.
Buyer	Buyer handles search for and negotiations with suppliers
User	Operator

However, B2B marketing is more likely to target the buyer only whereas B2C will appeal to each member of the buying group. Overall C is thus the better answer.

115

Tutorial note

You might not have heard of these terms before, but you should try to relate what the terms might mean in the context of the activities of a sales force. The terms should give you a reasonable clue as to what they mean.

(a) 'Hunting' in the context of sales force activities means going out to look for new customers to 'catch'. When the sales force focuses on 'hunting', they are looking for new customers and new business. In contrast, 'farming' means developing existing customers. When the sales force focuses on 'farming', they are looking for ways of selling more to existing customers.

(b) With 'selling', the sales force is concerned primarily with making the initial sale to achieve immediate sales revenue. 'Servicing' refers to the fact that after a customer has purchased products or services, there might be a requirement for after-sales support. With servicing, the aim is to keep the customer satisfied with the product and service, so that he will continue to keep on buying.

116 E-commerce is the use of the Internet to market and sell goods and services. An organisation can offer its products or services for sale on its web site, and customers are able to 'shop' on the site, place orders and pay for them by credit card (or other card). Special software checks the validity of credit cards and also gives security protection to the cardholder.

The advantages of e-commerce from a marketing viewpoint are that advertising and selling products or services on the Internet:

- provides an additional distribution channel and so adds to the marketing mix

- provides a convenient method of shopping for customers, and so meets the needs of some customers better than 'traditional' distribution channels

- is a fast and direct method of selling

- can be a low-cost method of selling.

It is probably easier to market services than products by e-commerce because with products, the problem arises of how to deliver them to customers who have ordered them. With some services, the service can also be delivered over the Internet, adding to the convenience of both buyer and supplier. Examples of services that may be delivered over the Internet are Internet banking and stockbroking services, buying software, Internet gambling, information services and on-line training.

117 Price is used in marketing to persuade the customer to buy on the basis that the product (or service) is being offered at an attractive low price in relation to the perceived quality of the product.

Price can be used in the following ways as a marketing tool for a consumer product:

- A discount may be offered off the normal price (for a limited period only).

- Customers might be offered 'two for the price of one' or 'buy four and get one free'.

- Special discounts might be offered to loyal customers.

- Customers may be offered 'money off' coupons.

- There might be a special low-price introductory offer for a new product.

- A company might advertise the fact that its products are cheapest in the market (for example: 'never knowingly undersold').

- Customers might be offered a long credit period for high-value items, or offered low-cost finance to buy the product.

- Products might be offered with a free extended warranty.

118 B2B marketing involves marketing to business buyers, whereas B2C marketing involves marketing to consumers. Business buyers and consumers are often attracted by different aspects of a marketing mix, and make their buying decisions in different ways and for different reasons.

Business buyers are generally more rational than consumers in their buying decisions and are often concerned with the 'commercial' aspects of purchase, in particular price (and credit terms), product quality and specifications and delivery times and reliability.

In business, the person who initiates a buying request (such as an inventory manager or a user department) is not the person who makes the buying decision (for example a buyer in the purchasing department), and for high-value items, a purchase might require special authorisation by senior management.

For marketing purposes, it is usually important to recognise who is most influential in a purchasing decision by a business, the buyer or a technical 'expert', and develop a marketing strategy accordingly – based on price, product specifications, displays at exhibitions and trade fairs, and so on.

In contrast, many consumer goods are fast-moving items, where the customer buys frequently, and often on impulse and in a convenient way. Consumers buy through different channels of distribution: whereas business buyers often respond to direct selling and through established supplier relationships, consumers buy through retail outlets catalogues or the Internet.

For consumers, buying decisions might be affected by advertising and sales promotions more than business buyers.

As a result of these differences, the marketing mix for business customers and the marketing mix for consumers are often very different.

119 The 'traditional' product life cycle goes through the phases of introduction, growth, maturity and decline through the course of its market life. The relevance of the product life cycle to marketing is that:

- marketing might be used to extend a stage in the life of a product

- a different marketing mix might be appropriate for different stages of the life cycle.

(a) Introduction stage. During this stage, the product is new and loss-making, and the task is to gain acceptance by customers. A key element in the marketing mix might be to find suitable and sufficient methods of distributing the product, and price is unlikely to be a significant item for marketing purposes – the product price will be fairly high.

(b) Growth stage. During the growth stage, the total market for the product is expanding, and the product becomes profitable. New competitors enter the market. Within the marketing mix, product design becomes important, and price is also more significant. The growth phase of a product's life might be extended by successful segmentation.

(c) Maturity. During this stage, total sales in the market reach a peak, sales growth ends and total annual sales remain fairly constant. This can be the longest stage in the life of a successful product. The task is now to sustaining profitability, probably by maintaining or increasing market share. Price is likely to be a major element in the marketing mix.

(d) Decline. During the decline stage, total sales of the product fall, and gradually manufacturers and suppliers drop out of the market. It might also be more difficult to segment the market into commercially-viable segments. Distribution (the accessibility of the product to customers) might become a more important element in the marketing mix, and product design innovations are much less important.

120 The main difference between product and production orientations is as follows:

A product-oriented company has a culture that is focused on making its products attractive and technically up to date. This can go to an extreme where the firm has excessive development expenditure (e.g. Rolls Royce's aero engine division) and can miss marketing opportunities which do not call for such extreme sophistication.

A production-oriented company tries to make as many units as possible and sees the way to profitability as being through economies of scale and production rationalisation (e.g. Henry Ford's statement that "you can have any colour you like, so long as it's black").

Both orientations are alike in that they share a danger of the firm failing to give enough attention to customer needs and wants. The product-oriented company may put in sophisticated features that nobody wants, whereas the production-oriented company may be unwilling to offer a full range of options as it wants to simplify production.

MANAGING HUMAN CAPITAL

121 D

A person starting a new job is often given induction and training. Induction is the process of familiarisation with the organisation and training involves the development of the individual's skills in the job. A probationary period (answer A) is a trial period during which the new employee is 'on probation' and has to prove that he or she can do the job well before being offered the job on a permanent basis.

122 D

A key word in the question is 'effective'. Effective appraisal requires a dialogue between the manager and the person being appraised (the 'appraisee'). Any problems with the appraisee's work or performance are identified and should be discussed and resolved constructively. Answer C, in contrast, describes an ineffective appraisal process.

123 C

Vroom developed an expectancy theory model, which suggested that the motivation of an individual to do anything is the result of 'valence' (the strength of the individual's desire to achieve a given outcome or reward) and 'expectancy' (the probability that achieving the given outcome will lead to the reward.) This has nothing to do with knowledge (answer A), satisfaction (answer B) or the quality of work performed (answer D). An individual will be motivated to act in a way that provides the 'best mix' of valence and expectancy.

124 B

Job rotation involves the movement of an individual from one post to another in order to gain experience of all the different tasks or activities in an organisation or a department. For example, an accounts clerk might be moved from the payables ledger to debt collection work and then into cost accounting in order to gain a broader experience of the work in the accounts department. Answer B describes job rotation more accurately than answer D. Answer C describes job enlargement.

125 C

A grievance procedure is a procedure that an individual can follow if he or she feel 'aggrieved' or wronged by something at work, and the problem has not been resolved by the normal channels. It is not a procedure where the employee is assumed to be in the wrong (so answer B is incorrect), nor is it an arbitration procedure or a collective bargaining arrangement.

126 C

An assessment centre brings together a group of applicants for a job or a number of jobs (for example, graduate trainee management positions) and the applicants are put through a variety of intensive assessments in a period of one to three days.

127 B

The correct answer can probably be worked out by common sense. A test cannot be contradictory, although the *results* from tests can be, so answer A cannot be correct. The fact that tests are general in nature does not means that test result will vary over time, so answer C is not correct. This leaves a choice between the tests being unreliable or unstable. If test results vary over time, this means that the tests are unreliable, but there is no reason to suppose that they might be unstable.

128 A

F.W. Taylor was a pioneer of the 'scientific school' of management in the US. He believed that work processes could be analysed and divided into component elements, and that greater efficiency would be obtained by getting employees to specialise in one small aspect or component of the overall process.

129 C

Succession planning involves 'grooming' an individual to take over in a key position after the present job-holder retires or moves on. This should ensure that the person who will take over has been given the necessary training and development programme to take over and do the work competently (answer C). A new person in a key job will not necessarily continue to do things in the same way as his predecessor; therefore answer B is incorrect. Succession planning is connected to promotion policy, where successors are appointed internally: however, the purpose of succession planning should not be to create promotion opportunities and answer A is not correct.

130 B

Recruitment is the process of attracting individuals into applying for a job. Employment agencies do this, usually by advertising or notifying the vacancy to individuals on their books. Screening is the process of vetting applications and removing those that are inappropriate and unlikely to be successful. The remaining applications are then passed to the company, whose responsibility it should be to select candidates for interview and make the selection.

131 D

Performance appraisal is partly designed to discuss performance with under-performing employees, and not all appraisal systems include discussions about pay: answers B and C are therefore incorrect. Performance appraisal should be for the assessment of performance, not personality. However, if there are no objective criteria for performance assessment, the appraisal will be subjective, and could lead to disagreement (or even argument) between the appraiser and the individual being appraised.

Other reasons for an ineffective appraisal scheme might be because:

- the appraisals focus on the personality of the appraisee, not performance in the job

- the system is not operated as intended, for example because managers have insufficient time for the appraisal interviews

- a lack of suitable training, so that there is inadequate 'follow- up' to appraisal interviews in which training and development needs are discussed.

132 A

If the employee's claim is correct, the employer would be liable for constructive dismissal, which is a form of unfair dismissal. A contract with a sub-contractor is subject to contract law, not employment law: the sub-contractor could claim breach of contract. It is probably considered reasonable to dismiss an employee who can no longer perform his job, such as a lorry driver who cannot drive (in the UK, on the assumption that there is no other job that the individual can do). Dismissal on the grounds of redundancy is also legal, although the employer must comply with redundancy procedures and legislation.

133 B

Although it is difficult to separate personal development from training, personal development might be defined as work-based learning and self-education (items I and IV). Giving employees time off to study is a form of training. Developing leadership skills is personal development when it occurs in work, but a course in skills is training.

134 A

Job evaluation is used to assess what the value of a job is worth to the organisation, and so what an appropriate level of *basic* pay ought to be. With knowledge work, it is often difficult to carry out a reliable, objective job evaluation.

Benchmarking can be used to establish a pay level by looking at basic pay in similar jobs in other organisations (so answer B is not correct). If there is a scarcity of knowledge skills, this will put upward pressure on basic pay levels, but does not create a serious problem for setting pay levels (so answer C is not correct). Performance evaluation is an issue with performance-related pay, but not basic pay (so answer D is not correct).

135 D

The answer here might seem the most obvious one to choose. However, it is useful to be aware of development action plans. There should be a plan for each individual within a performance appraisal scheme, and the plan should be kept up-to-date and referred to regularly.

136 A

Answer B describes teleworking (or telecommuting). Answer C describes flex-time. Answer D describes reduced hours working or part-time working.

137   D

References from a former employer are notoriously unreliable as a guide to future performance, or the candidate's character and abilities. The former employer is usually unwilling to criticise the individual, and concerned about any liability that might arise. However, a reference (on headed notepaper) should confirm that the candidate did actually work in the job, as stated in his/her job application, and that the employee was not dismissed for bad conduct.

138   C

Questions about likes, dislikes and attitudes are part of a personality test. An intelligence test measures intelligence and an aptitude test measures the ability of an individual to do the job. A situational test puts the individual into a 'mock' work situation and tests what he or she does. Situational tests are commonly used in group selection procedures.

139   D

Job evaluation is primarily a process by which the value of a job is assessed and a suitable rate of pay is decided accordingly. If different jobs are evaluated with the same scoring system, the rates of pay for the different jobs can be set in relation to each other, according to their respective total scores in the evaluation exercise.

140   A

Herzberg argued that the quality of management and working conditions are hygiene factors, and the level of responsibility is a motivator. He also argued that pay is a hygiene factor, particularly basic pay. However, pay can also be used as an incentive/motivator, for example by offering the prospect of a cash bonus for achieving a performance target.

141   B

To forecast the supply of employees over a planning period, a starting point for the forecast should be the numbers currently employed and their current skills, and the expected rate of labour turnover. These can be used to forecast how many of the existing work force will still be with the company and what their skills might be. Holiday entitlements are not a factor in making a supply forecast (but might possibly be relevant to forecasting the *demand* for additional staff).

142   B

If a job is offered for a probationary period, the employer can inform the job holder at the end of the probationary period that the position will not be converted into a full-time job. The employee must then leave. Using a probationary employment period avoids legal and regulatory problems, which will occur if the employer uses redundancy or dismissal as reasons for getting rid of an unwanted employee. Offering a lower rate of pay does not solve the problem of whether the individual is suitable for the job; it simply keeps costs down.

143   D

Lawrence and Lorsch (1967) found that organisations in a stable and predictable environment are most efficient if they have a traditional hierarchical management structure. However, organisations in a rapidly-changing environment or facing rapidly-changing technologies are most successful if they have a flexible structure in which authority is delegated and authority is decentralised. The greater the uncertainty and unpredictability in the environment, the greater is the need for delegation to specialised 'sub-systems' within the organisation.

144 B

Handy argued that the three elements in the motivational calculus for employees together determine the strength of the individual's motivation to put in effort to do the task well.

- Needs consist of the Maslow factors (the hierarchy of needs), together with the individual's character traits and outside influences and pressures.

- Results: an individual will assess what the effect will be of putting additional effort into the work.

- Effectiveness: the individual will then assess the extent to which these results will achieve his/her needs.

Needs, results and effectiveness are therefore all elements in the individual's motivation to put effort into the work.

145 B

In a virtual organisation, more individuals spend more time working from home or other distant locations, linked together by computer networks and (mobile) telephones. There will be fewer meetings between individuals, because informal/casual meetings are not possible. Formal meetings will have to be scheduled and will often be inconvenient to attend.

There is likely to much more team working, with empowerment of employees. This will mean having to give more trust to employees. There will probably also be much greater use of external consultants (outsourcing) and temporary staff.

There is no obvious link between working in a virtual organisation and motivation.

146 C

McGregor's Theory X and Theory Y are attitudes based on social science research, and McGregor regarded them as two distinct attitudes. Theory X is based on assumptions such as the dislike of individuals for work, which means that they have to be controlled and threatened by their supervisors and managers. McGregor believed that Theory Y was difficult to apply in some working conditions, such as mass production operations, and that it was much better suited to the management of managers and other professionals.

147 A

Likert argued that the motivation to work should be supplemented by modern management techniques, not by old systems of rewards and threats.

148 A

Herzberg's main 'motivators' are achievement, recognition, growth/advancement to higher levels, interest in the job and responsibility for the task. Hygiene factors are the company, its policies and administration, pay, security, working conditions, interpersonal relationships, the nature of supervision and status.

149 D

Answers A and B refer to profit-related pay and answer C describes either piece work payment or payment by the hour/day.

150 B

Likert argued in favour of a participative style of management as being the most effective. The least effective, he believed, is 'exploitative authoritative'. Answer D describes the contingency approach to management and leadership: Likert did not belong to this school of thought.

151 C

'Greater emphasis' presumably means that the style of management needs to be used much more. When employees are given more involvement in decision-making, and there are fewer levels of management, the participative style of management is both more appropriate and more necessary. Employees might be empowered, and any form of authoritative leadership will probably be ineffective.

152 C

Answer C should be the obvious and logical answer. In the past, management in some organisations has tried to justify unethical behaviour by saying that it did it in the interests of the organisation. This is an attempt to justify improper behaviour. The argument should not be accepted. However, in some countries, unethical behaviour is justified on these grounds – for example, attempts at bribery or corruption.

153 A

Job analysis should be carried out as an early stage in the recruitment process. Management should consider what a job consists of (job analysis) in order to establish the required skills or competences of the person who should be recruited to do the job. Interviewing, testing and the use of assessment centres are all part of the selection process.

154 B

If you are not familiar with the work of Devanna, you need to identify the solution by means of logic and analysis. An HR cycle indicates a continuous and repetitive process. The components of the cycle need to be in a logical order. It is illogical that job design should follow appraisal, development or performance: answers C and D are therefore incorrect. You might think that both answer A and answer B are possibly correct. However, 'involvement' is an issue for manager and subordinate, not the HR department. On the other hand, the development of individuals through training, job rotation and promotions is an element of HR. Answer B is correct.

155 A

F.W. Taylor was a pioneer of the 'scientific school' of management in the US. He believed that work processes could be analysed and divided into component elements, and that greater efficiency would be obtained by getting employees to specialise in one small aspect or component of the overall process.

156 A

Recruitment agencies are commonly used by organisations, and much training is carried out by external training specialists. For the re-location of staff from one geographical location to another, external specialists are also used. It is much more difficult to outsource staff development, where a detailed knowledge of individuals and their progress and experience within the organisation is required.

157 C

This approach identifies the competences (or 'competencies') that the job holder should have to perform the job well, and the individuals responsible for assessing candidates (such as an interviewer) should be asked to focus on whether each applicant appears to have the required skills or competences. For example, questions in an interview can focus on these areas of interest.

158 A

Answer A is the only one that is comprehensive enough. B is wrong as the assessment centre may be run by an outside firm, C is wrong as the candidate attends the assessment centre and D is wrong because the range of tests includes more than just psychological testing.

159 D

The choice is really between C and D since these issues do not relate to Greiner's model of succession planning. Whilst C seems appropriate and could even be deemed to be correct, D is the best answer. This is because, in a modern interpretation of scientific management, statistical process control would be part of monitoring the one best way of working in an automated manufacturing process, and work analysis is the foundation of work study, a principle feature of scientific management and the real focus for which answer to select.

160 A

Some students may have argued for answer D, but A is the best answer as standard questions ensure that each interviewee gets the same questions whether or not the interviewer likes them.

161 D

The correct answer is D, by definition. It is called the 'psychological contract' because (1) it is not a written contract but more implied, and (2) it truly exists or at least was understood to exist in the minds of those in the employer-employee relationship.

162 A

McGregor suggested the ideas of Theory X/Y so the answer has to be A or B. (Self-actualising man is by Schein and hygiene factors are Herzberg's ideas). Answer A is the correct version of Theory X as given by McGregor.

163 C

Person specification looks at the candidate to be recruited rather than at the organisation or the job itself.

164 C

A is wrong as they are different processes, D is wrong as job analysis may occur before anyone has been recruited to do the job. B has some merit as performance appraisal will be partly based on matching the employee's behaviour with the job analysis. C has more merit as selection would definitely include job analysis and then assessing a candidate's suitability for that role. The performance appraisal could refer to the candidate.

165 C

Content theories (e.g. Maslow, Herzberg) focus on 'what' motivates, rather than the process of motivation (e.g. Vroom, Adams). As such, needs are more often the focus than feelings. Most theories look at individual motivation rather than group motivation.

166 A

Outplacement refers to practical support from professional consultants designed to help people who have to leave a company, whether through redundancy or severance, move to the next stage in their careers.

167 B

Taylor developed the idea of 'Scientific Management', which included an emphasis on efficiency and suggested that financial rewards would motivate best.

168 D

Part A section 5.3 of Ethical Guidelines if you're really keen, or commonsense otherwise. None of the other options are reasonable.

169 C

The key aspect of 360° feedback is that managers are assessed on how their subordinates view them.

170 (a) Job enlargement is the re-design of a job so that the job holder has more responsibilities or a greater range of tasks to perform. Job enlargement might be appropriate where employees are under-utilised, and management are seeking ways of improving efficiency.

(b) Job rotation is a process in which individuals are moved from one job to another within a department or organisation, in order to give the individual experience in and knowledge of a wide range of jobs. Job rotation is used as part of a training or development programme for individuals.

(c) Job enrichment means making a job more fulfilling for the individual job-holder. Job enrichment will involve introducing new elements to the work that motivate the individual, and will hopefully encourage him or her to enhance performance.

171 The Internet can be used by a company or other organisation to carry out a test on potential recruits (for example, psychometric tests). Specialised software for providing tests and assessing results is available. The web site holding the test software might be held on a server within the company itself, or the company might use a testing system of a specialist organisation.

Candidates for a job can be asked to take a test, and the decision about whether or not to offer him/her a job will depend partly – or wholly – on the results of the test. Certain controls will be necessary, however, to prevent misuse or abuse of the system. For example, there will need to be a check on the actual identity of a person taking the test, otherwise an individual could possibly take a test on behalf of someone else, such as a friend.

172
- Hard HRM stresses the rational and quantitative aspects of managing human resources and improving performance.

- Soft HRM recognises that human relations management must be consistent with the organisation's strategic objectives, but places emphasis on employee development, placing trust in employees, participation and collaboration.

173 The other two types are:
- external contractors providing specialist services and non-essential services, and

- temporary staff and part-time staff, who are used to meet staffing requirements during busy periods.

174 A psychological contract between an individual and an organisation is a 'contract' in the mind of the individual. In return for the organisation satisfying some of the individual's needs, the individual in return will give some of his/her energy and talent to the organisation.

Handy's three types of psychological contract are coercive, calculative and co-operative.

- In a coercive contract, the individual is forced to work in the organisation without his consent. Examples are a prisoner in prison and, in some cases, a student at school.

- In a calculative contract, control of the rewards that satisfy the individual's needs (pay, promotion, and so on) is in the hands of the organisation's management. The individual decides how much effort it is worth putting into the job to get the rewards.

- In a co-operative contract, the individual identifies with the objectives of the organisation and works hard to attain them – in return for fair rewards, and a voice in the selection of targets or objectives and in the means of achieving them.

175 Employers should want all workers to have certain key skills, because this will mean that all new employees will already possess these skills and should therefore be able to perform to a certain level of competence without the need for further training. Key skills identified in the UK by employers and the government are:
- communication skills (including literacy where appropriate)

- IT skills

- skill in applying numbers

- problem-solving skills

- an ability to work with others

- a willingness to improve learning and performance.

176 Teamwork and participation can be effective in achieving improvements in work when the team members:
- co-operate spontaneously

- feel that they are participating freely in the work, and

- feel that they are working without coercion from management above them.

Workplaces are social environments, and individuals are motivated by more than just economic self-interest. A worker is a person conditioned by the social demands from both inside and outside the work place. Informal groups within the work place exercise a strong social control over the work habits and attitudes of the individual worker.

Peer group dynamics are important. However, a badly motivated team can develop a negative outlook on their work, for example if they are distrustful of management.

A task for management is to achieve a positive attitude to work by focusing on work teams and building up a positive outlook amongst teams to the work they are doing.

Section 5

ANSWERS TO SECTION B-TYPE QUESTIONS

177 SPEC

(a) An IT system should improve the efficiency, effectiveness or economy of an organisation. Efficiency would be achieved if the IT system enables the organisation to accomplish its tasks with fewer resources or in less time. Effectiveness would be achieved if the organisation is able to use the IT system to meet its objectives more successfully. Economy would be achieved if the IT system allows the organisation to operate at lower cost.

The benefits of an IT system for providing information are that it should be able to provide better-quality information so that management are better-informed for decision-making. The information system might be better because there is more relevant information available, or because it is more reliable, or because it is available in a more timely way (for example, available immediately through access to a central data file).

(b) Diagrams and tables are used by systems developers to analyse current systems and design and document new systems. They supplement narrative descriptions of a system, or provide a more understandable alternative to narrative descriptions.

(i) A data flow diagram is used to describe the processes that occur within the system. It shows the external sources from which data is obtained or to which data is sent. It also shows how data flows within the system from one operation to another, what operations are carried out on the data and the data files that are used for storing and retrieving data.

(ii) An entity-relationship model is a static model of the system. It describes the 'entities' within the system, which might be people (eg employees) or objects (eg invoice), places or an activity. The model also describes the relationships between entities in the system, usually as one-to-one or one-to-many relationships. An entity-relationship model should be supported by descriptions of the attributes of each entity. These models are commonly used for database design.

(iii) An entity life history describes all the events that happen to an entity within the system throughout the entity's 'life'. It is another method of presenting the logic of how a system will operate.

(iv) A decision table presents the logic of a decision, and indicates what actions should be taken in dealing with a transaction or operation given each possible set of circumstances that might exist. Tables can be used to illustrate aspects of a system's logic, but not the system as a whole.

(c)   Beer and Nohria argued that there are two approaches to the management of change, and managers commonly adopt one or the other at different stages through the change process. They called the two approaches Theory E and Theory O. Theory E focuses on the economic value of change, and management decisions are based on how shareholder value will be increased. It is a 'hard' approach, which shows little or no concern for the employees affected by change. Theory O is a soft approach to change based on 'organisational capability'. It is based on the view that the best way of implementing change is through a learning process of the employees, and with close involvement of employees in making decisions about changes. Whereas Theory E would consider that employees can be persuaded to accept change through offers of financial rewards, Theory O would consider that the effective way of introducing change is through employee motivation.

      A significant aspect of the argument of Beer and Nohria is that whereas in many organisations, either Theory E or Theory O is adopted by management at any particular time, the most successful way of implementing change is to apply both approaches simultaneously.

(d)   Mass marketing is marketing to a large 'audience', with the intention that the marketing message should reach a very large number of people. An example of mass marketing is television advertising. Mass marketing is most appropriate for consumer products that are purchased by a large number of households.

      Direct marketing is marketing directly to targeted potential customers. To use this method, it is necessary to have a file or list of actual or potential customers, for example a customer list extracted from a customer database. Examples of direct marketing are face-to-face selling and direct mail. Direct marketing is appropriate where the aim is to target known customers or customers who might be likely to buy, by offering something that might be of interest to them.

      Interactive marketing is marketing where there is a two-way exchange of information between the seller/marketer and the target customer. An example of interactive marketing is telemarketing, where an organisation telephones customers on a pre-selected list and tries to engage them in a conversation about its products.

(e)   A marketing decision support system is a system that can be used by marketing management to assist them with making decisions. The DSS will include a variety of management aids, such as forecasting models and statistical analysis models.

      Market research is crucial to the creation and operation of a marketing DSS. Market research is used to obtain relevant marketing data from a variety of sources, such as market research exercises, test marketing exercises, sales force opinions and external data records. A marketing DSS can be used to analyse the market research data, and provide information that should help marketing managers to reach well-informed decisions.

(f)   Three legal aspects of marketing are as follows:

- Health and safety legislation. There might be requirements for minimum product standards, or legal requirements for providing customers with information about the product. From a marketing perspective, it is important to ensure that customers are aware that any required health and safety standards are met by the products, and where appropriate, information should be provided with documentation or packaging for the products.

- Data protection legislation. It is important to ensure that any information held on a customer database is not in breach of data protection legislation.

- Legislation on mis-selling or mis-information. The marketing function should ensure that the selling and advertising/promotion of the company's products does not breach legislation on mis-selling or misleading/incorrect information.

178 NEW SYSTEM

(a) The main disadvantage of buying off-the-shelf software is that the software is unlikely to provide all the features that an organisation might want, and that could be written into a bespoke system. Consequently, the benefits from an off-the-shelf system might be much less than the benefits from a bespoke system would be. This could have implications for the competitiveness of the organisation. (It might be possible to arrange for the software supplier to write an adapted version of its software for the organisation, but this would add to the cost of the software and delay its implementation, due to the need for writing amended programs and testing them.)

With off-the-shelf software, the user has no control over system amendments and new system versions. The content and timing of new software versions is decided by the software house.

If system support is required for users of the new system, it might be possible to arrange a help desk facility with the software house, at a cost. Alternatively, the software user will have to train its own specialist IT staff in the new system and establish its own help desk internally.

(b) A prototype is a working version or model, but not the finished item. When prototyping is used for system development, an initial working model is produced and implemented operationally. Experience with the prototype should enable the system user and system designers to identify both weaknesses in the system design and also additional or amended user requirements for the system. Through experience with the system, the user should be able to identify the system requirements more clearly. Another prototype is then developed, incorporating the improvements and amended requirements, and the new prototype is implemented operationally. There is an iterative process, with a succession of prototypes developed and introduced, until the final system version is produced.

Prototyping enables a system to be implemented more quickly, because it becomes operational with the first prototype, before the system development is completed.

Prototyping should also result in better systems, because the system requirements will have been refined and improved with the practical experience and lessons obtained from working with the prototypes.

(c) Operations strategy is a vital element in the overall strategy of a firm. It concerns how the firm provide its products or services for delivery to the customer. The objective of a commercial firm might be stated as meeting customer needs with products or services, in order to increase the value of the firm over the long-term and the wealth of its shareholders. Meeting customer needs is critically important, particularly in competitive markets.

Operations strategy is concerned with the products or services that are made, and how new products are designed and tested. Product development is an element in both operations and marketing management. It is important that new products should meet customer needs more effectively than competitors' products. Operational strategy for computer-aided design might contribute to this aim.

Operations strategy should also be concerned with how efficiently, effectively and economically products are made or services are provided. Aspects of operating performance include quality, speed, dependability and cost. The management of quality is important because with better quality, customer needs are met more effectively, and costs are reduced. Speed of throughput means that customer needs can be met more quickly. Lower costs mean that the company's objectives of increasing shareholder wealth should also be more achievable.

The way in which the supply chain is managed can also be vitally important for meeting customer needs. Greater value can be obtained by improving the operation of the entire supply chain, for example by creating long-term strategic relationships with suppliers and outsourcing non-essential operations, so that the firm can focus on its core skills.

(d) The marketing mix 'traditionally' consists of the 4Ps: product, place, price and promotion. 'Product' refers not only to the physical product itself, but also to the services that are provided in association with the physical product. 'Place' refers to the way in which a product is delivered to the customer, and the channel of distribution that is used.

The planned new customer order and delivery system can be used to provide a stronger marketing message to business buyers.

The new computer system could strengthen the 'product' or the 'place' depending on how the benefits of the new system are classified. If the new system is successful, customers will be offered a much more reliable delivery system, where the company can verify immediately whether items are in stock and provide a 'guaranteed' delivery date to the customer.

The company's customers are all business buyers, and reliability of supply appears to be a key requirement. The sales and marketing team should be able to promote this improvement and make the products appeal more strongly to potential buyers.

(e) Staff training for a major new system should be organised in stages.

(i) Initially, the company should ensure that some of its staff are familiar with the new system. The best way of achieving this is to assign a member or several members of staff to the development team, to work with the system developers throughout the entire system development phase. These individuals should acquire a sufficient understanding of the system to prepare user documentation and training materials.

(ii) It might be appropriate to introduce the new system gradually, so that training in the new system can also be gradual. Selected operational staff should be given some 'class room' training in the new system.

(iii) Practical training cannot be carried out, however, until the system is sufficiently developed. Typically, this is after system testing, or after the development of the first prototype. Before the system goes 'live', there should be user tests. The purpose of user tests is partially to test the system itself, but also to provide user staff with experience in using the new system. Any operational difficulties that arise can be identified and resolved.

Training should therefore be a combination of formal training, practical training and user instructions (in documentation and/or as a help facility within the software). Operational staff working on the system for the first time should also be supervised carefully. The systems development team might also be used to check output from the system, identify any difficulties that individual members of staff are having with the system, and help to resolve them. This might be described as 'on-the-job' training.

(f) If staff are to be made redundant, company policy should be to avoid compulsory redundancies if possible. This can be achieved by discussing the situation with staff representatives, with the aim of inviting staff to apply for voluntary redundancy, and finding ways of re-training and re-deploying staff in other parts of the organisation. It might be a legal requirement that staff should be offered suitable alternative jobs within the organisation, if these exist, when their job is no longer required.

If a need for redundancies can be foreseen in advance, the company should try to avoid replacing staff who leave through 'natural wastage' (retiring or moving on to another job). Although this might result in some staff shortages in the short term, it will reduce the need for redundancies in the future.

For the sake of good management-employee relations, it is essential to discuss the need for redundancies openly and honestly with staff and their representatives.

The company should follow all the required legal procedures for making staff redundant, where redundancies are unavoidable.

It might be appropriate for management or supervisors to discuss redundancy one-to-one with the individuals affected, and offer assistance to staff with re-training in new skills for employment in a different organisation.

179 HUBBLES (PILOT PAPER)

(a)   **Slide 1:**

Features of a selling orientation

Focus on selling

Getting customers to buy what we produce

Importance of the sales function

Features of a marketing-led organisation

Focus on customer needs and wants

Developing products to meet those needs

Involvement of all employees

Notes to Slide 1:

A company that 'sells' its products is sales-oriented. The company offers a range of products that it tries to sell to customers, using strong selling techniques, backed by advertising and sales promotions. The philosophy is that a good sales force can sell almost anything.

A marketing-oriented company focuses much more on what customers need and want, and they try to develop products or services to meet those needs in a better way than competitors. A marketing-oriented approach involves all employees in selling, not just the sales force. For example, product design, production quality and customer service all matter, because these are elements on the overall 'package' offered to meet customer needs and expectations.

(b)   **Slide 2:**

Developing the marketing concept:

Focus on customer needs and wants

Re-training of employees

Market research

Identify gaps in the market

Develop a product package to fill the gaps

Notes to Slide 2:

To apply a marketing concept, Hubbles must concentrate much more directly on customer needs and wants. All employees should be trained to adopt this new culture, and the lead must come from senior management. To focus on customer needs, it is essential to find out what customers need and want. This information can be obtained by carrying out market research, and why some consumers prefer the products of competitors to those of Hubble.

Hubble should use market research to identify gaps in the market, or gaps and weaknesses in its own product range, and it should develop new products or aspects pf the overall 'product package' to fill those gaps and rectify the weaknesses.

(c) **Slide 3:**

Components of marketing mix:

Product

Place

Price

Promotion

People

Notes to Slide 3:

The marketing mix is the mix of activities and product features that make up the approach to marketing a product to customers. The elements of a marketing mix for a product are the product itself, place, price and promotion. People is a fifth element in the mix that can be added.

'Product' refers to the products features, including product quality. 'Place' refers to where and how the product is sold. Price refers to all aspects of sales price, including discounts; and promotion refers to the advertising and sales promotion techniques that are used to market the product. For a service industry such as retailing, 'people' are also significant in the marketing mix, because the company's employees deliver the service and have an effect on customers' perceptions of the service and their satisfaction with it.

(d) **Slide 4:**

Marketing mix and re-gaining competitiveness:

Product: changes in product design

Place: improving sales outlets, developing new sales outlets

Price: use discounting to attract more customers

Promotion: more advertising or sales promotion initiatives

People: train employees in user-friendly service

Notes to Slide 4:

There are many different ways in which a marketing mix can be changes in an attempt to regain competitiveness. Changes could be made to any element in the marketing mix. Changes might be made in the range of products offered, or in the design of products, to make them more attractive to customers. The 'place' could be changed, either by opening new retail outlets, improving the facilities and layout at existing retail outlets, or trying to sell through a completely new distribution channel, such as on the internet. Sales prices could be reduced to attract customers with lower prices. More in-store promotions might be used, or an advertising campaign, to boost promotion. Employees in the stores could be trained in customer-friendly service techniques, to improve customer satisfaction with their 'experience' in visiting Hubbles' stores.

(e) **Slide 5:**

HR Department contribution

Recruitment

Training

Procedures

Pay and conditions

Notes to Slide 5:

An HR Department can assist the Purchasing Department in the same way that it can assist other departments within an organisation. It can provide services and support in areas where the HR staff have expertise, and take away administrative duties from the management of other departments.

Recruitment. HR can assist with the recruitment of staff, for example by advertising vacancies and using recruitment agencies. HR staff can also assist with interviewing and assessing applicants.

Training. HR staff can develop and implement training programmes for staff in the buying department, to improve their skills.

Procedures. The HR Department can assist other departments by developing a variety of procedures, such as appraisal procedures, grievance procedures and career development planning.

Pay and conditions. The HR Department can assist in the development of rates of pay and working conditions for staff in the buying department, and negotiating with the representatives of employees on terms and conditions.

(f) **Slide 6:**

Purchasing Department and better performance of the organisation

Purchasing good-quality products

Obtaining better prices

Monitoring delivery times

Efficiency in buying administration

Notes to Slide 6:

A Purchasing Department: contributes to effective organisational performance in several ways.

Professional buyers can ensure that products obtained from suppliers are to a satisfactory specification and quality.

A central Purchasing Department should be able to negotiate lower prices for bulk purchasing.

The Buying Department can monitor delivery times, and ensure that suppliers are chased if they fail to deliver on time.

The Buying Department should apply better administrative techniques to improve the efficiency of buying, such as Electronic Data Interchange or Just in Time purchasing.

180 HEVE TRANSPORT

(a) Off-the-shelf software packages have several advantages compared with bespoke (purpose-written) software.

- Off-the-shelf packages are cheaper to buy than bespoke software costs to write.

- Off-the-shelf software is available for immediate use, whereas (even with prototyping) bespoke software takes time to design, write and test before it is available for use.

- With well-established off-the-shelf packages, the software should be well-tested and (almost) error-free. With bespoke software, there is a high probability that there will be errors in the software when the system is introduced, that will not be discovered until later.

- With off-the-shelf software, there should be good user documentation or help facilities in the software itself. With bespoke software, these would have to be written and developed – at a cost – and might not be of good quality.

(b) Prototyping means developing one or a series of 'working models' of the new computer system that is being developed, and implementing each successive prototype before the development work on the system is finished.

The main advantages of prototyping are that:

- Prototypes can be used to test the new system and identify faults and weaknesses.

- A new system will be introduced much more quickly if prototypes are used rather than if system implementation does not occur until the system development has been completed, and the finished system has been tested.

- By using prototypes for 'live processing', the user is able to re-assess the system requirements, and use the experience with the prototypes to make changes. As a result, when the finished system has been completed, it should be more efficient and closer to what the user really wants.

(c) The stages in systems development are as follows.

(1) Feasibility study. A feasibility study is carried out into a new system. An outline design for a new system is prepared, and the costs and benefits of the new system are estimated and assessed. A feasibility study is then prepared, recommending whether the new system should be developed and implemented.

(2) System analysis. If a decision is taken to develop a new system, the next stage in the development work is to carry out an analysis of the existing system. This work is done by systems analysts. The analysis establishes the objectives of the current system, how it operates, the processing volumes that it handles and processing efficiency, and the strengths and weaknesses in the system. This analysis provides a basis for assessing how a new system might meet the needs of the computer user better than the existing system.

(3) System design and development. The systems analysts design a new system, and prepare specifications for the system. The specifications include details of the individual programs and files that the system will contain, the hardware it will use, the nature of communications networks, processing volumes and speeds, and so on. With a large computer system, the systems analysts might begin by preparing an outline system specification, and when this has been approved, go on to prepare more detailed system specifications.

The detailed system specifications are used by programmers as their starting point for writing programs. When the programs have been written, program tests and system tests are carried out, before the system is 'handed over' to the user for implementation.

(4) System implementation. The system is brought into operational use.

Review and maintenance. Some time after implementation, a review should be carried out to establish whether the new system is meeting the user requirements, and whether actual costs and benefits are as planned. System maintenance involves correcting errors in programs that become apparent after implementation, and adapting the system over time to changing requirements of the user.

(d) (i) Program testing checks whether a program written for a system works properly and meets the specifications for the program, and that there are no programming errors. The test is carried out with test data, and the actual output checked against expected output.

(ii) The output from one newly-written program might be incompatible with another newly-written program and into which the output will be transferred. In other words, the separate programs written for a new system might be incompatible with each other. Systems testing is designed to test that the system as a whole functions as specified, and that the programming is consistent and compatible. Only after successful system testing can a new system be considered ready for implementation.

(e) Flexible employment means working on a casual or temporary basis. An organisation that uses flexible employment is able to adapt its work force quickly to its immediate needs.

Problems with flexible employment for HR management include the following.

- There might be problems with having continually to recruit casual and temporary staff to meet current staffing requirements.

- There will be problems with work continuity due to the continually-changing work force.

- There might be problems in creating effective work teams.

- If members of staff need training, there will be a problem in deciding how much training to give to temporary staff.

- There might be resistance by full-time employees and their trade union representatives to an excessive use of casual/temporary staff.

- Problems might arise with differences in pay and conditions for temporary staff compared with full-time staff.

- It is difficult (or impossible) to monitor the performance of casual/temporary staff.

(f) Flexible working is arranging and scheduling work so that employees can choose different hours of work, to suit their personal or family needs. (Alternatively, employers might vary the hours of their employees in order to meet customer needs.)

The factors to consider when setting up a flexible working scheme are as follows.

- Ensuring that management and the entire work force accept and welcome the flexible working arrangements.

- Establishing basic rules and procedures for flexible working, and allowing for their impact on terms and conditions of employment. For example, policies might be established for hours during the day when an employee must be in attendance (such as 'core hours' in the middle of the day), and establishing rules for holiday entitlements for employees who do work a variable-length working week.

- Making sure that the total work load can be handled by the employees in attendance.

- Making sure that the needs of customers can be met at all times by staff in attendance.

- Assessing the potential effect of the absence of key individuals from work at particular times of the day or week.

- Establishing arrangements for scheduling meetings and training courses so that the maximum number of employees will be able to attend.

181 STAND PRODUCTS

(a) Kanter argued that in order to build a creative organisation, management should have a change culture and develop a change strategy, based on participation by employees and empowerment of employees to make decisions for change. She argued that the following guidelines should be applied by management:

(i) to develop an acceptance of change (a change culture) within the organisation

(ii) to encourage new ideas from employees at all levels within the organisation

(iii) to enable employees and different groups within the organisation to interact and share ideas

(iv) to be tolerant of failures, because not all innovations will succeed

(v) to give recognition to creative activity and reward employees for innovation.

(b) An external trigger for change is an event or a change in circumstances or conditions that prompt an organisation into making changes. It is often helpful to categorise external triggers for change as:

- political change triggers, which are significant political events or developments

- economic change triggers, which are changes (possibly long-term changes) in economic conditions

- social and cultural change triggers, which are changes in social conditions or cultural outlook, such as a greater expectation of retiring at an older age

- technological change triggers, which are significant changes in technology such as improved systems for communications or transport

- environmental change triggers, such as a diminishing stock of key raw materials

- legal change triggers, which are significant changes in the law affecting what a company may or may not be allowed to do.

(c) Greiner identified five stages of growth for an organisation. Each successive stage in an organisation's growth is triggered by a crisis affecting the efficiency of the organisation's management.

- The first stage of growth occurs when the organisation is small. A successful organisation grows by being creative and innovative. The leadership is entrepreneurial. However, as the organisation grows over time, the established methods of control and decision-making used by the entrepreneurial leadership cease to operate efficiently, and there is a growing need for management systems for organisation, planning and control. This leads to a crisis of management.

- The crisis of management results in a move to new growth stage, which Greiner called growth through direction. There is an organised structure with formal management systems, and a management hierarchy develops. However, as the organisation continues to grow, these simple management structures cease to be effective. 'Local' managers feel that they understand the business better than their bosses, and can run the business better if they are given more authority. This results in a crisis of autonomy.

- A crisis of autonomy triggers the next stage in growth, which is growth through delegation. More authority is delegated to local managers, and a decentralised management structure emerges, for example with profit centres. As the organisation grows, and more authority is decentralised however, senior management begin to lose control over the organisation, and a crisis of control occurs.

- The crisis of control leads to the fourth stage in growth, growth through co-ordination. During this growth stage, central management reasserts control over the organisation as a whole through internal reporting systems and communication systems. Central management co-ordinates the activities of the different local management structures. However, formal reporting systems eventually result in a culture of bureaucracy in central management, which local management resists. This results in a crisis of red tape.

- The fifth stage in organisation growth, which overcomes the crisis of red tape, is growth through collaboration. Structures are less formal, and there is greater emphasis on collaboration between head office and local management in problem-solving, and there is a strong culture of participation in decision-making and team-work.

Stand Products appears to be at the stage where a crisis of control is occurring.

(d) Compulsory redundancies occur when (1) the employer no longer requires any employees to carry out work of a particular kind (or work of a particular kind in a particular geographical area) and (2) the employer therefore ceases to employ them and puts them out of work, against their wishes.

Compulsory redundancies might be avoided by:

- voluntary re-deployment of employees to other jobs in the organisation

- a voluntary transfer scheme to re-deploy employees to another part of the organisation in a different geographical location

- re-training arrangements so that employees can do other work requiring different skills

- voluntary early retirement arrangements

- a job share scheme, so that two former full-time employees might share a job, each working part-time.

(e) The concept of the supply wheel, developed by Cousins, is based on the view that organisations are moving away from managing the flow of goods into the organisation (traditional purchasing) towards the management of the supply process and the overall supply chain. A company is only as strong as the weakest link in the supply chain. For some companies, such as companies that are moving towards a virtual organisation, most or all of the supply chain is outsourced.

Corporate strategy and supply strategy are at the centre of the supply wheel. Depending on the strategies that are adopted, there are implications for several connected items:

- the structure of the organisation and its supply chain: for example, how much of the supply chain will be outsourced?

- developing a portfolio of supply relationships, and managing them

- developing the required skills and competences to manage the supply chain: for example, the need is now recognised for professional purchasing staff

- cost-benefit analysis to assess the benefits of supplier relationships: for example, some suppliers agree to an 'open book' approach to sharing information on costs

- developing performance measures for the assessment of purchasing and the collaborative relationships with suppliers: for example, having jointly-agreed measures of performance for the supplier and the supply relationship, and using a balanced scorecard approach that includes performance measurements for supply.

(f) - A quality objective. Quality standards can be set for an operation, which can then be judged by measures of quality, such as wastage rates, defective items, customer complaints, and so on.

- A speed objective. This is concerned with how quickly an item should be delivered to the customer after receipt of an order. Actual performance can be measured, and compared with an objective or target.

- A dependability objective. This is the objective of delivering an item to the customer (internal or external) exactly when promised, and without delays or cancellations.

- A flexibility objective. This is the objective of being able to adapt operations to meet variations in customer requirements or operational circumstances.

- A cost objective. This is the objective of performing the operation without exceeding a target cost level, and measuring actual costs against the target.

182 HILO CONSULTANCY

(a) A customer database is a file containing data about a company's customers. It can be used by a company to build relationships with its customers, by identifying their needs and buying characteristics. When a company understands the characteristics of its customers, it can design different ways of communicating with (marketing to) different types of customer, in order to sell more successfully.

The information held for each customer on a database might be, in addition to name and address, demographic data obtained from order forms, warranty cards, enquiries and responses to surveys. Information about a customer can be built up over time, from both customer service contacts and market research activities.

Customer databases can then be used to make decisions about:

- when to contact the customer (for example, a car dealer should contact a customer before the due date for an annual service and check-up)

- which products should be marketed to the customer (so that direct mail shots, for example, can be targeted more efficiently)

- which benefits should be stressed to the customer (on the basis of the product attributes that the customer seems to find the most important).

A customer database can therefore be used to create customised marketing programmes, that should be more cost-efficient and effective. For example, a customer database can be used to develop a customer loyalty rewards scheme, or for promoting new products.

(b) A high performance work arrangement might be defined as an arrangement which relies on all members of the organisation for their ideas, intelligence and commitment to making the organisation successful.

The arrangements will include some or all of the following features:

- more job complexity

- multi-tasking and multi-skilling

- the continual development of employee skills

- a minimum hierarchical structure of management

- a distribution of responsibility to employees, often through work teams

- much more use of horizontal communications (direct communications between employees or work teams)

- pay incentives for performance and for acquiring new skills

- more focus by the organisation on 'core activities'

- greater use of outsourcing or sub-contractors.

A high performance work arrangement might be given another name, such as 'employee empowerment'.

(c) A project-based organisation is one that is structured mainly as a large number of projects, many of them inter-related, using knowledge workers in project teams. The management structure is small and many of the project teams might use external consultants and temporary workers.

The main problems for the HR management in these organisations concern the relationships between the organisation and its knowledge workers. Particular HR problems are as follows.

- Career development. Since the management structure is small, the organisation cannot offer prospects of promotion as career development to most of its employees.

- Competence development. HR management need to ensure that their knowledge workers sustain and develop their knowledge and skills in a changing environment. However, personal development and training needs might be more difficult to identify.

- Pay. There are often problems in establishing a fair and satisfactory pay scheme for knowledge work.

- Trust. There are potential problems for management, who need to trust employees to a very large degree, since the organisation 'empowers' its employees.

- The HR management will also need to negotiate short-term contracts with external workers and temporary workers.

(d) Schein argued that if a manager wants to motivate employees successfully, the way that the manager thinks that employees behave should match they way that they actually do behave.

The four types of employee behaviour he identified were as follows.

- Rational-economic man. This individual's prime motivator is self-interest and maximising personal gain. The implication is that this type of person will be motivated by a pay system that rewards employees for performance.

- Social man. This individual's prime motivator is to satisfy social needs through relations with others at work. The implication here is that this type of employee will be motivated by a 'task culture' and teamwork.

- Self-actualising man. This individual's prime motivator is similar to the self-actualising needs identified by Maslow. This type of employee is motivated by demanding, challenging and rewarding work.

- Complex man. The motivation of these individuals is even more complex. Managers need to identify the motivators of each individual in order to get the best out of them.

(e) The International Standards Organisation (ISO), which is a network of national standards institutes, developed the ISO 9000 series to encourage the achievement of high quality standards within organisations. Organisations obtaining ISO 9000 certification are those which can demonstrate that they:

- fulfil the quality requirements of customers

- where appropriate, meet regulatory requirements with regard to quality

- enhance customer satisfaction

- achieve continuous improvement in pursuit of these objectives.

The quality principles on which the ISO 9000 series is based are:

- customer focus: the focus of the organisation should be meeting customer needs and giving customer satisfaction

- leadership: management should give a lead to all employees in creating a quality culture within the organisation

- involvement of people: the quality improvement process should involve everyone

- process approach: the approach to improving quality should focus on an analysis of processes

- system approach to management: management should recognise that processes within an organisation are integrated, and a systems approach to process management is required

- continual improvement: there should be a continual search for ways of improving

- factual approach to decision-making: management decisions should be made wherever possible on the basis of factual evidence

- mutually beneficial relationships with suppliers.

(f) The ISO 9001: *2000 guidelines* are designed to enable an organisation to establish a management system that provides confidence in the conformance of its products or services to established or specified quality requirements or standards.

The approach required is a process-based approach.

- The first step in a quality management exercise should be to establish the processes that will be investigated. The processes might be processes for managing the organisation, for managing the resources of the organisation (inputs), its realisation processes (processes that produce the output of the organisation) and its processes for measurement, analysis and improvement.

- The next step is to identify the processes within the organisation. This should begin with defining the purpose of the organisation and its policies and objectives. Having done this, the individual processes should be identified, and the sequence in which they occur or the inter-relationships between them. For each processes, there must be a 'process owner' and specified process documentation.

- Having identified the processes, each process should be planned according to the required quality standards. For each process this involves:

  - defining the process activities (inputs, outputs and activities to convert inputs to outputs)

  - defining the monitoring and measurement requirements (for measuring effectiveness and efficiency for items such as supplier performance, waste, failure rates, the frequency of incidents, on-time delivery, customer satisfaction and conformity with requirements

  - verifying the process and its activities against the planned objectives.

- When plans for each process have been made and verified, the planned process should be implemented.

- The process should be subject to continual analysis, comparing actual performance with the defined requirements. Where possible, statistical methods of analysis should be used, because these will be objective. Weaknesses in the process or opportunities for improvements should be identified.

- Corrective action should be taken and process improvements should be made.

183 PMK MANUFACTURING

(a) Taylor argued that the objectives of management should be as follows:

- the development of a science for each element of an employee's work (based, for example, on time and motion study)

- the scientific, selection, training and development of workers

- the development of a spirit of co-operation between managers and workers, so that scientifically-devised procedures can be applied to work practices

- the division of work between workers and managers in almost equal shares, with each group doing the work for which it is best-suited. This implies a formal, hierarchical organisation structure, systems of abstract rules and procedures and impersonal relationships between staff.

(b) Feedback is information that is collected from a system (as 'measured outputs' of the system) and reported back to a system controller. The feedback is compared with a standard or target, and if the measured results differ from the standard by more than a tolerable amount, the controller takes appropriate control action to adjust the 'inputs to the system'.

- Negative feedback is information indicating that actual performance of the system is worse than the standard or target, so that corrective action might be needed.

- Positive feedback is information indicating that actual performance of the system is better than the standard or target, so that it might be appropriate to take measures to ensure that the favourable results continue or are made even better.

An example of a feedback system in management is a budgetary control system. Actual results of a business or operation for a given period are measured and information is fed back to management comparing actual results with the budget. Where the differences are considered significant, suitable control measures might be taken by the managers responsible.

(c) The ISO 9004 quality standard defines continuous improvement as an eight-step method:

- Involve the entire organisation.

- Initiate quality improvement projects or activities.

- Investigate the possible causes of quality problems.

- Establish a cause-and-effect relationship for quality problems.

- Take corrective or preventative measures to deal with the problem.

- Confirm the improvement.

- Sustain the gains.

- Continue the improvement.

(d) BPR was defined by Hammer and Champny (1993) as 'the fundamental re-thinking and radical re-design of business processes to achieve dramatic improvements in critical, contemporary measures of performance such as cost, quality, service and speed'.

They argued that organisations should re-organise their operations in a radical way. Instead of having separate departmental functions, for sales, engineering, machining, finishing and so on, operations should be organised around business processes that meet customer needs.

Hammer identified four main principles of BPR:

- Re-thinking business processes in a cross-functional manner, and structuring operations around the *outcomes* of the process rather than on functional lines (the tasks that go *into* the process).

- Seeking improvements in operations through a radical re-design of processes.

- Where possible, organise operations so that the people who use the output from a process should also be the people who perform the process, because they will then be more concerned with high standards of performance for the process. This means reducing the number of internal suppliers and internal customers.

- Giving the authority to make decisions to people where the work is done, so that those who do the work also control it.

In order to achieve the full potential of BPR, these principles should be applied to the entire organisation, not just to parts of it.

(e)   The operational requirements for a system of JIT production are as follows.

- Zero inventories. Producing output to meet customer demand as and when it arises.

- High quality and reliability. If items are defective and rejected as sub-standard, production will be disrupted and sales to the customer delayed, since there will be no items available to supply from inventory.

- Speed of throughput-production. JIT relies on fast throughput in the production process in order to meet customer orders quickly.

- Flexibility. Production operations must be flexible, with very small batch sizes, so that production can be switched from product to product as customer demand arises.

JIT also has the objective of reducing costs, by eliminating the costs of holding inventory, by avoiding defective output and by achieving fast throughput in production.

(f)   Reck and Long (*Purchasing: A Competitive Weapon* (1988)) promoted the concept that close relationships with a small number of key suppliers, all carefully selected, gives purchasing a strategic relevance that adds to the competitiveness of the firm. Purchasing should not be concerned with getting the lowest prices from suppliers. Instead, it should be about developing strategic relationships with suppliers in order to add value to the supply chain. The most effective firms in a competitive market are therefore those that have strategic relationships with their key suppliers.

Reck and Long identified four stages of development that purchasing must pass through to become a 'strategic weapon' for the firm.

- Stage 1 is a passive stage. Purchasing has no strategic direction, and the purchasing function simply reacts to demands from other departments or functions within the firm. Suppliers are selected on the basis of price and stability.

- Stage 2 is an independent stage. The purchasing function adopts the latest purchasing techniques, but purchasing strategy is still independent of overall corporate strategy. However, the firm recognises the need for more professional purchasing staff, and that there are opportunities for the purchasing function to contribute to profitability.

- Stage 3 is a supportive stage. During this stage, the purchasing function supports the competitive strategy of the firm. Suppliers are considered a resource to be developed and used, and the purchasing function continually monitors markets, products and suppliers.

- Stage 4 is an integrative phase, when the purchasing function becomes fully integrated into competitive strategy. Relationships with key suppliers are mutually interdependent. Purchasing contributes to the development strategy, and possibly has representation at board level within the firm.

184   SOFT DIVISION

Tutorial note

Kanter listed 'ten rules' for discouraging innovation. You are not required to know what these are, but your answer should list ideas that are similar to those suggested by Kanter.

(a)
- A senior manager might treat any new idea from a subordinate with suspicion, both because it is new and because it comes from a 'lower' person.

- A senior manager might insist that when a subordinate needs approval for something requiring the manager's personal approval, he must go through several different layers of management first, and obtain signed approval from each of these managers.

- When an individual or department suggests a new idea, the senior manager might invite other individuals or departments to criticise it. Everyone is therefore given an opportunity to criticise everyone else's ideas.

- The manager is critical of many things and does not give praise.

- The manager regards problems as a sign of failure: this discourages subordinates from reporting problems in their area of responsibility and suggesting ideas to resolve them.

- The senior manager controls everything strictly.

- The senior manager makes decisions about reorganisation in secret, and springs them on employees without warning.

- The manager makes sure that requests from employees for information are fully explained and justified.

- The senior manager, in the name of delegation of authority, gives subordinates unpleasant management tasks such as making other employees redundant.

- The senior manager never forgets that he is the boss, and as the boss, he knows everything important about managing a business.

(b)   Demand forecasting of employee numbers and skills might use any or several of the following methods.

- Management's judgement about the likely future requirements for each category of employee.

- Trend analysis. Future employee requirements might be forecast by projecting historical employee numbers and growth rates into the future, using statistical analysis. (Adjustments can be made for any expected improvements in productivity.)

- Ratio analysis. Employee numbers might be calculated as a ratio or proportion of another key figure in the business plan. For example, the forecast growth in employee numbers might be linked to the expected growth in sales turnover.

- Work study methods. These use estimates of the standard times to do certain work and estimates of work volumes. Staff numbers can be calculated from these standard times, allowing for expected working hours, idle time, holidays, absenteeism, and so on.

(c)
- Natural wastage. The company might decide not to recruit replacements when one of the employees leaves (retires or resigns).

- If any of the employees are on fixed-term contracts, the company can decide not to renew the contracts when (and if) they expire.

- A voluntary early retirement scheme might be offered.

- A scheme for re-training the employees to do other work might be devised.

- If these arrangements fail to avoid the need for some redundancies the company may begin the redundancy programme by looking for individuals who are willing to take voluntary redundancy (on favourable terms), rather than making compulsory redundancies.

(d)　Psychometric tests are tests, often using questionnaires, that assess the mental abilities and aptitudes of an individual (verbal, numerical and spatial reasoning) and also personality traits and the individual's interests and values.

The main advantages of these tests are that:

- many are well-established, and have been tried and tested over time

- they provide an objective assessment of an individual, based on the individual's own responses to questions

- they can be validated, by comparing a recruit's scores in a psychometric test with his or her performance in the job.

The main disadvantages of psychometric tests are that:

- there are some doubts about the value of personality testing for recruitment and employee assessments

- psychometric tests do not directly test an individual's competencies for a particular job

- individuals taking a test in a language that is not their first language could be at a disadvantage

- experts in psychometric tests are needed to analyse test results properly, and they can be expensive.

(e)　(i)　An appraisal system is used to assess the performance of an individual in his or her work. The purpose of the appraisal might be either:

- to consider the future training and development needs of the individual, or

- to assess performance with a view to rewarding the individual, in a performance-related pay scheme.

(ii)　There are several potential problems with a performance-related pay scheme. These are:

1　deciding what aspects of performance should be used for the assessment

2　identifying performance measures that recognise longer-term as well as short-term benefits for the organisation

3　preventing employees from focusing on targets linked to pay-related performance, to the exclusion of all other aspects of performance

4　making the scheme fair for everyone

5　deciding *how much* to pay for performance.

(f)　Corporate social responsibility refers mainly to the issues a company might (or should) consider with regard to employees' rights, human rights, the environment and sustainable growth, contributing to the general welfare of society and acting in an ethical way in business.

The marketing department of a company with a CSR policy needs to consider the positive or negative consequences of the products or services the company sells, how the products have been made, to whom they are sold and how they are advertised or promoted.

For example:

- products should be manufactured to the required legal standards for health and safety: where appropriate, health and safety facts should be displayed on the packaging for the products or on the product itself

- packaging should be 'environment friendly', for example consisting of bio-degradable materials

- the company might need to consider how its suppliers manufacture their goods: for example, a well-known brand of footwear suffered damage to its reputation from reports that the shoes were supplied by manufacturers using child labour

- advertising should be honest

- sales promotions might be linked to charity donations or charity events.

Public awareness and investor awareness of CSR is growing, and marketing departments will probably need to give increasing attention to this area, and its consequences (positive or negative) for their company's reputation.

185 GOURMET COMPANY

(a) Contingency theory states that:

- there is no single best way to organise and manage a business organisation, and

- the most appropriate way to organise depends on the circumstances.

The termed 'contingency theory' was originated by Lawrence and Lorsch in 1967. They argued that the development and structure of an organisation depends on the amount of uncertainty and the rate of change in its environment.

Different parts of an organisation may face different environmental uncertainties and changes. To deal with these various different environments, an organisation creates specialised sub-units, each with different structural characteristics. For example, sub-units might have different levels of formalisation in the management structure, and different degrees of centralisation/ decentralisation of authority. The greater the differences in the environments of each sub-unit, the greater the extent of differentiation in their structures needs to be.

Lawrence and Lorsch also argued when an organisation develops separate sub-units or departments to deal with differing environmental circumstances, problems arise with effective co-ordination between the sub-units. They therefore argued that the efficiency and success of an organisation depends on a combination of:

- the extent to which they are able to create sub-units to the level required by the environment, and

- the success with which these different sub-units can be integrated effectively.

(b) (i) A continuous inventory management system involves maintaining a continuous record of current inventory levels. Materials and parts are re-ordered when the quantity held in inventory falls below a specified reorder level or when there are insufficient items remaining in inventory to meet the expected future requirements for production.

A periodic inventory system involves checking inventory levels from time to time (periodically) and placing orders for fresh quantities to bring the inventory level back up to a specified maximum amount.

An ABC system of inventory management classifies inventory items into categories A, B and C, according to their importance (volume of usage and cost). Closer control is applied to the most important items (probably using a continuous management system) and least control is applied to the minor, low-value items.

(ii) MRPI schedules production and materials purchasing requirements on the basis of actual and expected demand for the firm's end-products. Materials are purchased to meet production requirements when there are insufficient quantities in inventory. MRPI therefore requires a continuous inventory management system for major inventory items. However, an ABC approach is also consistent with MRPI.

(c) The JIT philosophy can be applied to the provision of services as well as to manufacturing products. The aim should be to provide a service to the customer immediately, when the customer wants it. This requires:

- avoiding waste in providing the service

- eliminating wasteful effort

- getting the service 'right first time' so that it does not have to be done again

- holding minimal inventories of materials needed to provide the service

- avoiding unnecessary movements (motion) in providing the service.

A key aim of JIT in service provision should be to reduce queues to zero. Waiting is wasteful, inactive time. All time spent waiting in a queue in wasteful. To meet customer needs, it is important not to waste the customer's time.

(d) A user-friendly computer system is a system with a Human-Computer Interface (HCI) that makes the system easy to use and understand. The main aspects of the HCI in a system are the methods of input for data, and the interaction between the human user and the computer when the system is in operation. For many systems, the interaction works through on-screen dialogue and prompts.

A customer will very little experience of computer systems should be expected to operate the system without difficulty.

The most user-friendly input method will depend on the nature of the system. The choice of input method or methods should be made on the basis of convenience speed and, as far as possible, avoiding input errors. For customers in a food store, checking out their own purchases and making their payments, the main input methods will probably be a bar code reader for pricing the purchases, and some form of plastic card reader for payments. Some form of key pad or touch screen might also be appropriate.

A user-friendly interface should also be provided by the user's screen. The screen should display clear instructions and where necessary prompt the user into the next step of processing. It will also clearly display the cost of the purchases.

(e) Concept screening is the process of vetting a new product idea, to assess whether the product is likely to meet the standards required to give it a chance of success in the market. Product ideas are generally screened from three perspectives.

- A marketing perspective. This considers the features of the product, and the customer needs or requirements that the product will meet. This leads on to a consideration of the probable size of the market, the market share that the firm might achieve and whether sales demand is therefore likely to be high enough.

- A financial perspective. A new product idea should be evaluated financially, and the expected returns should exceed the costs. The assessment might use investment appraisal techniques, notably DCF analysis and risk analysis.

- An operations perspective. The screening process will also consider the implications for operations, and in particular whether the firm has the production capacity to make the new item, and whether significant change swill be needed in operational systems and procedures.

(f) Branding is an element of both the 'product' and 'promotion' elements of the marketing mix. It is used for several purposes.

- It helps to differentiate the products of one manufacturer (or retailer) from those of competitors. Customers can identify with a brand, and associate each brand with a particular price/quality mix.

- Consumers might develop a loyalty to a particular brand. A company might be able to take advantage of brand loyalty to extend its product range to new products with the same brand name.

- Customer loyalty to a brand can give a manufacturer more control over its marketing strategy, and in its negotiations with distributors.

- Retailers might be more willing to display products with a recognised brand, rather than lesser-known brands.

- Branding can be used to reduce the importance of price in the marketing mix. Customers might be willing to pay more for a 'quality' brand.

- Advertising is made easier, because advertisements can focus on selling the brand rather than the product itself. Where rival products do not differ significantly from each other (for example, in the case of many basic food items), this can be important.

- Branding helps with the self-selection of products by customers in supermarkets and other retail stores.

186 MARKETING-LED

(a) Market segmentation is the division of a total market into distinct groups or sections. Buyers within each group should share common characteristics that will make them similar in their needs and preferences for products or services, or similar the way in which they might react to a particular marketing initiative or marketing mix. A challenge for the marketing management is to segment the market in a useful way.

To be useful, a group of buyers or potential customers must respond differently from buyers in other market segments to the way a product is priced, or to the quality or features of the product, or the way it is promoted, advertised or distributed.

Markets might be segmented, for example, on the basis of:

- demographics (age, socio-economic characteristics, and so on)

- lifestyle

- product usage and purchasing habits

- differing customer needs.

Products can then be designed, priced, promoted and made available in such a way that it will appeal to a targeted segment of the market.

For example, the markets for clothes and fashion, and for motor cars, can be segmented according to age and other socio-economic characteristics (such as wealth, culture) or according to lifestyle.

(b)   There are different ways of segmenting a market according to lifestyle. One approach is to split the market according to the circumstances in which the customers for the product of service live through the stages of their life. For example, a simplified segmentation of the market might be:

(1)   single person, not living at home

(2)   young married couple or couple living together, no children

(3)   young couple with children under seven years old ('full nest 1')

(4)   older couple with older dependent children ('full nest 2')

(5)   older couple with no children living at home ('empty nest')

(6)   single older person living on his/her own.

Other segments of the market might be identified in a similar way, so that all potential customers for the product or service can be classified into one of the market segments.

This approach to market segmentation might be useful for marketing holidays. For example, young single people, older married couples with dependent children and single older people all seek different types of holiday at different times of the year. Different holidays packages can be devised and marketed to each segment of the market.

(c)   A relevant example is a meal in a top-quality restaurant, such as a restaurant with one or more Michelin stars. For a meal of this kind, product (the food and drink) and the place (the surroundings and atmosphere) will be important. In addition, however, significant elements in the marketing mix could be as follows:

- People. The quality of service from the waiters and the excellence of the cooking depend on the people doing the work, and the customer will be aware of this 'people' element.

- Processes. In a restaurant, processes refers to the customer's experience of the meal, and the processes that the customer is taken through from the time of entering the restaurant to the time of leaving. The meal should be a memorable experience.

- Physical evidence. The customer might also appreciate physical evidence of the fact that the meal is high-quality and something 'special'. Physical evidence of the service might be provided by expensive tableware (cutlery and glasses etcetera), or the uniforms of waiters and other staff, or even the restaurant's 'logo' or name on the menu.

187   V COSMETICS (MAY 05 EXAM)

Examiner's comments

Most sub questions were handled will by candidates. Several candidates illustrated their answers with examples drawn from well known companies (for example, Virgin).

Common errors

- Responses exceeding the limit required.

- A lack of understanding of the concept of ethics and its relationship to the proposals.

- Unclear understanding of direct marketing.

(a)   Using the 4Ps marketing mix, the approach can be explained as follows:

Product

- Range of cosmetics.

- Strong brand name, implying a quality product at a competitive price.

Promotion

- V typically spends little on advertising relying instead on the strength of its brand name.

- The cosmetics associates will also promote the products to friends at cosmetics parties.

- Internet and mobile telephone technology will also be used to communicate details of the products to potential customers.

Price

- Competitively priced against high street brands.

Place

- Will not be on sale in shops.

- Customers can order using the Internet and their mobile telephones.

- Customers can also buy from the cosmetic associates.

- Little information given about distribution.

In all of this it is key that the marketing mix variables are blended to satisfy customer needs.

(b)   The human resource implications of using 'cosmetics associates' are as follows:

- Selection and recruitment: applicants must be trustworthy, presentable, engaging and reflect the image of the company. This is particularly important, as the company brand name is the main aspect of the marketing mix.

- Training: associates need to be trained in:

    –   features of the product range

    –   how to organise and run the parties

    –   sales techniques

    –   the firm's administrative procedures for handling orders and payments.

- Remuneration: the usual method for associates would be commission (e.g. 25% of sales revenue generated) but V may have to offer a basic salary as well to attract suitable candidates.

- Retention: having built up contacts, V does not want associates leaving to work for themselves or a competitor.

- Supervision: there needs to be a system so V can check that associates are not damaging the firm's reputation by hard selling or poor customer care.

(c)   The main features of direct marketing are as follows:

- 'Direct' means that there are no intermediaries – V would deal directly with the end consumer.

- Often claimed to be cheaper as no need to share profits with intermediaries.

- Should enable better control of the sales process.

- Very common with internet companies e.g. Amazon.

(d)   The advantages of the Internet are:

- Potential to reach huge numbers of people.

- Will reach the right sort of people – V's customers are likely to be younger, more affluent and thus more used to buying online.

- Cheap as avoids the costs of a physical site.

- Can use existing websites.

- Facilitates e-commerce so customers can buy online.

- Speed of communication.

- Convenient for customers.

- Allows a customer to compare products easily.

- Can build up information database about customers.

(e)   V might use the Internet and mobile phone technology as follows:

The Internet

- The website should be engaging, have competitions.

- Promotion could involve banner ads, *sponsored search engine results* and affiliate websites.

- Competitive price approach *will fit with people's expectations* when shopping online.

- Customers can order online.

- Customers can buy using credit cards via a secure server.

- Details could be passed onto associates.

Mobile phones

- The method again fits with the sense of fun associated with V's image.

- Promotion via text messages and alerts

- Details could be passed onto associates.

(f)   The main ethical issues are:

- Are associates being treated fairly, especially with regard to remuneration if it is commission only?

- Is it ethical for associates to visit people's homes to sell the product?

- Will associates feel under pressure to sell to their friends even though they might not want to use the products?

- (Mis)use of customer database.

- Is it ethical to 'cold call' people on their mobiles?

- Whether the product has been or will be tested on animals.

- Does the manufacture of the product use non-renewable resources like oil?

- Where will the product be manufactured – if in a third world country then V will have to ensure local workers are treated fairly and not exploited.

188 CFO

(a) **Operating systems**

The operating system is the system software that manages the control activities of the computer. It can be seen as the chief manager of the computer system, controlling:

- which resources the computer system will use

- scheduling the use of those resources and monitoring their activities

- the links between other hardware devices, such as keyboards, printers or faxes, and makes sure they are ready to use

- the efficient storage of data, files and directories, monitoring storage space within a computer and how best this should be used

- coordination of different parts of the computer so that many tasks can be done simultaneously.

Three main features of an operating system are:

Multi-programming / tasking

The operating system allows multiple computer programs to use the computer's resources at the same time. For example, a user can be inputting new or updated data relating to a customer on the customer database, whilst at the same time the user can be printing off a separate report on weekly activities.

Graphical User Interface

Users interact with the operating system through the user interface of that particular operating system. Modern operating systems, such as Windows use a graphical user interface (GUI) to represent common commands and computer operations. GUI uses a range of icons, buttons, symbols, pull down menus and bars to represent programs and files, which can be activated using a mouse or cursor.

Security and password controls

Operating systems will have strict password control systems to prevent unauthorised access to data and files. The operating system can be programmed to ensure that users can only access approved areas of the system.

(b) **Benefits for CFO**

The benefits of the above features are as follows:

Multiprogramming/multitasking

This should improve efficiency throughout the firm. For example, a user in Business Unit B may wish to use the mortgage customer database to refer to customer information, whilst also preparing a spreadsheet report on overdue mortgage accounts. Multi-tasking will allow the user to display both programs on screen at the same time and work on them both simultaneously, without having to close one program down to work with the other.

Graphical User Interface

CFO is likely to have a number of separate programs relating to the full range of insurance products they offer. If all of these use the same GUI, then users will be able to navigate their way around all parts of the system without too much difficulty or need to re-learn, thus improving productivity and efficiency. It should make it easier, for example, for staff to sell additional products to customers when they are on the phone.

Security and password controls

For CFO, security of data is critical. A great deal of confidential customer information will be held on the system and customers will want to be assured that their data is not at risk. If customers lack confidence in the CFO systems, then they are less likely to do business with CFO.

(c) **Updated website**

The importance of the new website to CFO is as follows:

Business Unit A

Business Unit A has lost customers in recent years by being slow to introduce technological delivery of its products. The new website is thus critical to future success as more and more customers will use the Internet to research and purchase financial services products. Business Unit A must respond to its customers' expectations.

Customer satisfaction will be key in maintaining its position in the market. The additional features proposed for the website should enhance customer satisfaction and improve customer interaction with the company.

For example, one of the new website functions will be the ability to produce online decisions for credit and discount facilities. This should improve speed of response for the customer, as the system, rather than the operator, can now make a decision.

The updated website will also allow cross selling of products between the five call centres as customers will be able to see all products online. This is likely to be key to future growth for CFO.

Business Unit B

Business Unit B staff are more interested in a stable desktop environment and user friendly operating system, than a state-of-the-art website.

(d) **Benchmarking**

Benchmarking is a method of comparing the operational performance of a company with other companies, often competitors that are considered to be the 'best in class'. The main types of benchmarking are:

- **Internal benchmarking** is comparing the performance in key areas in one part of an organisation with the performance in one or more other parts of the same organisation.

- **Competitive benchmarking** is comparing your performance in key areas with the performance of your most successful competitors.

- **Process benchmarking** or activity benchmarking involves identifying and making comparisons of processes, activities, products or services of other organisations in a different industry.

- **Generic benchmarking** looks at conceptually similar processes, more for ideas than targets – for example, Xerox looked at how the US mail order company L.L. Bean handled large items such as canoes when trying to improve its own transportation of photocopiers.

(e) **Advantages of benchmarking for CFO**

Competitive advantage

Being a member of the Forum for Quality in Lending, CFO can compare itself against other mortgage providers. This way it can identify the key aspects of other mortgage providers that customers most value can identify where it needs to improve to stay competitive. This will give it a competitive advantage over those mortgage providers who are not part of the benchmarking group.

Reducing complacency

The benchmarking group will use a range of key indices to compare organisations, including customer satisfaction. This forces CFO to be outward looking and focus upon improving customer satisfaction.

A change in culture

Organisations who undertake benchmarking tend to be more dynamic and forward thinking. They are more open to change and to improvement in delivery of service.

Traditionally, Business Unit B has been less dynamic and innovative, but it may have to change now that it is part of the Forum for Quality in Lending.

Allocating resources

Benchmarking allows organisations to allocate scarce resources to those areas most in need of improvement. CFO could use the indices provided by the benchmarking forum to identify its main areas of weakness and could ensure that those processes were the first to be allocated resources such as money, staff time and expertise.

Provides a good marketing tool

Being part of an industry-wide and recognised quality body will be a key marketing tool for CFO and should help to retain existing customers and attract new customers.

(f)   **Staff training**

Improvements in staff training in CFO could improve the quality of customer service as follows:

Training in products sold

- More knowledgeable staff will be able to find the most suitable products for customers. This is critical in an industry with a poor record of misselling.

- Staff will be able to deal with customer concerns and queries more quickly and with fewer referrals.

- Staff may be able to sell additional products to customers, for example, a customer wanting a mortgage may also be open to buy insurance. For this to work, it is vital that staff in unit B are aware of unit A products and vice-versa.

- Customers will feel that staff understand their needs better and will thus feel more confident in their recommendations.

Training in technology

- It is vital that call-centre staff are fully fluent with new systems to avoid delays when dealing with potential customers.

189   MOTIVATION ASSUMPTIONS

(a)   (i)   *Maslow's need-based theory* – Maslow developed a model of human motivation which was composed of five levels of distinct human needs, arranged in an hierarchical order. These are:

- physiological needs (food, water, air, etc)

- safety needs (security, stability, freedom from physical danger)

- social needs (belongingness and love)

- esteem needs (achievement, recognition)

- self-actualisation needs (self-fulfilment or realisation of one's potential).

According to Maslow these needs exist in a hierarchy, whereby human behaviour is motivated by the attempt to satisfy that need which is most important at a particular point.

Furthermore, the strength of any particular need is determined by its position in the hierarchy and by the degree to which any lower-order needs have been satisfied. The lower-order needs (physiological and safety) are dominant until satisfied, whereupon the higher-order needs come into operation.

(ii)   Herzberg's motivation-hygiene theory – also known as the two-factor or dual-factor theory. The motivation-hygiene theory explains human motivation in terms of factors which act as satisfiers and dissatisfiers. According to Herzberg, those factors that act as satisfying agents, and therefore are motivating forces, include achievement, recognition, advancement and growth in the job. These are known as job contentment factors or satisfiers in that they lead to job satisfaction, but not job dissatisfaction should they be absent. These motivating factors stem from the performance of one's work.

The second group, referred to variously as the maintenance or hygiene factors, include money, status, job security, supervision, company policy and administration and working conditions. Unlike the first group, these hygiene factors are not motivators, but their absence leads to job dissatisfaction. Thus for Herzberg human motivation should be viewed in a two-dimensional way, with the presence or absence of certain job factors leading to satisfaction and dissatisfaction.

(iii)   *Theory X and Theory Y* – McGregor identified that managers have a rule of thumb to describe how people can be motivated to work.

Advocates of Theory X would view their subordinates as an 'untrustworthy, money-motivated, calculative mass' who have an inherent dislike of work and will avoid it wherever possible. This rational-economic view of man was adopted by classical theorists such as Taylor and Fayol.

If there are subordinates with these attitudes then they would have to be driven, threatened and coerced to get them to expend adequate effort towards the achievement of organisational objectives. Economic incentives including payment by results and group and individual bonuses would be the only form of motivation and workers would be exhorted to 'work hard, obey orders and we will look after you'.

At the other extreme, followers of Theory Y believe that people like and gain satisfaction from work – it is as natural as play or rest. This self-actualising concept of man is that adopted by the behaviourists who claim that even the unskilled, occupied in the most menial tasks, seek self-actualisation and a sense of meaning and accomplishment in their work, provided that their basic needs are more or less fulfilled.

McGregor did not put this forward as a theory of motivation as such, but as a description of how managers think in the lack of a more scientific understanding. Each theory has implications for management style – Theory X suggests close supervision and control; Theory Y suggests delegation.

(b)   The effect that the changes at R Company will have on the sales people could be as follows.

(i)   *Commission consolidated into higher salary* – if someone has been doing particularly well out of the previous incentive payment system, he/she will not like this change – it may even demotivate them. Less effort is now required by them to make the same amount of money. Those who will be motivated by this change are those who work in a sales area where commission was low; they may see the system as fairer overall.

The effect of the change will depend on the staff's individual needs. Those who are starting out in their career may find more money motivates them – they are aiming to satisfy their basic needs. Those who are wanting to fulfil their self-fulfilment needs may not necessarily be greatly affected by a salary change. Younger people and those who also have a mortgage and family to consider are usually motivated by money. They will react either positively or negatively to this change depending on the effect it has on their pay packet.

Herzberg argued that salary was a hygiene factor, so the change will only motivate if staff felt underpaid before.

The salary change is more likely to increase motivation for McGregor's Theory X employees than Theory Y.

(ii) Non-contributory pension scheme – this would seem to satisfy an individual's security needs. However, a younger person who sees old age as a long way off is less likely to be motivated by this offer. An older person seeing their working days coming to an end may find it more rewarding and feel grateful to the R Co for providing it. However, because they are older they do not have so much time left in employment and will receive less pension than the younger members.

One could argue that a pension would be a hygiene factor, using Herzberg's ideas, so the change will only motivate staff who felt aggrieved at the previous policy.

Theory Y staff are more likely to have a long-term perspective on their careers so will value the pension change more.

(iii) More prestigious cars – this is a status symbol and shows the member of staff and other people how highly they are regarded by the R Co. It should help to fulfil their ego needs. We must remember that for each section the extent to which the individual is motivated will depend on his/her own needs. For example, if someone already has a Porsche of his/her own, being given a company Rover is not likely to motivate them.

It is debatable whether a company car would be seen as a motivator, conveying status and recognition, or a hygiene factor, regarded as a "right".

Increased holidays – this seems a good offer except for those people who live and breathe work. Young single employees who are looking to make a name for themselves will find this less attractive than employees with a family who want to spend more time with their children.

Theory X staff will definitely value not having to work as much!

190 MONDAY NEWSPAPERS

(a) Market positioning involves deciding how the products or services of the firm should be marketed relative to rival products and services. Within the total market, a firm might choose to present its products as the market leader or least cost product. Positioning a product as market leader generally means that it has to be marketed largely on the basis of price.

An alternative approach is to position the product as something that appeals to a particular segment of the market. The product might then be sold on the basis of its differentiating features rather than price.

Even within a market segment, it is necessary to position a product relative to rival products. The product needs to be presented as something that places it in a distinctive part of the market segment. Again, price can be used to position the product as the low cost item in the segment. Alternatively, products might be positioned at the 'top end' of the market, offering higher quality but at a higher price.

Product features (product differentiation), quality and price are the most obvious ways of positioning a product, and promotion can be used to present a product image to reinforce the market position. However, it might be possible to position the product using distribution channels to make the differentiation. For example, Amazon positioned itself in the market for book selling by offering books for sale online at the buyer's convenience. With newspapers, it has been possible in some cases to position a new newspaper as a 'free' paper made available at railway stations to commuters: free newspapers are now another segment of the total market for newspapers.

(b)   The marketing mix for national newspapers is an appropriate combination of the 4Ps: price, product, place and promotion. Newspapers might compete with rival titles on the basis of price. One newspaper producer might offer a price that is always lower in price: alternatively, there might be a short-term lower price offer in an attempt to increase sales. Newspapers recognise the general importance of price as a key factor affecting sales demand, and publishers continually attempt to reduce and control costs.

Newspapers differentiate themselves as much as possible on the basis of 'product'. In the UK, there is a segregation of the market into the tabloid popular press, the 'quality titles' and the 'middle market titles'. Within each segment there is competition, and newspapers often seek to achieve product differentiation by means of 'exclusives' and eye-catching front page headlines.

National newspapers perhaps compete less on the basis of 'place' in the marketing mix. However, regional newspapers market their local emphasis, and free newspapers need to provide their product through a convenient distribution method (such as arranging to make them available at railway stations in the morning, or delivering to homes free of charge).

National newspapers also compete through promotions, although the costs of mass advertising need to justify the expected benefits from higher sales. Where mass advertising is used to promote newspapers (for example, through poster advertising or TV advertising), the advertising message often focuses on the product content. However, public relations is another important element in the promotion of newspapers: newspapers can often sell more copies by creating national news themselves, and promoting their involvement.

(c)   The information about the total market size of the national newspapers market, analysed on a regional basis, and the market share of each newspaper, needs to come from the newspaper publishers themselves. Newspapers provide details of their circulation figures and make them available to external users. This is essential in the newspaper industry because newspapers obtain much of their income from advertising and promotion features. Knowing how many copies of each title is sold is a critical factor in the selection by advertisers of a newspaper for advertising, and it is also a key issue in the negotiation and agreement of advertising rates between newspapers and advertisers.

Independent verification of circulation figures is necessary to protect advertisers against the risk that newspapers will provide dishonest or misleading circulation figures. In the UK, an Audit Bureau of Circulations (ABC) provides independent verification of circulation figures, which newspapers provide monthly. These figures are audited, either by the ABC's own staff or by the external auditors of the newspaper publisher.

(d)   Newspapers use the Internet and e-mail to improve their communication systems and to offer new services to customers.

- The Internet and e-mail are used to obtain information for publishing. For example, a public relations department or PR agency will normally use e-mail to issue new press releases to the major newspapers.

- Newspapers can use the Internet to access data, such as official statistics and published government documents, or to identify contacts within organisations. E-mails might be an efficient method of communication as an alternative to telephone calls.

- Some newspapers provide archive services via the Internet, so that users can access back copies of newspapers, or look up specific articles that have been published in the past.

- Newspapers might also offer a web site service, either free of charge or at a subscription price to subscribers, offering additional information not contained in the published newspaper.

(e) Sales demand fluctuates according to the day of each week. There are two editions each day. It is unlikely that Monday Newspapers can do anything to alter the pattern of sales demand between days of the week, or between early and late editions. It would therefore appear that production scheduling should be planned to meet sales demand. Printing on the large presses will be in one large batch for each edition, and the batch size will be the estimated sales demand for the day, with possibly some extra copies to allow for spare copies for distributors to meet unexpectedly high demand.

MRP I can be used to plan complex production processes and monitor inventory levels for a wide range of raw materials, parts and sub-components. However, printing newspapers is probably a fairly straightforward production process. The main raw materials are paper and ink, and the product is not complex. It is therefore unlikely that an MRP I system would provide significant benefits for the company.

There are some similarities between printing newspapers and JIT production requirements. Although Monday Newspapers might wish to hold inventories of paper and ink, it will not hold any inventories of finished goods, and will not have any work-in-progress at the end of each day. This is because daily newspapers lose their value at the end of the day on which they are published. It is also important to ensure that the production process is efficient, with a minimum of breakdowns and waste.

However, in many respects, newspaper printing is not well-suited to JIT. JIT production applies the concepts of flexible production, with an ideal batch size of one, small machines and small work groups. Since the company produces a fairly standard product, large batch production on large efficient machinery is probably a much more appropriate production process for newspapers.

(f) The marketing reasons for publishing three colour supplements are probably as follows.

- If rival newspapers also publish colour supplements, it might be necessary to publish supplements to remain competitive with rival newspapers in the same segment of the market.

- Supplements give the consumer more product for the same price and, by providing more value for money, the newspaper publisher might hope to sell significantly more copies.

- Specialist supplements on sport, cooking and 'living' will provide the newspaper publisher with an opportunity to sell more specialist advertising, such as advertisements for sports equipment and cooking items.

- It might also be possible to obtain revenue from sponsored articles in the supplement, where the contents of an article promote a manufacturer's products. For example, XYZ Airlines might be prepared to sponsor an article on air travel in which the airline is featured in a positive way.

In summary, the potential benefits are greater competitiveness for the product and higher revenue from sales of newspapers, advertising and sponsorship.

191   ROUND THE TABLE (NOV 05 EXAM)

Key answer tip:

The question asks for guidance notes, so avoid lengthy paragraphs and use bullet points.

(a)   Why a level capacity strategy might be difficult for a firm wishing to adopt a just-in-time (JIT) strategy

Level capacity

- With a level capacity strategy, the aim is to maintain processing capacity at a uniform or level amount throughout the planning period, regardless of fluctuations in demand.

Just-in-time

- JIT systems aim to hold minimal stocks, producing goods just in time to be used or sold.

Problems

- At times of low demand, a level capacity strategy will result in increasing stock levels, contradicting the JIT aim of minimal stock.

- At times of high demand, a level capacity strategy will result in falling stock levels – possibly to zero. If the demand continues to be high, then production will have to be increased to meet customer requirements on time. The level capacity approach would prevent this happening, thus the JIT system will fail to deliver.

- These problems highlight the fact that JIT is a pull system responding to demand, whereas a level capacity strategy is a push system focusing on production.

Conclusion

- Unlikely to be compatible unless demand is very steady.

(b)   The impact of demand strategies on marketing

Demand strategy ('demand management')

- An organisation might attempt to 'manage demand' with the aim of stabilising demand and making it more predictable.

- If demand is fairly stable and predictable, capacity levels can then be planned accordingly.

Implications for marketing

- An aim of demand management is often to encourage customers to use a service in an off-peak period rather than at peak times. Examples of demand management are:

  - on the railways or buses, offering off-peak tickets at much lower prices

  - lower prices for 'off-season' holidays

  - lower prices for telephone calls at off-peak times.

- A company might use advertising to boost demand during low demand seasons, such as encouraging consumers to eat more ice cream during the cold months of the year.

- In some cases, an organisation might seek to boost demand in low-sales periods by offering a completely different product or service with the same resources. For example, mobile vans used for selling ice cream in the hot months might be converted to selling hot meals such as burgers and hot dogs during the colder months.

(c)   Chase strategies and flexible organisations

Chase strategies

- With a chase demand plan, the objective is to match capacity as closely as possible with demand. If demand increases, capacity is increased, and if demand falls, capacity is reduced.

Flexible organisations

- Flexible organisations seek to build in the ability to change rapidly in response to changing market conditions.

Relationship

- In order to achieve a chase demand strategy, resources must be flexible.

    –   Staff numbers must be easily increased or reduced in numbers, possibly by hiring temporary and part-time staff, overtime or sub-contracting.

    –   Variations in equipment capacity must be achievable by methods such as equipment hire.

- In capital-intensive operations, a chase demand plan is unworkable, because equipment cannot be easily increased or decreased at short notice.

(d)   Differences between service organisations and manufacturing organisations

The main difference between service and manufacturing organisations is that the former cannot hold stock to act as a buffer between demand and capacity. This has the following implications:

Level capacity strategies

- If demand is less than capacity, there will be idle resources – management must accept that there will be idle resources for much of the time. This is often evident in operations such as retailing, and the hotels and restaurants business.

- When demand exceeds capacity, the operation will have to turn away some of the customers.

Chase strategies

- Trying to match capacity with demand is often very difficult for service industries, especially if staff are highly skilled.

- Additional capacity can be gained by the use of temporary staff or freelancers, but at the risk of quality suffering.

Demand strategies

- Many service operators try to manage demand to increase staff utilisation. This can include price discrimination to attract customers to quiet periods when staff would otherwise be sitting around with nothing to do.

- Many restaurants offer special menus mid-week and at lunchtimes.

(e) Software to improve inbound logistics

What are inbound logistics?

Inbound logistics are the activities concerned with sources of funds (working capital, investment), relationship with suppliers, supply sources and costs, receiving, storing and distributing the inputs to the organisation system (materials handling, stock control, transport, etc).

Software applications

Inbound logistics can be improved by use of the following:

- MRP I applications – Materials Requirement Planning (MRP 1) is a computerised system for planning the requirements for raw materials and components, sub-assemblies and finished items. It is a system that converts a production schedule into a listing of the materials and components required to meet that schedule, so that adequate stock levels are maintained and items are available when needed.

- ERP applications – Enterprise Resource Planning (ERP) was developed from MRP. In an MRP system, the effects of any change in sales demand are calculated by the system, and new schedules for manufacturing and materials procurement are produced. An ERP system performs a similar function, but it integrates data from all operations within the organisation.

- JIT applications – to help manage stock.

- E-procurement software to speed up the buying process and thus reduce the need for buffer stocks.

- Allowing suppliers access to an extranet, where they can see scheduled production and ensure that items are made and delivered in time.

- Warehouse management applications to speed up finding and delivering stock items.

- Delivery and distribution applications to improve the efficiency of delivering raw materials and components to where they are needed in operations.

- Software applications to assist in quality control checking of bought items.

(f) Computerised assistance that could be used by those selling cars and wanting improve demand

The following computerised assistance could help boost demand:

- Website-based selling that could reduce the overheads associated with a traditional showroom and allow the firm to offer lower priced vehicles. A website has the additional advantages of always being open and being able to show more detailed information, involving product reviews and comparisons.

- Viral marketing – the recent Citroën advert with a car performing a Justin Timberlake-style dance routine was originally a small video file that the firm hoped people would email to their friends as it was very original when it first came out.

- Maintaining a database of previous customers so they can be contacted directly to encourage them to replace their old cars with a new one.

- Use of emails to advertise ('spam').

- If 'computerised assistance' extends to enabling greater flexibility in the production process, then the sales staff can offer customers a greater range of choices without significantly delaying delivery times.

- The company can ensure that its stock is listed on various car search websites to enable customer and dealer to find each other. This is particularly useful for secondhand and rare cars.

Section 6

ANSWERS TO SECTION C-TYPE QUESTIONS

INFORMATION SYSTEMS

192 PROJECT MANAGEMENT

(a) Project management differs from functional management in that it is the management of resources which are attempting to achieve specific objectives within set timescales and budgets. Functional management, on the other hand, is concerned with providing an on-going service.

A project has boundaries and it is one of the activities of the project management team to set and keep the project within those boundaries.

A project will be initiated to develop or try something new and accurate costs are therefore difficult to estimate. It is also difficult to estimate benefits or eventual outcome and projects must therefore be carefully controlled and monitored.

The project management team would need, first of all, to identify the standards for:

(i) the organisation of the project, including any user involvement

(ii) estimating, resourcing and scheduling the project including drawing up a project plan

(iii) quality control

(iv) the activities performed and their assessments

(v) the end product produced or developed.

Each project will be different, but it is still necessary to identify suitable technical standards relating to what is being developed.

The development of a computerised administrative system is used to illustrate an approach to project management. The stages are as detailed below.

Organisation

Creating a project board who will be responsible for the project and who will have authority over it. The board will be responsible for:

(i) approving plans

(ii) monitoring progress

(iii) allocating resources

(iv) assessing results, and

(v) recommending continuance or termination.

A project manager will be in charge of the project itself and he will report back to the project board.

The project manager is responsible for:

(i)   defining individual responsibilities

(ii)   preparing state or phase plans

(iii)   setting objectives

(iv)   collating information from project teams

(v)   controlling team activities, and

(vi)   reporting to the project board.

The project manager would have a number of project teams with team leaders reporting back to him.

Planning

At the beginning of a project outline technical plans will be needed to identify the major technical activities.

When the technical plans have been produced, identification of required resources can then take place. These resources include 'expert' staff who may be required at particular times or for particular activities.

The project itself will be broken down into a number of stages, with each stage being monitored and then assessed at its completion. In this way identification of deviances from the expected plan can be fully analysed.

Controls

At the end of each stage the project manager will report to the project board, who will compare the actual achievements against the expected achievements.

These comparisons will allow the project board to estimate the likelihood of the project being successful, completed within the specified timescale, and completed within the specified budget.

Activities/end products

The activities of the project should result in the end project being quality assured, as each activity is fully monitored throughout.

A quality assurance test would be performed before each stage or before the final project was deemed to be completed.

Review

At the completion of the project the management of that project would be reviewed. Although no two projects are the same, experience gained throughout the course of the project should be fully assessed and documented in order that similar types of projects may benefit in future.

(b)   The management of a project is very complex. Activities need to be scheduled and planned in order to make the most effective use of the resources available.

Some activities are reliant upon other activities having been completed before they themselves can be started. All activities therefore need to be properly planned to assess the order in which they need to be undertaken. A critical path will exist throughout the project. Network analysis identifies the dependence of one activity on another.

Computer-based packages now exist which aid the project manager to identify the critical path. If activities differ in their actual time from their estimated time, these differences can be entered into the computer and a recalculation of the critical path takes place.

Project evaluation and review techniques (PERT) allow for probability and risk assessment to be input and resource requirements to be more accurately estimated.

PERT packages aid project management because they allow for fast recalculation of the critical path. Project managers may also perform 'what if' calculations in order to assess possible outcomes for alternative assumptions.

Computer aided software engineering (CASE) is another tool of the project manager. CASE tools incorporate the use of products such as 4GLs which automate part of the programming function. 'Case tools' is the generic term for this support.

Project management is also aided by the use of standard packages such as word-processing, desktop publishing, etc. These packages prove most useful in the rapid preparation of clearly laid out reports and manuals.

(c)   It might be less expensive to use in-house staff. A third party vendor would add a margin to the costs of the programming time. Provided in-house staff are available there would be no net cost to using in-house staff.

In-house staff should have a clearer insight into the needs of the organisation and the manner in which its systems are organised. This might mean that the resulting software is superior to that which might be produced externally.

Writing the software in-house means that the organisation has control over the documentation and source documents. These can be filed and will be available to assist with upgrades and developments. If a third party supplier retains any of these files then it might become difficult to maintain the system in the future.

Writing a new system will be a major undertaking. Most organisations would find that this would overwhelm their in-house resources. The ongoing maintenance of existing systems would be set aside during this period, possibly causing problems elsewhere in the organisation.

193   E-MAIL

(a)   Communication by e-mail impacts on work practices in a number of ways. It affects the speed of communication, it adds to the choice of media to use when sending messages or conducting meetings and it accommodates teleworking to suit different lifestyles. There are also negative aspects to the communication channel. It encourages 'chatting' and other non-essential communications and some people use a type of shorthand, which does not seem very business-like.

The **speed of communication** with e-mail is one of the major impacts on work practices. There is an almost instant delivery of messages, documents, reports or letters. The technology allows the same message to be sent simultaneously to a group of people, such as a committee, and there are no significant time delays, whereby one person receives the information before another. This particular feature reduces ambiguities and helps facilitate co-ordination.

Because people receive their messages as they are sitting at their computers working, there is also a tendency for them to **reply more quickly** than they would to a circulated hard copy. This means that delays in waiting for information can be reduced or eliminated and time can be spent doing more productive work. Unfortunately, when people send messages that require a response, there is an expectation that it will be instantaneous. When there is a delay it generally creates a certain amount of impatience and frustration.

Another impact of e-mail on work practices is that it **increases the choice of communication channel**. Many tasks can be completed more quickly and effectively than would have previously been the case without e-mail facilities. It has advantages over traditional forms of communication. Documents no longer need to be despatched by courier. It is more economical than sending letters because it costs less to send an e-mail than the cost of a postage stamp, especially when fast delivery is required. It can be more secure than sending a letter or memo because access can be denied by the use of passwords. Electronic delivery and read receipts can be requested, and a record can be kept of messages, which gives it an advantage over telephone calls.

Because e-mail allows information to be disseminated more readily via circulation lists, bulletin boards and discussion databases, **the need for meetings is greatly reduced**. Until quite recently companies had regular committee-type meetings just to distribute information. These types of meetings can be very costly and do not always achieve what is required. The use of e-mail can be a far more efficient and reliable way of keeping everyone informed. There are still some types of meetings which it is not possible to replace by e-mail, but the arrangements for them e.g., the distribution of agenda, can all be distributed more efficiently with e-mail.

The downside to all this is that it has obvious implications for employment and the requisite skills of the work force. There can be a tendency for employees to become attached to their computer screens and avoid social contact. This could be undesirable if employees are unable to work together.

The Internet, with its e-mail facilities, is a part of many people's lifestyle and is no longer considered a form of communication for business only. It has enabled teleworking, with many more people working away from the office environment, changing the entire focus of work. The **virtual organisation** allows individuals to work on a project or task and communicate with other members of the team, using e-mail, as though they were sharing an office. It no longer matters where people are located or what time suits them to be working. The Internet allows e-mail messages to be sent anywhere in the world at any time of the day or night for the cost of a telephone call. The message is sent to a mailbox and this can be accessed when the recipient logs on to their computer.

There are bound to be **some disadvantages** associated with communication by e-mail. Because it is very easy to use there may be several messages going backwards and forwards between individuals in a short space of time. People are tempted to use their e-mail facility as a chat line for social as well as work purposes. They can also waste time by distributing items that are not related to work, such as screen savers and games.

Another disadvantage is that messages sent via e-mail tend to be much more informal than traditional hard copy letters and can also be more informal than a telephone call. They are inclined to be very short, without any frills such as salutations. Certain groups have developed a type of language that is only used in e-mail communications. This language uses keyboard characters to denote certain words or phrases. Unfortunately, this trend will have an impact on the language used at work. Employers have been complaining for a long time that school leavers have poor literacy skills and cannot write a business letter. With fewer reasons to practice these skills because of new technologies, formal letter writing will become redundant.

(b) Like all forms of communication, e-mail has its place and is very useful and efficient. However, there are a number of occasions where it would not be an appropriate form of communication. They include interviews and meetings of a personal or confidential nature, group discussions and training sessions.

E-mail messages are inappropriate for interviews of a personal or confidential nature. One-to-one interviews for a job or an appraisal could not be conducted without the parties to the interview being together. Part of the interview technique is to see how people react to different types of questioning and this could not be handled by e-mail. Disciplinary and grievance interviews are similar but raise sensitive issues, which do not lend themselves to being reduced to short e-mail messages. Some messages are so sensitive that even face-to-face communication is difficult. No one would want to find out some bad news via an e-mail.

Although there are ways of making messages secure and delivering them to the right person, there can be security problems associated with sending messages over a computer network. Within an organisation, messages can be delivered to the wrong person via the internal e-mail system because they have a similar name to the intended recipient. Messages sent via the Internet may pass through several servers en route to their destination and at any of these servers the messages could be read, intercepted or copied.

Discussion groups, conferences, meetings and training sessions are all occasions when e-mail would not be a suitable method of communication. It would only take ten people in a discussion group, using e-mail to send items to each other to be discussed, for the messages to become very confused. People participating in the discussion could soon lose track of how it is progressing. Because there is a mixture of oral and visual communication involved in some conferences and training sessions, they are unsuitable for e-mail. It is very difficult to show the subtleties of body language other than at face-to-face meetings.

(c) Use of company email for personal correspondence could create serious problems for the organisation. If a member of staff sends a message that is deemed offensive or defamatory, then it may leave the organisation open to adverse publicity or even legal action.

The receipt of personal emails may involve staff receiving files from unrealiable sources. These could contain viruses that could cause systems crashes.

Personal use of company email may put a strain on the organisation's communications bandwidth, slowing down legitimate correspondence.

Reading and replying to personal emails may be a distraction from employees' duties unless they restrict such activities to breaks.

194   SMALL CHAIN

(a)   Essentially, there are four approaches from which to choose:

Direct changeover

The existing system is abandoned for the new at a given point in time. Prima facie this seems an economical approach, but this is balanced by the risk that the new system will not work perfectly. Furthermore, there will be no safety net, in terms of existing procedures and staff, with which to recover the situation. It is not suitable for large systems crucial to the well-being of the organisation. If the new system bears little or no similarity to the old, this may be the only route. In the context of the department store, it should be obvious that this is not a viable option; if the new system collapses, then the store potentially loses all sales until it is remounted.

Parallel running

This involves the running at the same time of both old and new systems, with results being compared. Until the new system is proven, the old system will be relied upon. A relatively safe approach, which also allows staff to consolidate training in the new system before live running commences. It is expensive, however, because of the extra resources required to run two systems side by side. Parallel running is necessary where it is vital the new system is proven before operation. In the case of the Point of Sale (POS) system, this would be the most suitable method of changeover.

Phased changeover

Here the new system is introduced department by department, or location by location. This is less drastic than direct changeover, and less costly than parallel running, although each department may still be parallel run. For the department store group it might well be a sensible approach to introduce the new POS system into just one store, initially, and parallel run at that store first, before switching to phased changeover, and subsequently to implementation at all other stores.

Pilot changeover

This is another compromise approach, involving the running of the new system, or functions/subsystems thereof, on a sample of users, transactions, files, etc. in parallel with the new system. This might be followed by full parallel running, or a switch to phased changeover. Care must be taken with the choice of sample. The nature of the new system here, makes it unlikely that this approach could be adopted.

Whichever approach, or combination of approaches, is adopted, good management control, including thorough monitoring, will be essential if the new system is to be successful.

(b) **Checklist of implementation** activities should include:

- development of a changeover timetable
- involvement of all affected personnel in planning
- advance notification to employees, followed by periodic progress bulletins
- development of training programme
- consider possible needs for external resources
- delivery of Point-Of-Sale (POS) equipment
- testing of equipment
- installation and testing of software
- completion of documentation
- training for systems operators
- system trials
- changeover period
- acceptance of new system
- operational running.

(c) **Systems evaluation**

This is a vital and important part of system implementation. Its objective is the systematic assessment of system performance to determine whether the established goals are being achieved.

A number of criteria are commonly used to measure the performance of the systems:

Time, i.e. the time required for a particular action to be performed. Response time is the time that elapses before a system responds to a demand placed upon it; for the POS system, this must be measured in seconds. Turnaround time is the length of time required before results are returned; for a POS system, little processing is done, and this may not be significant.

Costs, sometimes the only measure applied, are used to determine whether the various parts of the system are performing to financial expectations, and include labour costs, overheads, variable costs, maintenance costs, training costs, data entry costs, data storage costs, etc. For the POS system, all of these should be considered.

Hardware performance should be measured in terms of speed, reliability, maintenance, operating costs and power requirements. The performance of the POS devices in the various store departments, the central computer servicing the POS system and any networking components must be evaluated.

Software performance should be measured in terms of processing speed, quality and quantity of output, accuracy, reliability, maintenance and update requirements. Again, this is necessary for all software involved in the POS system.

Accuracy is a measure of freedom from errors achieved by the system and can be measured in several ways; but it is important that the type of errors as well as volume is analysed to ensure that serious errors are quickly identified. In the POS system, it is essential, for example, that the prices charged to customers are accurate.

Security means that all records are secure, that equipment is protected and that unauthorised or illegal access is minimised. It is important that the central database containing product prices is not corrupted, for example.

Morale is reflected in the satisfaction and acceptance that employees feel towards their jobs. Absentee rate and employee turnover are two factors that can be used to assess morale of the POS operators in the stores.

Customer reactions are an important factor in the context of the POS system; large numbers of complaints from customers would indicate that the system is not performing satisfactorily.

All the data gathered from the various components of evaluation should be studied to assess the success or otherwise of the system and, if the latter, to help pinpoint the reasons why performance is not reaching expectations.

(d)   The new system might offer the opportunity to reduce staffing. The fact that information is being gathered automatically and in real time from the POS means that there will be less need for clerical analysis in support of inventory control, preparation of sales reports, etc. The prospect of such changes may be a source of uncertainty and unrest in the period leading up to the change.

Sales staff could find the introduction of the new system unsettling. In the short term they will need to adapt to the technology. This could prove stressful if it leads to delays in serving customers. In the longer term, the system could speed up the flow of customers, reducing the need to employ as many sales staff.

The new system will pemit far more accurate and responsive inventory management. Staff theft is a serious problem in the retail industry. The new system will make staff theft far more transparent and obvious. Detection and prevention of theft is desirable, but it can also lead to poorer staff relations, with honest staff feeling aggrieved if intrusive measures are taken to reduce the extent of any detected problem.

195   IN-HOUSE SOLUTION

Developing a large in-house computer system calls for a large investment of resources. The major risk is that the investment is a failure, and the system fails to deliver the expected performance or provide the expected benefits. There have been reported instances, for example, of major new computer systems for government departments simply failing to function as intended.

A key requirement is good project management. A responsibility of the project manager should be to ensure that the system requirements are properly specified and that the system is designed to meet its requirements. The system should also be implemented on schedule and within its budget.

(a)   The specification of the requirements for an in-house system is a critical element in the system development. Unless the requirements are fully and accurately specified, the developed system will fail to provide complete user satisfaction. There are two ways of dealing with this problem. One approach is to take extreme care when the system requirements are specified prior to starting the system design work, and to ensure that the computer user agrees with the formal system specification. A problem with this approach is that it may be difficult to specify system requirements completely at such an early stage, especially when the new system will be large and complex. A second approach is to develop the new system by an iterative process, using prototypes. Each successive prototype of the system can be implemented and tested in practice, and the user can use the experience with each prototype to review and revise the system requirements for the next prototype. Prototyping should therefore help to ensure that the final system meets the user's actual needs as closely as possible.

(b)   There is a risk that the system will not be designed properly, and that the designers will fail to meet the system specifications. The systems analysts should be required to demonstrate their understanding of the current system, and that their new system design will meet the users' requirements. The project manager should therefore ensure that the process of analysing the current system and designing a new system is documented clearly. Techniques such as data flow diagrams and entity-relationship models can be used to demonstrate the logic of the system, so that the user can confirm that the current system has been properly analysed and the new design appears appropriate.

An in-house system development should also involve representatives of the computer user. For example, individuals employed by the computer user may be assigned to the project development team. A responsibility of these individuals should be to check the new system design and discuss detailed operating features with the systems analysts.

The new system should also be thoroughly tested before it is implemented. Each individual program should be tested individually, to confirm that the program logic is correct and the program has been written correctly. A systems test should then check to ensure that the individual elements or programs within the system are compatible with each other, such that the output of one program can be read as input to another program.

(c)   The project manager should have responsibility not only for ensuring that the system is designed properly, but also that it is completed on schedule. There are techniques to assist with project scheduling control, such as critical path charts or Gantt charts (which can be produced with standard project management software). Critical path analysis allows the project manager to monitor progress on the system development activities, and identify those that are time-critical and those that can be delayed without affecting the overall completion time for the project.

The computer user might want to introduce a new system as quickly as possible, and there is a risk that completing a finished system will take too long. A solution to this problem would be to develop the new system in an iterative fashion, using prototypes. An initial prototype can be designed and implemented much more quickly than a fully-finished system. The user can therefore use the new system operationally before it is completed.

(d) There is also a risk that the new system will cost more to develop than planned. Higher-than-expected costs might affect the financial justification for the new system. The project manager should therefore exercise effective cost control. An appropriate method of doing this would be a simple budgetary control reporting system, with regular reports of actual costs to date against budgeted costs, for each phase of the development. Ideally, the regular reports should also include re-assessments of the remaining costs to complete the project. When the project costs appear to be exceeding budget, the project manager should take appropriate control measures.

(e) The computer user might have difficulty in learning how to use the new system, and there might be strong resistance from employees who are reluctant to use it. Successful implementation of a major new system requires the close involvement of everyone affected. At an appropriate time during the system development, employees of the computer user should be introduced to the system, trained in how to use the system, and asked for their opinions on how the system might be operated in practice. The choice of system changeover method might also affect the ease of implementation, and the extent of user acceptance. A pilot test or phased implementation of the new system might give the users more time to familiarise themselves with the change.

(f) A system development should not end with its initial implementation. There is a strong likelihood that some features of the system will not operate as intended, and that the users' requirements will continue to change. There might also be serious errors in the programs that do not become apparent until after the system is in operation. These problems will affect the efficiency of the system unless arrangements are in place for system maintenance. IT staff should be designated to provide post-implementation for the system, assisting with the post-implementation review and providing whatever maintenance and updating is required.

196 DATABASE

(a) A database is a file of data, or several inter-related files of data, structured in such a way that the data can be accessed, used and updated by different applications. A database is therefore a common set of data files for multiple users.

A database management system is software that manages and controls a database. It controls access to the data files from multiple users and provides data security. A DBMS can be defined as software that stands between data files and the applications using those files. A DBMS therefore de-couples the data and the applications.

As a result of de-coupling, it is possible to write amendments to individual application programs without having to make amendments to the data files. Similarly, it is possible to make changes to the data on file independently of any changes in applications. The physical layout of data on the database can be altered without having to change the application programs that use it.

(b) Three benefits of a database management system, compared with separate application systems, are:

- centralised data management

- data independence, and

- systems integration.

In a database system, the data is managed by the DBMS and all access to the data is through the DBMS. This contrasts with conventional data processing systems where each application program has direct access to the data it reads or manipulates.

When applications are designed as separate computer systems, the programs written for each application are usually based on a detailed knowledge of data structure and format in the data files. Any change of data structure or format would therefore require appropriate changes to the application programs as well as to the files. If major changes are made to the data, the application programs would probably have to be rewritten.

In contrast, in a database system, the DBMS is an interface between the application programs and the data. When changes are made to the data representation in the database, the data maintained by the DBMS is changed but the DBMS continues to provide data to the application programs in the same way as before, transforming the data as necessary for the application program. This provides data independence. Every time a change is made to the data structure, the programs already using the data before the change will continue to work.

With a database and DBMS, all files are integrated into one system. This reduces data redundancy (unnecessary duplication), making data management more efficient. In addition, a DBMS provides centralised control of the operational data.

Databases therefore have several distinct advantages over separate data files for different computer applications:

(i) The data is input once only, and is available to all applications. If separate files are maintained for each application, data that is common to more than one system must be input once into each system. Single input is quicker and the number of input errors will be fewer.

(ii) Databases also avoid the duplication of data on files, thereby saving storage space in the computer system.

(iii) A database provides data integrity. All users of data for any computer application use the same data. This provides consistency, and avoids the possibility that different computer applications might use inconsistent data.

(iv) Access to data on file is available to a wide range of users, simply by specifying the data required.

(v) A database provides flexibility for computer users. Since there is a common set of data, new computer applications can be written more easily, without having to construct new files.

(vi) A large database can provide opportunities for in-depth analysis of the data ('data mining') to extract new information by identifying patterns in the data that were not previously apparent.

(vii) The cost of system maintenance should be lower, since data is updated only once, not several times for different applications.

(viii) The data on a database has to be structured (modelled) logically. Modelling should help to give system designers and users a better and clearer understanding of the data that they use.

(c) An EIS provides senior executives with the means to prepare ad hoc reports in order to identify opportunities and to evaluate proposals. Ideally, it will offer a decision-maker the means to 'drill down' through a report to obtain increasing levels of detail as and when required.

A database will offer the means for an organisation to provide the data required by its EIS. The flexibility inherent in a database design will make it easier to use the EIS to its full potential.

For example, management might wish to prepare, say, a set of accounting statements for a particular segment of the business even though this had not been anticipated in the design of the routine reporting system. Once the statements have been prepared then the managers will be able to call for more detail (e.g. an analysis of a particular category of sale).

Offering data in this flexible way means that it will be relatively easy to produce reports and documents, including graphs and charts, to assist in discussion and analysis.

The overall system will make it far easier for managers to ask 'what-if?' questions. It will be relatively easy for managers to evaluate the implications of potential changes arising from brainstorming meetings or proposals from consultants.

CHANGE MANAGEMENT

197 ZED BANK (PILOT PAPER)

(a) Lewin suggested that a process of change within an organisation should go through three main stages: 'un-freeze', 'movement' and 're-freeze':

- The process of 'unfreezing' involves persuading employees that the current situation is unsatisfactory and that change is desirable. Unless employees believe that the current situation is unsatisfactory, they will not want to change anything. However, in addition to persuading employees to be dissatisfied with the current position, it is also necessary to offer an attractive alternative that employees will prefer, but which can only be reached by means of change.

  It is therefore essential at this stage of the change process that management should have a clear idea of the new situation they want to create, so that they can explain it to employees and convince employees that the new situation is desirable.

- The process of movement or change cannot happen until employees are willing to give up the existing situation and know what they would like to have instead. This is the process of continuing to win the support of employees, whilst implementing the planned changes. It is generally argued that in order to make the process of change easier to implement, employees should participate in the process, by contributing ideas and suggestions about what should be done. Employees should also be kept fully informed, so that they know what is happening, and do not feel that unwelcome changes are being imposed on them.

  The movement process also requires management to identify the areas where resistance to change is strongest, and to take measures to reduce the resistance and obtain greater acceptance for the changes.

- The final main stage in the change process is 're-freeze'. Having achieved the desired changes, management should try to ensure that the new situation survives, and the organisation does not revert to its old ways and old systems. The re-freeze process is therefore designed to reinforce the change. This might be achieved by close supervision and management but the most effective way of sustaining change is to keep the support of all employees. One way of doing this might be to offer cash bonuses or other incentives that are linked to achieving target performance levels.

(b) (i) Incremental change means step-by-step changes over time, in small steps. When incremental change occurs within an organisation, it is possible for the organisation to adapt to the change without having to alter its culture or structures significantly. Employees are able to adapt to the gradual changes, and are not unsettled by them.

In contrast, transformational change is a sweeping change that has immediate and widespread effects. The effect of transformational change is usually to alter the structure and culture of the organisation, often with major staff redundancies and the recruitment of new staff with new skills.

The spokesperson for the bank has argued that the change will be incremental. Since the change will take place over a long period of time, staff will have time to adapt to the new structure. There will be no compulsory redundancies and staff will be re-trained in new skills. Although some branches will close, others will remain open, and customers will be offered additional facilities through on-line banking.

The trade union leader believes that the change will be much more dramatic. He might believe that many employees will leave the bank because they are unable to adapt to the new service, or because they are unwilling to re-locate from the branches that are closed down. The bank might push through the branch closure programme more quickly than it has currently proposed, and staff redundancies could be made compulsory if there are not enough individuals willing to take voluntary redundancy.

Essentially, the two individuals take differing viewpoints because they are looking at change differently. The spokesperson for the bank wants to persuade employees to accept the change, and even welcome it. The trade union representative wants to warn employees about the potential consequences, and has therefore stressed the risks.

(ii)   Participation might make the changes appear less threatening to employees because they will know that their views will be taken into account in the transition process. The fact that they will be able to enter into a dialogue will reduce the risk of them refusing to cooperate with the proposals.

Involving the employees will, ideally, create a sense of ownership on the employees' part. That will enable Zed Bank to draw on their insights and experience of the company in making the changes as effectively as possible.

There are, however, drawbacks to participation. It can slow the rate of change because time must be allowed for consultation and feedback.

Participation will only work if there is a sense of mutual trust and loyalty. If staff members are distanced and resentful then their input to the transition will have little or no value. If management is not willing to trust staff and take their input seriously then there will be 'pseudo-participation' which will tend to create greater resentment than failing to consult.

Employees have to be willing to engage with the changes and work towards bringing them about. Otherwise their participation in the process might be used to delay or disrupt the changes rather than bring them into effect.

In this case, the fact that some members of staff will be affected more than others might create the possibility of some groups of employees feeling alienated by both the bank and their colleagues. For example, staff in the branches that are due to be closed may be more likely to lose their jobs or have to make significant changes to their working patterns than those employed in large, city-centre branches.

198 ORGANISATIONAL DEVELOPMENT

(a)   Organisational development (OD) emerged in the 1960s and is commonly associated with the work of Warren Bennis. OD is concerned with change in organisations, and Bennis believed that to implement change, a major educational programme was necessary to change the attitudes of employees 'so that they can better adapt to new technologies, markets and challenges, and to the dizzying rate of change itself.'

OD is also associated with management consultants, who act in the role of 'agents for change'.

The basic approach begins with the recognition that the organisation is having difficulty in adapting to change, and employees are generally hostile to the idea of change. Management consultants, in their role as change agents, diagnose the problems.

Another feature of OD is that to educate employees into accepting and welcoming change, it is essential to involve them in the identifying what the problems are, what is causing them and how the problem might be resolved.

It is essential that during the diagnostic phase, trust is built up between individuals and groups within the organisation, and with the consultants. In the case of B Company, for example, trust needs to be re-established between operations staff and quality control staff; therefore it is essential to bring them together in the diagnostic and problem-solving exercise.

A number of different ideas might be considered about how each problem might be dealt with. Agreement then needs to be reached about which ideas should be tested, and how the tests should be carried out. It might be decided, for example, to implement a suggested solution on a trial basis, and monitor the results before trying to extend the solution to the rest of the organisation.

The actual techniques of carrying out diagnostic and problem-solving exercises, and the types of 'solution' favoured by OD experts, can vary considerably.

(b)   The approach described above can be applied to the B Company. However, the company is facing a large number of problems, and each will have to be diagnosed.

The management consultants hired to assist in the programme should carry out an initial survey of the situation. It appears that the company has a variety of problems arising from environmental change. Even the demands from staff for higher pay might be linked to high pay rises in the economy generally.

All the 200 employees in the organisation should be involved in the programme, and having carried out their initial study, the consultants, together with senior management, should probably hold a general meeting with all staff and explain the perceived problems and the purpose of the programme.

An immediate concern has to be the low morale and lack of co-operation between departments. This has not been a problem in the past, and there may well be particular reasons why the deterioration occurred. In discussing the company's problems with staff, these motivational issues need to be recognised and considered.

The consultants might begin by trying to identify and analyse the company's problems on a departmental basis, trying to win some trust and obtain some co-operation from all the individuals. The investigation needs to consider what the problems are in implementing the new hygiene regulations, why changes in consumer tastes have had an adverse effect on business, what problems are being caused by the activities of competitors, what has been the perceived reasons for and impact of the material price increases, and why employees feel the need for higher pay.

As trust develops – which it needs to do if the programme is to succeed – the issues of low morale, and poor inter-departmental relations can be considered more openly. When the time is appropriate, the consultants should bring together people from different departments so that they can discuss and diagnose the problems they have experienced.

Since the key issues seem to be internal, getting employees to recognise the nature of these problems and their causes will be a critical element of the OD programme.

The consultants should make sure that at all times during the OD programme, all employees feel that they are a part of the exercise and that their views will be heard. Since it is difficult to listen to the views of 200 individuals face-to-face, opinion surveys might be used, and the results of the surveys reported back. It is also important, as the programme progresses, to keep everyone informed about ideas that are emerging and solutions that are being proposed.

The lack of faith in management is also another problem that has been identified and that is probably a fundamental issue. The OD consultants need to use a method of persuading management to recognise their failings, and to consider how they should be acting instead. A series of face-to-face interviews with management, in which they are informed about the negative feedback from employees about their abilities, might be a useful method of bringing the problem into the open for discussion and resolution.

The problems arising from the environment will not be resolved until the problems of morale, co-operation and conflict are resolved. Working towards solutions to the external problems can provide a way of recognising and resolving the internal problems. The conflict between operations and quality control might be very difficult to resolve, and the consultants will have to make sure that the two sides discuss their grievances freely with each other. (The consultants should be well-trained and experienced in conflict resolution.)

The consultants should also keep in view the goal of educating the work force into recognising the need for change and welcoming the idea of change in order to get better.

The consultants might consider that the problems of poor co-operation between departments calls for a radical solution, and a solution might be encouraged that is based on a radical re-organisation of operations around processes rather than functions. (This would be a form of business process re-engineering.)

(c)   The company should ask several consultants to tender for the contract. Consultants should be approached on the basis that they have a reputation for being experienced in the area of organisational development.

Tenders should be scrutinised for relevant indicators that the consultants will bring about successful change, such as:

- prior experience of the food industry

- a logical and sensible proposal for the approach to be taken to B Company

- a realistic timeframe and budget.

The shortlisted firm should be asked to meet with the board in order to discuss the proposals. This meeting should include the senior members of the consultancy team who will participate in the project. The board should not finally grant the contract unless it is satisfied that there is a rapport with the consultants.

199   K COMPANY

(a)   Learning organisations are those that encourage questions and explicitly recognise mistakes as part of the learning process. Edler, Burgoyne and Boydell define the learning organisation as 'an organisation that facilitates the learning of all its members and constantly transforms itself'.

Peter Senge identifies five core competences for any company that wants to become a 'learning organisation':

- Building a shared vision or common sense of purpose, so that all members of the organisation are pulling together all the time, instead of only being brought together by an external crisis.

- Achieving personal mastery of the issues to be learnt through continuous self-development and learning, and passing this learning onto others through the organisation's cognitive systems and memories. In this way, the organisation maintains and develops it own norms, values, behaviours and mental maps over time, even though the individuals who first 'learnt' them are no longer there.

- Utilising mental models, so that individuals can both identify the assumptions that they bring to a situation, and develop alternative ways of doing things which will have a significant impact.

- Team learning, so that not only individual team members but the team collectively learns how to tackle difficult situations and decisions without losing the benefits of team working.

- Systems thinking, so that a situation is analysed for how it fits together as a whole, rather than just as a set of separate problems to be solved separately. In particular, this involves an understanding of how the organisation as a whole fits together and functions, so that the effect of an issue which impacts on one part of the organisation can be analysed in terms of its impact on the whole.

Building up a learning organisation should be undertaken in stages. Initially the emphasis will be on bringing all the organisation's workers round to an understanding of the importance of such matters as continual improvement, quality and benchmarking as ways to achieve improvements in 'how we do things round here'. Bureaucratic brakes on such improvements should also be removed at this point.

In the next stages the organisation's managers in particular can be encouraged to think of new ways in which the organisation could function – for instance, new technology, new markets, and new ways of delighting the customer.

The final stage is achieved when the processes undergone in the first two stages have become a way of life for everyone involved in the organisation. The important point about this stage is that it should be maintained in the long term so that the organisation can benefit fully from all the effort that has been put in. In other words, building a learning organisation is a continuous process rather than a project which can be implemented and then left. This is of particular importance for K Company as it operates in conditions of permanent, rapid change.

The implementation of the ideas implicit in the learning organisation is a significant effort which K Company probably feels it cannot afford to fail in. The company should also be aware that cultural changes will be required.

(b) The idea of the assessment centre is part of a philosophy that grew out of the obvious shortcomings of the application, interview and references alone as selection techniques. Assessment centres allow assessment of individuals working in a group or alone by a team of assessors, who use a variety of assessment techniques depending on the requirements of the client.

The first step towards setting up an assessment centre is to make sure that the jobs on offer have been fully analysed into a set of competences, against which a set of criteria can be developed. The assessment centre activities can then be designed so as to test these competences against the criteria. The activities can include, as well as interviews and 'psychometric' tests, hands on simulations, in-tray exercises, role-play and presentations. There may even be outdoor, team-building exercises.

Since assessment centres became a more widely used technique it has been shown that they are much better at predicting a successful match between the selected candidate and the employer. The wider the range of techniques used, the more successful the result in terms of a good match.

Because there is such a wide range of assessment methods used at an assessment centre, it is argued that the approach is more thorough and therefore more successful than the more traditional approaches. If nothing else, the process takes longer and allows the potential employer to see the candidates over a longer period of time, and therefore 'get to know them' in a number of situations. This contrasts well with the very time-constrained, artificial interview situation. The methodology must be rigorous however, or else there is the temptation to select the person who just seems the most sociable etc.

The big disadvantage of assessment centres is the cost of setting them up, administering them, staffing them and producing the results. Many smaller companies simply cannot afford them , although recruitment consultants can stage them on behalf of a client if there is a one-off, very important appointment to be made. If this is the situation for K Company then selective use of assessment centres will probably be very beneficial.

(c) Vision statements are often a source of cynicism and alienation. Organisations frequently pay lip service to an idea but do not really mean it.

If there is a genuine vision and shared culture then the members of an organisation will work together in that direction because they want to, not because they have been told to or are responding to some artificial stimulus.

It is extremely difficult to impose a leader's convictions on an orgabisation, no matter how heart-felt and sincere those convictions are.

A successful vision has to be shared by everyone. Achieving this needs to involve everyone. The leadership challenge is to uncover and define a shared picture of the future that fosters genuine commitment rather than mere compliance.

200 F STEEL COMPANY

Key answer tips

There is a lot of material in the scenario and you should be careful in part (a) to include all of it, and analyse it carefully. The most obvious model to use here is Lewin's unfreeze-change-refreeze force field analysis, although you could have adopted a contingency approach instead.

(a) The situation outlined for F Steel Company can be usefully analysed using Lewin's force field analysis, whereby the facts are identified as being either forces for change or forces for resisting change, and either internal or external.

Force	*Internal force for change*	*External force for change*
Newly-appointed CEO	*	
High costs and low productivity	*	
Rising exchange rate		*
Subsidised steel companies		*
Weak domestic demand		*
Strong overseas demand		*
Late deliveries	*	
Customers complaining about quality	*	*

	Internal force resisting change	*External force resisting change*
Trade union attitude	*	
Complacent managers	*	

(b) Lewin's force field analysis, which identifies both forces for change and forces for resistance to change, is probably most appropriate for the CEO to use a change management model.

The main point of the model is that it highlights those forces for change in the right direction that should be encouraged, and those forces for resistance that should be diminished.

The model is not that straightforward, however. For instance, the fact that the force should be for change *in the right direction* is important; obviously the fact that costs are high and productivity is low is a force for change, but if it were encouraged the company would end up in liquidation! In addition, not all forces for change can be encouraged. External forces for change in particular are not always open to influence from the organisation. For example, it is unlikely that F can do anything at all about the exchange rate, as this is a macro-economic factor. Weak domestic demand for steel also probably cannot be affected by one producer, at least in the short term. The existence of subsidised steel companies overseas is difficult to affect, though in the long term pressure can be brought to bear on governments to level the playing field.

The main thrust of force field analysis therefore is to concentrate on those internal factors that can be influenced in the right direction. In turn these may affect external factors, such as customer complaints and the share of the strong overseas demand taken by F.

On the basis of this analysis the CEO should attempt the following steps for change:

- **Unfreeze**: develop understanding of the need for change, and reduce the factors that maintain and reinforce undesirable current behaviour. As the main forces for internal resistance are the attitudes of trade unions and managers, the CEO can unfreeze their behaviour by laying out clearly how far the company is threatened by the competition, and getting them to understand that without change the survival of the company, and therefore of jobs, is uncertain.

- **Change**: develop the desirable new attitudes and behaviour in all employees so that change is effected. This might be a lengthy and difficult process, as the facts can be difficult to communicate in a positive fashion that will encourage people to change their behaviours, Seminars, question and answer sessions, examples of other companies who have changed successfully, and committees of workers putting forward ideas, are all mechanisms by which change can be both encouraged and implemented. As well as employee involvement, the threat of redundancies and penalties, and the opportunity for rewards and new ways of working, should be made clear. These will need to be discussed and agreed by the trade unions. As the point at issue is effectively the survival of the company, it should be possible to achieve this. Negotiation is also required with the managers, and it may be that some of them will have to be made redundant if they continue to resist change.

- **Refreeze**: ensure that the new behaviours are firmly embedded by means of supporting mechanisms such as pay and conditions. The company should be sure to implement whatever promises regarding rewards and opportunities it made during the change process, but more importantly the pressure for constant improvement and continued change must be kept up.

(c)   Peters suggests that the following five areas of management are important for success in a chaotic business world:

- **An obsession with responsiveness to customers.** If the F Steel company's managers had been paying attention to their customers' needs and wishes then they would have paid more attention to the different attitudes of their customers from their new markets. Matters such as prompt delivery and quality would have received more care.

- **Constant innovations in all areas of the firm.** The managers of the company must accept that the world has changed and that they must adapt. This might mean new products, more attention to quality, or innovation in employee relations.

- **Involve everyone in everything.** The employees and their unions have to accept that they must adapt their working practices if they wish to retain their jobs. It will be much easier to change this attitude if the company takes the union leaders into their confidence and work together with them to develop new working practices that will create wealth for everybody.

- **Leadership that loves change.** The complacency shown by management indicates a desire to leave everything substantially as it is, without making changes.

- **Control by means of simple support systems.** The problems with delivery times and quality need to be resolved. Ideally, the sources of the problems should be identified and resources invested in dealing with them, rather than creating an unhealthy attitude.

201 R & L (MAY 05 EXAM)

Examiner's comments

This was a popular question and most candidates answered (a) in particular well. Some candidates drew purposeful examples from similar organisations including the recent MG/Rover experience.

Common errors

- A large number of candidates described change management theories in part (b) without relating them to the scenario or addressing the central issue of how resistance might be overcome.

(a)   R & L has built up a reputation as a good employer and will want to preserve this strength while still reducing the size of the workforce. To do this it can take the following initiatives:

Consultation

If there is a trade union at the firm, then union officials should be involved from the very beginning in designing a programme to reduce the size of the workforce. Once the union agree that job cuts are needed now to protect jobs in the future, then their help should be forthcoming.

Even if there is no a union, then employees should be consulted at all stages of the process. This will reduce hostility from workers and will be seen by the outside world as the firm acting more reasonably than imposing changes on the workforce.

Initial steps

One of the first steps R & L should take is to review future staff turnover or 'natural wastage' to see how much of the 50% reduction can be met by staff leaving anyway and/or retiring. Experience could indicate figures for the former and a review of HR files should indicate the numbers for the latter.

An immediate halt on recruitment would also reduce future job losses.

Reducing labour hours without reducing the number of workers

R & L can protect some jobs by reducing the hours people work rather than losing employees. This can be done by a mixture of the following:

- job sharing schemes
- part-time working
- a shorter working week
- reducing the amount of overtime offered.

Reducing the number of employees without compulsory redundancy

R & L's reputation will be damaged most by forced, compulsory redundancies, so the firm will wish to keep these to a minimum. Worker numbers can be cut without redundancy by the following:

- 'encouraging' anyone over retirement age to retire

- offering early retirement to workers over a certain age

- outsourcing non-core functions to outside suppliers who agree to employ some R & L workers as part of the deal.

Retraining

It may be that there are areas of the firm where more staff are needed. Rather than recruiting from outside the firm, training should be offered to existing staff so they can be moved within R & L.

Support

Employees who are affected by the changes should be offered support. This could take a number of forms:

- counselling and support for those facing early retirement or redundancy

- retraining offered in new skills necessary to get jobs in other firms

- training and help in preparing a CV, how to fill in application forms and interview techniques to help workers find new jobs

- offering redundancy payments that are higher than the legal minimum.

(b)   **Kotter and Schlesinger** identified six main methods of dealing with resistance to change. These can be applied to the situation facing R&L as follows:

1   Education and communication

Resistance to change is often fuelled by rumours and suspicion so improved communication can help by clarifying the situation. It is rarely sufficient on its own unless the rumours were totally unfounded. For example, knowing that you will be made redundant takes away the anxiety whether or not you will lose your job but does not take away resistance to the cuts.

Given R & L's desire to continue to be and be seen to be a good employer, this would be a suitable strategy and would involve meetings with employees to explain why job losses are necessary and the different options available (as discussed in part (a))

2   Participation and involvement

Key stakeholders who have both significant power and significant interest in the changes should be involved in the change process. This will facilitate better acceptance of the changes and commitment to work through problems together.

In the case of R&L this is another highly suitable method and should involve consulting trade union representatives and workers generally and incorporating their ideas. The union for example, may promise to stop workers going out on strike if the firm promise to keep compulsory redundancies to an absolute minimum and agree to generous redundancy payments.

3   Facilitation and support

Facilitation and support are designed to reduce employee anxiety and involve counseling and training. It is particularly appropriate when employees are going to have to adjust to fundamental changes.

With R&L this is also a highly suitable strategy given the major changes envisaged and the desire to be a good employer. All of the initiatives discussed under the heading of 'support' in section (a) would be appropriate here.

4   *Negotiation and agreement*

There is frequently an element of compromise in change management so each party feels that they have gained something from the process. For example, if employees feel that they have kept their jobs, then they might be willing to accept reduced hours and pay.

This is another suitable strategy for R&L as it appears to have had good employee relations in the past so could count on goodwill in negotiations rather than outright hostility.

5   *Manipulation and co-optation*

This can involve misinformation, keeping employees in the dark about changes and buying off key players, usually to drive changes through more quickly.

For R&L this would not be a suitable strategy as workers would feel used and tricked, creating significant ill-feeling. Ultimately this would affect R&L's reputation may result in more staff leaving and does not fit with R&L's desire to be a good employer.

6   *Explicit and implicit coercion*

In extreme cases some firms resort to force and the threat of force to push through changes. This could involve sacking any workers who could cause problems, intimidation and threats. This is a particularly dangerous strategy when a strong trade union is present, as it will usually result in confrontation.

This is not suitable for R&L as it does not fit with the stated aim of continuing to be a good employer and may be both illegal and unethical.

202   T COMPANY

(a)   **Triggers for change**

Organisational change can be driven by both external developments and/or internal organisational factors. The key triggers for change in T Company are as follows:

External triggers	*Internal triggers*
• Government decisions to deregulate the telecommunications industry • Technological developments in wireless technology (mobile phones!) • Development of broadband Internet technology • Shift in consumer tastes away from fixed line telephones to mobile phones.	• Senior management decisions to enter the mobile telephone market and, later, broadband Internet services • Managers' decision to sack workers • Workers' decision to take industrial action to preserve jobs • Trade union's decision to support the actions of T Company employees.

The key difficulties that the T Company is likely to face in making all the necessary changes are as follows.

Existing culture

The inherited bureaucratic culture of the organisation with its rules and procedures is likely to act as a barrier to change.

Employees' resistance to change

Employees will resist change due to:

- fear of being unable to cope with the new technology
- unwillingness to throw away existing skills and learn new ones
- fear of job losses
- fear that new jobs will be more specialised and more boring.

Action of trade unions

The threat of action by the trade union will make change even more difficult.

(b) **The change process**

Success to date

T Company has had a mixed record of success in the management of change to date.

The main success is that it has managed to change from being a provider of only fixed line telephone services to one that now also provides mobile and broadband Internet services. This is despite the old bureaucratic culture and structure.

The main failures have been as follows:

- Attempts to downsize the workforce resulted in industrial action that cost T Company many millions.
- The current implementation of broadband services is also meeting with resistance. Engineers have threatened industrial action in support of a large pay rise.

Managing future change

There is no universal plan for the successful management of change as each situation is different. At best, there are useful models and principles to help in the design of the change process. One such model was developed by Lewin.

Lewin argued that some (usually external) forces are outside management's control and so management should concentrate on the internal forces driving change and those resisting change. Lewin suggested a three-step process to then manage the change as follows:

1 'Unfreezing' – which involves reducing forces that resist change. This involves providing people with an understanding of why change needs to occur so that they can more easily accept it.

2 'Changing behaviour' – in such a way that new attitudes, values and behaviour become part of employees' new ways of thinking.

3 'Refreezing' – introducing mechanisms, such as reward systems and structures, to ensure that the new behaviour pattern is maintained.

In the case of T Company, many of the forces for change are outside the control of the senior management. Management needs to accept the changes in the market place and adopt strategies to deal with the threats and opportunities the changes present.

Unfreezing

Management can use the threat of competition to persuade employees and the trade union that, unless changes are made, the very survival of the company and, therefore, the jobs of employees, are at risk. This should create dissatisfaction with existing methods.

Changing behaviour

Changing behaviour is difficult and will require a range of methods:

- effective communication of what needs to be changed and why
- regular meetings involving all employees
- negotiation with unions to ensure their participation in the change process.

The directors may be tempted to force changes through regardless of the reasons for resistance. The danger of this approach is that employees often return to the old ways of working once the pressure is removed.

Refreezing

- To consolidate changes made appropriate incentives and penalties must be put in place.

- Rather than sitting still there should be an emphasis on constant improvement to raise levels of productivity even further.

(c) The most obvious mechanism is the control and manipulation of organisational resources. Senior management can allocate resources in such a way that managers and departments are encouraged to embrace the new culture. This might be combined with the development of revised internal reporting systems so that resistance to change is highlighted and penalised in terms of performance measures.

Management might publicise its desire to change the culture within the company. Amongst other things, this could be raised as an issue by board members who are participating in interviews for promoted posts. Middle management might, therefore, be encouraged to align itself with the interests of this elite.

The company's systems need to be consistent with the whole process of change. If reporting and decision-making systems are based on the outmoded culture then it will persist and will, indeed, be viewed as the board's preferred approach.

The board might even resort to symbolic devices. Creating positive messages in support of those who embrace the changes and adapt to it will speed implementation more quickly.

203 Y

(a) Change in organisations has positive and negative attributes. On the positive side, it means experimentation and the creation of something new. On the negative side, change means discontinuity and destruction of familiar social structures and relationships. Despite the positive aspects, change may be resisted because it involves both confrontations with the unknown and loss of the familiar. Change presents those caught up in it with new situations, new problems, ambiguity and uncertainty. Many individuals, groups and organisations find change, or the thought of change, painful and frustrating.

Individuals – seek to protect a status quo because they have a fear of the unknown. They develop a vested interest in the perpetuation of particular organisation structures and accompanying technologies. Changes may mean the loss of jobs, power, prestige, respect, approval, status and security. In the case of 'Y', it may also be personally inconvenient for a variety of reasons. It may disturb relationships and arrangements that have taken much time and effort to establish. It may force an unwanted location or geographical move or alter social opportunities. There could be problems with learning new skills. Some employees will fear that they will fail and will be reluctant to take on retraining. Perceived as well as actual threats to interests and values are thus likely to generate resistance to change.

Groups – there will be groups of people who see their position threatened and who will combine to resist any threats to their position. In particular, the middle management groups, fearing de-layering, will feel threatened and will be looking to their trade union to protect their interests. There may well be calls for industrial action or action to obtain the highest possible severance pay or redeployment terms. Even without the help of a trade union, groups may collude informally to resist change. They may do this by withholding information or by not being wholly co-operative with those seeking to implement change.

Organisational – at this level there will be a number of factors that will make the change process difficult. These include the existing investment in resources and past contracts and agreements with various organisational stakeholders. It is especially difficult to renegotiate the terms of the contracts with stakeholders, such as the trade unions. However, the main factor is the existing structure and culture of the organisation. Firms that change from a role culture, in a relatively stable and a large-sized organisation, to a different culture that requires a flatter, more organic, organisational structure to cope with competition in the open market, will have problems in surviving such a dramatic change.

(b) There are a number of ways that change can be facilitated. Kurt Lewin developed a general-purpose diagnostic and problem-solving technique to bring about change and improve performance. His force field model suggests that in any situation there are forces that push for change (driving) as well as forces that hinder change (restraining). If the forces offset each other completely, it results in equilibrium and status quo. Change can be brought about by increasing the driving forces or by reducing the restraining forces. Lewin's force-field theory of organisational change is illustrated below:

Using this model, we can show that the major driving force for change is the increasing competition brought about by changes in the industry environment. There are few options for 'Y' except to respond to it by becoming leaner and more effective. Reducing management levels and its consequent reduction in staffing levels should help to cut costs. The strengthening of the telephone banking division should help the bank's competitiveness, as should the investment in IT and training.

Despite clear evidence of the threat to the future of the bank, the plans that management have produced do not seem to have convinced the employees. The management should attempt to communicate the message to managers and other employees more effectively. It is not clear from the scenario what methods have been used to communicate to the workforce either the seriousness of the bank's situation, or the rationale behind senior management's plans to combat this situation, but this must be an early priority for the senior management team.

J Kotter and L Schlesinger suggest education and communication, along with other means, such as participation, manipulation and coercion as specific methods for overcoming resistance to change.

Resistance may be based on misunderstanding and inaccurate information. When this happens, it is important to get the facts straight and to discuss and reconcile opposing points of view. Managers should share their knowledge, perceptions and objectives with those who will be affected by the change. This may involve education e.g. a training programme, face-to-face counselling, reports, memos and group meetings and discussions. However, the managers should tread carefully because bank employees generally have a high level of education and it would not help the case for change if management underestimated this.

A method associated with communication and education is that of facilitation and support. The management at 'Y' may be able to alleviate the fears of some individuals by the use of counselling and group discussion.

Participation is another way of reducing resistance to change, involving all employees from the start of the change process. Collaboration can have the effect of reducing opposition and encouraging commitment. It helps to reduce the fears that individuals may have about the impact of changes on them and makes use of their skills and knowledge. By presenting the problem the bank is facing to employees in a series of face-to-face meetings, and offering the possibility of participation in the decision-making and planning process, it may be possible to get more employees to buy into the planned changes.

Given that the decisions have been made at 'Y' and that resistance has already been encountered it may well be that the best way forward is now through a process of negotiation and agreement with representatives of the workforce. Trade union officials will probably represent the employees' side. A process of negotiation and bargaining may result in concessions from management, in terms of built-in safeguards and appropriate compensation for the union members. The bank could then be allowed to continue without further interference.

Management could always try the manipulation or co-optation approach. It can put forward proposals that deliberately appeal to the specific interest, sensitivities and emotions of key groups involved in the change. Alternatively, it can use information that is selective and distorted to only emphasise the benefits of the change. Co-optation involves giving key people access to the decision-making process, such as 'buying people off' with the promise of some kind of reward for going along with the proposed changes. These techniques may work in the short run but create other problems. Manipulation will eventually be discovered and will discredit the reputations of those involved. Trouble-makers who are co-opted tend to stay co-opted and may continue to create difficulties from their new position of power.

The last approach – the use of explicit and implicit coercion – is where the management abandons any attempt at consensus and may involve mass redundancies without right of appeal. This would have to be the approach of last resort since the image of the bank would suffer and the morale of the remaining workforce would be badly affected.

OPERATIONS MANAGEMENT

204   ELECTRIC PUMPS

(a)   The operations function in manufacturing electric pumps is concerned with converting raw materials into a finished product and delivering them to the customer. Operations therefore covers the following areas:

- Purchasing. The purchasing department are responsible for obtaining raw materials and parts from suppliers.

- Production. The production function converts the raw materials and assembles parts and components into finished products. Without more information about the nature of the pumps that the company produces, it is not possible to suggest what type of production process the company uses.

- Production planning and control. This function is concerned with scheduling production, and making sure that the materials, labour, machinery and other resources are available to manufacture the pumps. Production control involves monitoring production flow and dealing with any problems, hold-ups and bottlenecks that might arise.

- Product design or engineering. There will probably also be a separate section within operations that provides technical expertise. These experts might be responsible for new product design.

- Inventory management. Raw materials and finished goods inventory must be stored or warehoused.

- Logistics. Manufactured pumps must be distributed to customers. The customers for pumps will be industrial buyers, and the task of delivering them will probably be included within the operations function.

(b) If the O Company has not changed its methods much since the early 1970s its methods of operation are presumably old-fashioned, and it is perhaps surprising that the company has survived in what is presumably a competitive environment.

Since the 1970s, IT technology has developed significantly. Product design has been affected by electronics, and robotics are used extensively in production equipment (Computer-Aided Manufacture of CAM). Product design might also make use of computer software (Computer-Aided Design or CAD).

Production planning might be assisted by computer systems such as MRPI, which O Company presumably does not currently use.

Management planning and control is also assisted extensively by computer and communication technology. Computer systems can be used to monitor and control production flow.

Quality improvements are probably essential to restore the competitiveness of the company's products, as well as to reduce costs. The company could consider applying Just in Time production and purchasing methods. JIT helps a manufacturer to focus on lower costs and efficient production methods, including the elimination of waste and defective items.

Alternatively a Total Quality Management programme could be applied. (JIT and TQM share many common principles.) The aim should be to eliminate waste in production, possibly using statistical quality control techniques. Quality improvements also rely on employee involvement, and initiatives such as a continuous improvement initiative, a 5S approach or quality circles might be considered. An employee education and training programme is probably required. However, if the problems of the company are severe, a more radical approach to change and quality improvement might be attempted by means of a BPR exercise.

Internet technology can be used by the purchasing department to identify new sources of supply from different parts of the world (global sourcing). This might be particularly significant for O Company, since it should need electronic components for its products, and the cheapest and best-quality suppliers could well be located in other countries. Improvements in transportation systems and the smaller size of electronic parts makes global sourcing quicker and economical.

(c) Strategy deals with how an organisation achieves its objectives. For example:

- Where is the business trying to get to in the long term (direction)?

- Which markets should a business compete in and what kind of activities are involved in such markets (markets; scope)?

- How can the business perform better than the competition in those markets (advantage)?

- What resources (skills, assets, finance, relationships, technical competence, facilities) are required in order to be able to compete (resources)?

- What external, environmental factors affect the business's ability to compete (environment)?

- What are the values and expectations of those who have power in and around the business (stakeholders)?

Tactics are the most efficient deployment of resources in an agreed strategy.

Tactics follow on from strategy.

205 PRODUCTION SCHEDULING

(a)   When batch production is based on economic batch quantity sizes, each batch size for a particular product is the same. The batch size is the quantity that minimises total annual inventory costs, which are assumed to consist of inventory holding costs and batch set-up costs. However, the Economic Batch Quantity (EBQ) formula is based on the assumption that the demand for the item is constant each day, week or month, and in addition there are no costs from stock-outs.

A levelled scheduling system is based on different assumptions. It is assumed that demand is fairly predictable, over the short term at least, but might vary from one period to another. In the case of VB Production, weekly demand for each product is forecast to vary over the next four weeks. Production is therefore scheduled as a constant amount each week over the planning period. In the case of VB Production, this means that if the next four weeks are taken as the planning period, weekly production would be 4,750 units of Product A, 9,500 units of Product B and 6,000 units of Product C.

An advantage of a levelled scheduling system is that it may be possible to operate a continuous production process, with no lost time between batches (because the production process is continuing all the time). However, whether or not this is possible will depend on the output capacity of the production process, and whether or not the three products are made on the same machines or on different machines.

If the company moved from production of the three products in economic batch quantities to a levelled scheduling system, management would have to consider the following issues.

- With an EBQ system, there is usually an inventory re-order level, and a new batch of items is produced as soon as the inventory quantity falls to this level. With levelled scheduling, a system is required for ensuring that there is adequate inventory available to meet demand (unless stock-outs are acceptable). This could be a particular problem when the scheduled production quantities in any week are less than the expected sales demand. For example, if the scheduled weekly production of Product A is 4,750 units each week, 9,500 units will be produced in weeks 1 and 2, when total sales demand is expected to be 11,000 units.

- There should also be a good practical or economic reason for switching from batch production in economic batch quantities to levelled production scheduling. One potential reason is to achieve a continuous production process for all three products, with no down times between batches. However, if the three products would still be manufactured in batches, it is not clear whether levelled production scheduling would bring any benefits. Management needs to recognise that the most appropriate production scheduling system will vary according to circumstances.

(b)   With a levelled scheduling system, production is scheduled at a constant rate in each period to meet anticipated demand. It is a volume-based system of production scheduling, where the focus of attention is on quantities manufactured in each period. With JIT production, in contrast, production is initiated by actual demand rather than anticipated demand, and the focus of attention is on the rate at which items can be produced. Whereas levelled production scheduling is a volume based scheduling system, JIT is a rate-based system.

It is by no means clear how a JIT production system would benefit VB Production. Sales demand for each of the three products varies each week, but demand quantities seem fairly large. This suggests that sales orders for each product are received regularly. When orders for a product are received regularly, such that production has to be regular, some of the goals of JIT production become unachievable. For example, JIT production has an ideal batch size of one, and production is scheduled for specific orders as they are received.

To achieve JIT production when sales demand is fairly continuous, but sales volumes vary from week to week, there would need to be a system of regulating the production flow up or down in response to demand, so that sales demand can be met quickly without having any inventory from which to meet the demand.

JIT production involves more than simply responding to customer orders, eliminating inventory, production flexibility and speed of throughput. It is also concerned with quality and reliability in production and the elimination of waste. As with continuous improvement, the success of a JIT system requires the participation and involvement of employees, and a change of culture within the organisation, towards one of eliminating waste, flexible work practices and ensuring speedy throughput. A change to JIT would therefore need careful planning, the total commitment of senior management, and full co-operation from all the employees affected. This is likely to require some time to achieve.

206 PIPE DREAM:

(a)   The main features of TQM are as follows.

    (i)   The primary aim within a system of TQM is to meet the needs and requirements of customers and achieve full customer satisfaction. Juran argued that having identified its customers' needs, an entity should develop products that meet those needs and it should seek to optimise the product features so that they meet the needs of the entity as well as those of its customers. The entity should then develop a process for making the product, and should optimise the process.

    (ii)   TQM should be applied to all aspects of an entities activities, not just to production operations, and to all employees, whatever their job.

    (iii)   TQM must involve everyone within the organisation, and there must be a commitment to quality from everyone. To achieve this commitment, there must be committed leadership and a change of organisational culture. The concept of empowerment of employees is very closely associated with TQM: management must give more power to employees to make their own decisions, and should learn to trust them to do what is best.

    (iv)   All quality-related costs should be measured and managed. These costs can be classified as prevention costs, inspection costs, internal failure costs and external failure costs. An aim should be to minimise the total of these costs. In TQM, the view is that by investing in prevention, total quality costs will be minimised. In the long-run, it is cheaper to prevent poor quality than to look out for it or rectify the problem when something goes wrong. Crosby developed the concept of 'getting things right first time', so that failures do not happen.

(v) An entity must develop systems for monitoring quality performance and to support quality improvements. Deming is associated with developing systems of statistical quality measurement and statistical quality control. Establishing quality standards and monitoring actual performance against those standards has also led to the development of international quality standards (for example, the ISO 9000 series).

(b) The main problems with introducing TQM into operations are likely to be getting the total commitment of senior management and the willing support of employees. A radical change is needed in culture and in attitudes towards the customer and quality. For management, the changes must involve greater empowerment to employees and greater trust.

Since the cultural changes required are so large, it might take time to introduce a system of TQM successfully.

A starting point should probably be to win the enthusiastic support of management. Managers should be given training in TQM concepts and practices, so that they understand what TQM is about and what they, as managers, should be expected to do. Without the full support of management, employees are unlikely to be persuaded that TQM is worthwhile.

Although TQM and continuous improvement are not the same, it might be appropriate to adopt some of the concepts of continuous improvement. In particular, the entity might introduce '5S practice', to improve the quality of the work environment.

Employees need to understand the importance of meeting quality standards, and the entity should establish quality standards for its operations. Employees should be encouraged to achieve the quality standards, and actual performance should be reviewed against the targets. The principles of Six Sigma might be introduced, so that statistical quality control is applied throughout the production process, and the levels of waste and defective output are reduced to minimal levels.

Quality should perhaps be written into all of the entity's procedures and systems. A criticism of TQM is that it might become too bureaucratic and procedure-led. Nevertheless, the entity might benefit from reviewing its management of quality systems, in accordance with the ISO 9001: *2000 guidelines*.

(c) The emphasis in TQM is on the prevention of mistakes. Arguably, it could be almost as wasteful to incur additional costs on manufacturing goods to an unnecessarily small tolerance as it would to waste money on correcting defects or scrapping waste products. For example, if Pipe Dream's customers require pipes of a particular length, plus or minus two millimetres, there is no need to aim to manufacture pipes that are within a tenth of a millimetre of the specification. Making pipes that were that close to the target might offer advantages if there were no cost associated with doing so, but otherwise the company should develop processes that are intended to get all output to within the intended standards of output.

TQM is essentially about understanding the needs of customers (both internal and external) and working towards meeting those needs. For example, a motorist who wishes to purchase an inexpensive car might be prepared to tolerate the use of cheaper materials in trimming and decorating the interior of the car, but might still prize durability and reliability in the car itself. There is no need for a car manufacturer who is aiming at the cheaper end of the market to produce cars that are built to the same standard as those produced by the manufacturers of premium markets.

Tutorial note

It can be a matter of some confusion that concerns for customer requirements and for quality/no waste are common to several operations management approaches – notably TQM, JIT and continuous improvement. The question here asks about TQM, and the answer therefore does not mention continuous improvement, introducing a system of quality circles, kanban systems and the control of production flow, or lean manufacturing. Before you take the examination, it would probably be a good idea to establish clearly in your own mind which operations management practice you associate with each 'ideology'.)

207 URBAN DANCE

(a) There are three types of benchmarking that the company might consider: internal benchmarking, competitive benchmarking and activity benchmarking.

Internal benchmarking is based on the assumption that within an organisation, there are several different units performing very similar activities. In the case of Urban Dance, the company operates a number of dance schools. It is also assumed that some units will perform better than others, at least in certain respects.

The internal benchmarking process therefore involves comparing the performance of the different units with each other. The aim is to identify 'best practice', and the ways in which one unit is performing better than the others. It should then be possible to apply the best practice in the other units, and so improve the performance of the company as a whole.

In order to carry out any benchmarking exercise, it is important to identify key aspects of performance for measurement, and having done this, to establish one or more suitable measures. The benchmarking exercise involves measuring these pre-determined aspects of performance, and analysing the differences and their causes.

A limitation of internal benchmarking, however, is its assumption that best practice can be identified within the entity itself. In practice, this might not be the case. All the schools of Urban Dance might use similar sub-optimal practices and achieve sub-optimal performance. Comparing their performance might therefore fail to reveal any information of value.

Competitive benchmarking is based on similar general principles as internal benchmarking, but with the significant difference that one or more competitors are selected for comparison. The external benchmark should be a successful competitor, preferably a successful dance school company with schools in the same areas as the Urban Dance schools, or a company that attracts its students from the same 'pool' of potential applicants.

The aim of competitive benchmarking is to establish whether the competitor performs better in the key performance areas, and if it does, to consider ways of removing the 'gap', and bringing performance up to or above the level of the competitor. If the company is able to do this, it should become more competitive, and more successful.

However, the success of competitive benchmarking depends of obtaining useful information about the performance of the main competitors. Rival dance schools are unlikely to volunteer the information, and it would therefore be necessary to obtain information for comparison from whatever reliable sources there might be.

Activity benchmarking, also called 'best practice' benchmarking or process benchmarking, is based on the view that it is not necessary to compare practices with similar types of organisation. Useful information about best practice can be obtained by comparing particular activities within the entity with similar activities in different types of entity. For example, Urban Dance might establish performance measurements for student recruitment activities with similar activities of a music school, or an art school or a private boarding school. Activities relating to normal academic education might be compared with similar teaching in a normal but successful academic school.

Activity benchmarking can help an entity to identify weaknesses in particular areas of its activities. The entity therefore needs to be aware of weaknesses that exist, in order to look for another entity that would be willing to provide the benchmark for that particular activity. The co-operation of the other entity is also required, but this is realistically more achievable than with competitive benchmarking.

(b)   The following initial steps should be taken by management of Urban Dance.

    (i)   Senior management need to identify the fact that there are probably weaknesses in operations that can be identified and rectified by means of benchmarking.

    (ii)   A decision has to be made about what type of benchmarking would be most appropriate in the circumstances. If internal benchmarking is selected, management would be assuming that best practice was already being achieved in some if its schools. If competitive benchmarking is preferred, management need to recognise that one or more competitors are performing better, and that the differences in performance need to be identified. The choice of activity benchmarking would be appropriate only if management know which activities they wish to improve.

    (iii)   Having decided which type of benchmarking method to use, the company needs to plan the exercise. With internal benchmarking, the management of the individual schools will probably have to be consulted, and involved in the process. With activity benchmarking, an external organisation to act as the benchmark needs to be identified, and its co-operation obtained.

    (iv)   The key areas of performance for benchmarking, and the measures of performance that will be used, should also be planned, at least in outline.

(c)   Benchmarking has the potential to create problems if it is mismanaged.

Performance measures must be comparable, otherwise the results may lead to costly distractions and mistakes. For example, measuring performance standards in a an area such as dance will be subjective. Different instructors may mark to different standards and generate results that are not comparable.

Benchmarking may also be difficult when the inputs are different. For example, one school might draw heavily from a catchment area where the local state schools place a great deal of emphasis on dance. Students referred from those schools might appear to be progressing more rapidly than those at another school where the local conditions are very different.

Benchmarking also requires the ability to rank different outcomes so that targets are realistic. For example, a competitive benchmark comparing performance in dance and academic subjects might reveal that some schools perform better in the former and others in the latter. That might suggest that schools which focus on dance tend not to devote sufficient time and resources to academic subjects and vice versa. Urban Dance should avoid trying to equal the best performance in both areas unless it can find some means of dealing with the inherent conflict between the two.

208   VIRTUAL

If a company adopts a strategy of becoming 'virtual', its aim is to manage all the operations involved in creating products or services and delivering them to customers, without becoming involved directly in any of those activities. The small number of employees/managers within the virtual company simply focus on their core strengths, which might be to manage the supply chain. A virtual company has no obvious centre, and might consist of individuals linked by computer networks and telephones.

However, in order to deliver products to the customer, there must be operational activities. Resources have to be converted into finished products. If a virtual company does not perform these activities itself, the work must be outsourced to an external organisation. In theory, all activities could be outsourced, and the virtual company would then need to manage its agreements and arrangements with its external suppliers and service providers.

The traditional function of purchasing is concerned with buying items from external suppliers, and getting the best deal available, such as the lowest purchase price. With supply chain management, the approach is different. An entity looks not just at its immediate relationship with its suppliers, but at the entire supply chain from raw materials to finished product, and looks for ways of improving it and adding more value. This will often involve developing long-term relationships with key suppliers, and co-operating to improve elements of the supply chain, and new product developments.

In a virtual company, the entire supply chain is operated by external organisations. Managing this supply chain therefore involves persuading other organisations to deliver supplies efficiently, so that the desired end-product reaches the end-customer on time.

Global sourcing has been made more possible by the Internet and by improvements in the transportation of goods. The Internet allows an entity to identify suppliers in different countries more easily, and to obtain information about them. E-mail and other communication methods allow an entity to communicate with suppliers in any other country. Improved transportation systems mean that goods produced in one part of the world can be shipped to other countries at reasonable cost and within reasonable time frames.

In theory, a virtual company could manage a global network of suppliers and logistics firms, to produce consumer products and deliver them to markets anywhere in the world. However, the virtual company needs to remain an essential element within the overall value chain. It is crucial that the virtual company should remain in control of one or more vital elements of the chain: for example, it might retain control over sales and distribution channels and control over the brand name. With consumer durable products, it is probably also essential to retain a direct interest in product design activities.

A successful virtual company therefore needs to be efficient in managing the sequences of processes that go into making and delivering products or services. Key skills are therefore the management of outsourcing, the management of the supply chain or value chain, developing a successful global supply network, and remaining innovative and competitive.

209 PROCESS IMPROVEMENT

(a)   Business process re-engineering (BPR) is the analysis and design of work flows and processes within and between organisations. It involves the critical analysis and radical redesign of existing business processes to achieve breakthrough improvements in performance measures.

For example, an enterprise that has decided to focus on customer service as its source of competitive advantage will redesign its business processes with customer service as its primary goals.

(b)   Continuous improvement or kaizen is a management philosophy based on seeking gradual and small changes in all aspects of an entity's operations. Like TQM, it requires the commitment of all employees, and the development of a culture of quality and concern for the customer. Over time, the organisation will gradually change, adapt and improve its performance.

BPR, in contrast, is based on dramatic change, involving the restructuring of an organisation, its systems, its use of IT, its management systems and its performance measurement systems. Dr Hammer described BPR as a fundamental rethinking and radical design of business processes, to achieve dramatic improvements in critical performance measures such as cost, quality, service and speed.

Whereas the ideas for improvement with kaizen come from employees themselves, the initial ideas for radical change in BPR might come from external specialist consultants. Employees will need to be persuaded of the need for change, and to be involved in the change process, but it is not necessary to develop a culture of believing in change and quality improvement.

Whereas continuous improvement considers changes in any aspect of the organisation and its operations, BPR might be more focused on specific processes rather than all the business processes within the organisation.

BPR is probably more appropriate in circumstances where gradual improvements through kaizen might be too little and too late, or where the problems are fundamental such that small changes will not resolve them. Suitable circumstances might therefore exist when:

(i)   competitors are outperforming the company considerably

(ii)   there are conflicts within the organisation, particularly between functions and departments

(iii)   a very large amount of management time is wasted in meetings

(iv)   there is an excessive use of unstructured communications such as e-mails and memos, and relatively little structured communication

(v)   there are serious weaknesses and inefficiencies in key processes.

(c)   The practical approach to BPR varies to some extent between different specialist consultancy organisations. All agree that to implement BPR successfully, there has to be communication throughout the organisation, so that everyone is aware of the issues and why changes are being made. The broad approach, however, is usually as follows:

(i)   The first step is to investigate the current operations within the organisation, and in particular the operating procedures and the results that are being achieved. This investigation will also need to consider how environmental changes, such as technological changes and changes in customer preferences, are affecting operations. Where weaknesses in the organisation are identified, a decision has to be made about whether radical change is needed, or whether only small changes are needed. Where radical change is needed, the senior management will need to recognise that the changes could involve redundancies and closures of operations. It will also be essential to communicate the vision of what changes are needed to the organisation's employees, and the employees who will be affected must be educated in the need for changes.

(ii)   If a decision is taken to introduce change through BPR, a management structure for the project should be established. There should be a senior manager acting as leader and promoter of change. Management of the operations affected by the change should also be involved, with representatives in the BPR project team. The senior manager will probably appoint a 'process owner', who will be the manager responsible for how the process performs. The re-engineering team, possibly five to ten in number, will be responsible for diagnosing the current system and for oversight of the re-design of the process and its implementation.

(iii)   The re-engineering team should have the responsibilities for identifying opportunities for radical change. This should begin with an exercise to identify the key processes within the organisation. The key processes, which might include product development, customer support, order processing, the development of manufacturing capacity and customer communications, are unlikely to correspond with the traditional functional /departmental structure of the organisation. In identifying key processes, the investigators should be looking for opportunities for change, typically through changes in the use of information, changes in IT systems or changes in people. At the end of this stage of the project, the reengineering team need to decide on which processes should be given the priority for change, how the new process should be operated, what the key process characteristics should be, the critical success factors and the key performance measures.

(iv) Having identified which process to re-engineer, the team should look at the current process, and gain an understanding of why it is performed as it is at the moment. The objectives of the process should already have been clearly defined, and the current process should be assessed in terms of how far it meets those objectives, and how far it falls short.

(v) The actual re-engineering can then begin. The re-engineering team is responsible for developing new ideas for the process. These will often be based on new technology, new uses of information, and the re-design of jobs (for example, combining several jobs into one, and ensuring that procedures are carried out in a logical order and that work is performed where it makes most sense to do it). It is also important to consider what effect a change in the process with have on all other processes that interact with it.

(vi) Details of the re-engineered process need to be developed and the new process must be defined.

(vii) A strategy or plan must also be developed for moving from the current process to the new process. The employees affected by the changes should be kept involved. The new process will probably require a new organisation structure. The changes could involve re-skilling the work force, through re-training or new recruitments, and the introduction of new IT systems.

MARKETING

210 MARKETING FUNCTION: CONCEPTS

(a) Any discussion on marketing mix will include consideration of the 'Four Ps'. These are product, price, promotion and place (or distribution). Their main characteristics are as follows.

Product – is anything that is offered to the market for use or consumption. Factors to be taken into account will include quality, any branding, variety, special features, style, packaging and fashion. Generally, people want to acquire the benefits of a product so they will also be looking for the characteristics of guarantees, after-sales service and general reliability.

Price – is important because it is the only element that produces revenue. Normally this will be characterised by reference to being fixed to both market conditions and also costs of production. Other characteristics will embrace discount policy for quantity or early payment, as a 'weapon' in the introduction of a new product or complementing another line, and also trade-in allowances.

Promotion – is the way in which the product is drawn to the attention of the market place. It covers advertising in all its forms (e.g., press, commercial TV, outdoor hoardings, etc), personal selling, sales promotions and publicity through media coverage.

Place – the purpose of this is to get the product to the consumer, hence the alternative names of placement and distribution. Its characteristics are the channels of distribution and the physical distribution activities. It is also concerned with the location of sales outlets and the infrastructure of warehousing and transport facilities.

(b)   The scenario given is one where the skilful application of the four Ps has meant new life for an attraction with declining popularity. Working in the favour of the manager is the fact that with increased prosperity and leisure time for many people, there are opportunities to retrieve the situation and to exploit the attraction very profitably. Two obvious examples in the UK are Alton Towers and Madame Tussauds.

It is essential to recognise that one element on its own cannot be manipulated to give success. It is important that each element be considered as part of the overall approach and that the effect be co-ordinated to ensure improvement. However, for ease of presentation, it may be appropriate to consider each item individually.

Product – the manager must consider just what he is selling and what is so special about his product that encourages tourists to travel to visit the attraction, sometimes at very great expense e.g. a walk in the main street of Stratford-upon-Avon on any summer's day will confirm the worldwide interest in this particular product. Here, of course, the products are all associated with William Shakespeare and this is very skilfully exploited by the theatre, the Shakespeare Trust properties and all the other attractions that constitute 'the product'.

With this example, the basic concept underpinning what the tourist expects is self-evident. For a museum or theme park, the manager must carefully research the product. Does the visitor want an educational visit, an 'experience', a 'white-knuckle' ride or passive entertainment? Possibly the visitor might want all of these. There are many examples where museums have changed their image, so that instead of passively viewing relics, people can actively experience some of the items on display.

Once the manager has determined his underpinning approach, he can consider what other complementary facilities should be provided. Obvious ones are good rest areas, souvenir stalls, convenient catering provisions and possibly even hire of cameras (as in Tussauds). If the quality is good, there is every likelihood that the additional revenue earned would greatly enhance the profitability of the attraction.

Price – coupled with any changes or developments in the image for the theme park or the museum must be reconsideration of the pricing policy. Typical problems that need to be addressed are as follows.

(i)   How does the price level proposed compare with competing attractions? Will it be seen as value for money?

(ii)   Should there be one overall admission price covering all activities, or would a separate admission charge with extra tickets for rides and other attractions be more appropriate?

(iii)   Will the price level proposed and the estimated attendance ensure that a profit is made?

(iv)   What family schemes, concessions for children and senior citizens, or coach parties, should be arranged?

(v)   A popular development is the provision of package deals for admission and overnight accommodation, e.g. Legoland, Seaside Sun centres, etc. Would this be possible?

(vi)   Should there be different peak charges at weekend and bank holidays?

(vii)   Would the price level be acceptable both to home visitors as well as overseas tourists?

(viii) What price should be charged for franchises such as food and souvenir kiosks?

Promotion – here the concern must initially be with the development of the 'product' and the image it is to portray. Is it a family day out or an educational experience, or should the 'fun' aspect be stressed? Once decided, then the most appropriate means of promotion must be determined. Several outlets might be used. For example, press and commercial television advertising would be satisfactory to attract home visitors but are unlikely to be seen by overseas tourists. Hence, knowledge of what most people do on their first night of a holiday would be appropriate. After unpacking, many people congregate in the reception area of the hotel or campsite picking up leaflets for the local attractions - and this approach was found to be one of the most effective in promoting the new image of Tussauds. Where a small discount token is printed in the leaflet, than it is found that many people cannot resist this bargain.

Place – As the theme park or museum is in a fixed location, particularly in the short to medium term, then consideration of channels of distribution is inappropriate. There are other elements, which may be explored, such as exploitation of the location, and the provision of car parking and conveniences for public transport. Market segmentation is considered under this heading and here there can be opportunities to attract different consumers at different times. One example is the use of a holiday camp for different activities at varying times of the year: for example, holidays during the period April to September and conferences outside these dates. If the marketing manager reconsiders the approach under these headings and is bold in his approach, then popularity of the attraction will be high again. However, having once carried out this exercise, he must not 'rest on his laurels' as people are continually looking for new experiences and he must work all the time to maintain the position.

211 SEGMENTING

(a)   Market segmentation is a scientific, rational process of trying to match the needs of specific groups of customers with the organisation's products and services.

The idea is that different groups in society have different needs, aspirations, statuses, etc and that even a humble product like a bar of soap possesses different 'meanings' for the different groups.

The advantages for firms marketing efforts are as follows:

- The same product can be advertised in different media to target different customer groupings – trade journals for professionals, leisure magazines for general customers, local newspapers for local clients, websites for international buyers and so forth. This may be expensive (in time and money) but should increase sales to offset costs.

- Product packaging and branding can be changed to represent different products for differing segments. Expensive wrapping using gold and black can change the 'meaning' or status of the soap bar to move it 'up-market'. This need not be expensive, especially if the only thing that changes is the name. Some car companies use the same body or engine but brand the car differently - the manufacturers' name and model name are changed.

- The actual product can be altered or enhanced to suit the needs of different customer groups. This is an expensive option involving re-design and production re-tooling and should be part of ongoing development.

Thus, the advantages are in the efficiency and accuracy of the marketing plan and the increased returns to investment as against a 'one size fits all' undifferentiated strategy.

(b)   Three variables of the clothing market would be:

(i)   *Gender* – males and females have very different requirements and view clothes differently in terms of their perception of the 'meaning' these generate to others.

(ii)   *Age* – within the gender category, there are clear differences with regard to age, for example school uniforms or general school wear for secondary school age children; young people's leisurewear; older people's formal/business attire and leisurewear. Size also varies with age and so it is essential in clothing to differentiate by age.

(iii) *Lifestyle* – under the age category, leisurewear is more common for those not in work. Between 20 and 60 both men and women who work require more formal outfits and a greater number of these than children or retired people.

In terms of the paint manufacturer, these are two variables that can be used to segment the market:

(i) *End-user* – some businesses are virtually wholesalers and supply the general public, so these would require more stylish tins with colour charts and advice leaflets. Other businesses are strictly 'trade' and would require a narrower range without the enhancements.

(ii) *Size* – a big customer would require large batches with quantity discounts, a special salesperson allocated to them etc. A small high-street trader would require only occasional visits by a representative, but might need help merchandising/displaying the paints effectively. There would be hundreds of these and so a dedicated service would not be feasible – re-ordering would be made easier for the small trader for example.

(c) Online sales have grown dramatically, creating a body of potential buyers who are prepared to select goods from websites and pay for delivery. Niche and specialised products can be offered on web pages without detracting from more mainstream offerings. Customers will often search for particular items using search engines (e.g. Google) and so the company does not have to spend a great deal of money on actively promoting these offerings. Provided the items are capable of being delivered by post or courier, they can be sold by mail order. Thus, companies do not need to establish an expensive distribution network.

The phenomenal success of eBay has created a virtual marketplace that is ideal for many vendors. Some large companies have a significant presence on eBay and use it to sell reconditioned items or ends of lines. However, this marketplace could, potentially, be of value to any company that is keen to offer a non-standard product. The system for rating buyers and sellers even offers a degree of confidence in online sales that might not have existed otherwise.

212 GREEN COMPANY

(a) A company needs a reasonably reliable estimate of the total size of a market, both within the regional markets or market segments that it currently operates, and possibly in other regions and segments too. This will enable the company to assess its market share, and its competitive position within its markets. Knowing market share will also help the company to decide on an appropriate marketing mix.

For example, if the total market is large and the company estimates that it only has a small market share, it might consider focusing on one segment of the market, and developing a marketing mix that will appeal to customers in the targeted segment. On the other hand, if the total market is fairly small but the company has a large market share, the marketing strategy might aim at trying to protect the market share against competition.

If the total size of the market is known (and total sales within each market segment are also known), it is a simple task to calculate market share. The main difficulty is estimating the size of the total market.

The total size of a market might be estimated in a number of ways:

(i) In some industries, there might be a suppliers' association (a voluntary association of manufacturers). Where there is such an association, members might have agreed to an arrangement whereby each provides confidential information about their annual sales turnover to the association, which then calculates the total annual sales of its members. If the members operating this scheme represent a substantial proportion of total sales to the market, a reasonable estimate of total market sales can then be given by the association to the participating members. It is not clear here whether or not Green Company has such a manufacturers' association for its particular industry.

(ii) The company's sales team or marketing team can try to establish from their main distributors what percentage of the total sales of the distributors are for products of the Green Company, and what proportion of their sales are sales of competitors' products. This will enable the company to assess its share of the market in the sales distribution channels that it uses. Having estimated its market share, a total size of the market can be calculated. Since the number of distributors for the company's products is probably fairly small, a reliable sample could be asked to provide information. However, distributors are under no obligation to provide such information.

(iii) Some information might be obtained by the sales force simply by discussing sales and marketing issues with distributors, or providing information about distributors who do not sell the products of Green Company. However, this information would be difficult to convert into a numerical estimate of market size.

(iv) If the company's main competitors file annual accounts, some information about total market sales might be obtained from this source, by looking at the sales turnover data. However, it is unlikely that rival companies will provide sales information in their annual report and accounts in a form that is usable by their competitors.

(v) It might be possible to establish estimates of market size and market share from a market research exercise in which consumers are asked about their buying habits. However, for gardening equipment, it is by no means certain that reliable data could be obtained in this way, since consumers do not buy gardening equipment regularly, and are probably not as 'brand aware' as with frequently-purchased consumer goods.

(b) A company selling gardening equipment will sell mainly through distributors, such as garden centres. There are several ways that the company might use to forecast sales demand for the new products.

(i) The company could try to establish which of its distributors are likely to sell the new products, and what they expect their purchase quantities to be. This would be a form of survey of buyers' opinions. Opinions could be obtained by members of the sales force in discussion with their contacts in distributor organisations.

(ii) The sales force might be asked to give their view of the likely demand for the new products, based on their experience of the market and customers. The views of the different sales representatives can then be compared, and a 'composite' view of expected sales can be estimated.

(iii) It might be possible to obtain the opinions of potential customers, by carrying out a market test in a limited number of distribution outlets. Test marketing will help the company to judge what sales might be if and when the products are introduced to the entire market.

(iv) If the new products are similar to products that have been launched in the past, it might be possible to predict sales on the assumption that the growth in sales will be similar to the pattern of sales for new products in the past. However, this is probably an unreliable method of sales forecasting for new products, since there is no way of being sure whether the products will be well-received in the market.

(v)   It might also be possible to obtain an 'expert opinion' about sales by asking for the views of experienced managers within the company.

(vi) The company should assess social trends. Long-term changes in demand might be predicted by looking at the types of houses that are being built. If there is a trend towards smaller gardens then that might have implications for the types of gardening equipment that might sell well. If there are fewer gardening programmes on television or sales of magazines are declining, then that could signal a decline in consumer interest.

(vii) The company should investigate historical relationships between sales and factors that might have had an influence on sales levels. For example, if sales were depressed when mortgage interest rates were high, then that suggests customer demand is affected by disposable income. Forecasts of economic trends might then be used to identify potential changes in demand.

213   RESTFUL HOTELS

(a)   There are several ways in which pricing can be used as an element in marketing.

- Restful Hotels might be able to promote itself as a low cost hotel for the quality of service provided, but without putting the four star ratings at risk. The company could then market its hotels as the cheapest in their area for the quality of services provided. To succeed with this pricing strategy, Restful Hotels would need to control costs.

- There are difficulties in generating revenue at new hotels. It might be appropriate to use promotion (for example, web site advertising) to boost the business at these hotels. However, if price is used as a marketing tool, it might be appropriate to charge low room rates until demand is more established, or offering special room prices for a short period of time. For example, it might be possible to have sales promotions offering cut-price rooms at any Restful Hotel in the world to customers who book before a specified date.

- The company should also consider charging different prices in different locations, such as higher prices in city centre hotels than at holiday resorts, because the type of customer is likely to differ between the different types of location.

- It might also be possible to have differential pricing, with room prices varying according to the day of the week or the season of the year.

- Another form of price differentiation to win more customers might be to offer special price deals for pensioners or even students.

- To improve the 'value for money' marketing message, it might be more appropriate to offer more services free of charge (within the room charge), rather than to lower prices. Examples of free add-on services might be a courtesy bus from airport to hotel at holiday resorts.

(b)   The hotel market is segmented in different ways. One method of segmentation is to classify hotels according to quality (number of 'stars') and price. However, a policy of moving from a portfolio of four-star hotels, say to a portfolio of five-star hotels or a mixed portfolio of four-star and three-star hotels, will take time to implement.

If market segmentation is to succeed within a fairly short space of time in boosting total sales revenue, marketing strategy should probably focus on creating a stronger appeal to a sector of the market that does not currently take accommodation at Restful Hotels.

Sectors of the market for hotel rooms might be analysed, for example, as business users, conference participants, and holiday makers. If the hotel group does not currently attract, say, conference business, it might consider a marketing initiative to promote this type of business. If room occupancy is low at weekends, it might be appropriate to promote 'bargain' weekend breaks.

There might also be opportunities for focussing on customers for other services of the hotel, other than rooms. For example, the company might consider developing its restaurant service and promoting these to the general public.

(c) The company is aiming for the premium range of hotel accommodation. Cutting prices might attract some customers who were previously unwilling to pay market rates for a four star hotel, but might put off some of the company's existing customer base as staying at a Restful Hotels hotel will no longer have the same degree of exclusivity. It might also mean that existing customers are forced to share the hotel with a less select group of residents.

Reducing prices might create a loss of revenue and there is no guarantee that it will generate additional volume. The change in prices might have to be managed so that the reductions are offered in a discreet manner. For example, the 'rack rate' offered at the reception desk for any customer who contacts the hotel directly might remain unchanged, but the discount offered to travel agents could be increased so that the agents can enjoy a bigger commission from each sale. That might give them an incentive to send more customers to Restful Hotels.

The other big danger with cutting prices is that Restful Hotels might then trigger a price war with competing hotel chains. If competitors start to lose business they might cut their own prices, leaving Restful Hotels no more competitive than before but enjoying less profit from each and every sale.

214 TROY BOATS

(a) The elements or stages of brand positioning might be described as follows.

- Brand definition. The product supplier needs to create an awareness in the mind of consumers what the brand represents, and what type of product will be sold under the brand name. Initially, this will probably mean associating the brand with a fairly narrow range of products. Over time, however, an established brand might be extended to cover a wider range of different products.

- Brand differentiation. When consumers know what a brand represents, the next stage in developing the brand is to differentiate it from the brands of rival products. The aim should be to create a clear and meaningful idea in the minds of consumers how the company's branded products differ from those of rivals. If there is no differentiation, consumers will presumably base their purchasing decision on other factors such as price and convenience. Typically, brands might be differentiated on the basis of product features and price.

- Deepening a brand. With very successful brands, the brand eventually becomes associated in the mind of consumers with their own personal goals and values. This is known as deepening the brand. This process creates strong brand loyalties, and buyers of the brand will continue to do so. For example, a branded range of food items that are differentiated on the basis of 'organic' foods might become associated in the mind of a segment of the market with 'healthy eating and healthy living'. Brand extension becomes easier once a brand has been deepened.

- Defending the brand. Branded products are sold in highly competitive markets. Once a brand has been established and has become successful, it needs to be defended against rival products and new marketing initiatives by competitors.

(b)   To establish an Argo 0 brand, the company needs to decide first of all what range of boats should be sold under this brand name. The aim of brand definition should be to associate the brand name with a particular type of product. There might be a risk that if the company uses the brand name for all the boats that it makes, from small sailing boats up to large motor cruisers, customers will not define the Argo 0 brand clearly in their minds. An alternative approach to brand definition is to start by applying the brand name to a particular range of boats.

If the process of achieving brand identification is successful, the company can go on to create brand differentiation. Since there are no other branded products in the market at the moment, the company must decide how the Argo 0 boats should be presented to customers as being different from the boats made by any other manufacturer. The positioning of the brand in its market might be on the basis of price or quality, or particular design features.

If the company is successful in creating a successful differentiated brand, the next step is to try to deepen the brand. This might be possible by associating the Argo 0 brand with a particular lifestyle that customers would like for themselves, such as 'freedom to get away' or 'life of luxury and leisure'. If the process of brand deepening is successful, the company might be able to extend the brand name to other types of boat.

A successful brand needs defending, often by means of advertising and sales promotion. The company should develop a suitable marketing mix to promote its branded products, for example through regular magazine advertising, and displaying its boats at boat shows, exhibitions and trade fairs. Continual product improvement would also be desirable.

(c)   Creating a brand name requires some means of bringing the brand name and the qualities that the brand espouses to the attention of potential buyers and also to those who might be in a position to influence buying decisions (e.g. journalists). That could be a very costly process. For example, advertising in boating magazines is one option, but it could be a very costly matter and the adverts will have to continue for some time before brand awareness might be developed. The company could also establish a presence at major exhibitions and trade conferences, but that is also an expensive option and one that could generate very few immediate sales, requiring an ongoing commitment.

Potential customers might be wary of committing themselves to a purchase of this type from a relatively unknown supplier when there are better established brands in the market. This is not merely a highly expensive considered purchase, but one that might involve literally staking one's life on the product's reliability. Existing buyers might be happy to trade with Troy Boats because it is a well-established local supplier, but it might be very difficult to branch out into wider markets without this sense of local awareness.

215   BLACK COMPANY

(a)   If a company pursues socially responsible policies, these should apply to all aspects of its operations, not just to marketing. The factors that the company should consider will depend on its particular circumstances. However, its CSR policies should have regard to the following issues:

- Dealing ethically in business with customers and suppliers. Unethical business practices, such as misleading advertising, or taking excessive credit periods from suppliers, might have an adverse effect on the company's reputation in the mind of business associates and customers.

- Having regard for human rights, including employees' rights. The company should treat its own employees fairly. In addition, it should also consider the working conditions of employees in businesses that supply products from Central Europe. Adverse publicity about employees in these businesses working in unhealthy conditions, or in conditions of 'slave labour', could have a damaging effect on the reputation of Black Company.

- The company should also show concern for the environment, for example the need to avoid unnecessary pollution and wasteful use of raw materials. Black Company might therefore need to consider the packaging for its products and the disposal and recycling of the plastic containers for its successful range of sweets.

- The company should also have regard to the general welfare of society. With confectionery products, a major issue is the effect of food products on health. The company should consider investing in research to monitor the effects on health of excessive eating of its products.

(b) If a company has CSR policies, there could be valuable marketing advantages in promoting them.

- Since eating confectionery has potential implications for health, the company should consider presenting itself to the market as a producer with concerns for health. For example, the details on product packaging about the contents of the product might be presented in a more meaningful and clear way, so that customers who want to know what they are eating are given a better understanding. The company might also consider offering new products with more 'healthy' features, such as smaller sized chocolate bars and some sugar-free products.

- Advertising should be honest, and should not promote an unhealthy lifestyle for children and adults. The company might even consider using marketing to promote itself as a 'healthy living' producer, for example by sponsoring amateur sports events.

- The company should perhaps address the environmental problems of waste, particularly with product wrappings and packaging. There might be opportunities for presenting products in an attractive package, but using fewer packaging materials, or more environmental-friendly materials. The company might also review the sale of the products in plastic containers, and consider another way of presenting them. To gain a marketing advantage out of this initiative, the company should consider promoting itself as a manufacturer with concerns for the environment.

It is important that if a company uses marketing to promote itself and its products are socially responsible, the general public should believe the message. There way well be public mistrust of companies that claim to be socially responsible and environmentally aware, but are actually being dishonest with their marketing message.

If a company believes that is genuinely socially-responsible, and has implemented to promote CSR, it might be able to enhance its reputation through public relations.

(c) Black Company sells a product that is inherently unhealthy. Excessive consumption of confectionery harms teeth and promotes obesity. Consumers of the products should come to no harm if they use the product in moderation, but recent developments in public health campaigns suggest that companies that sell such products face a difficult challenge in retaining consumer confidence.

The product is aimed at children, who are deemed a vulnerable target market and who are seen to require a degree of protection. Companies who advertise in such media as children's comics and advertising slots during children's television programmes leave themselves open to criticism. The alternative is either to stop advertising or to advertise in media that are less likely to attract the target audience.

The product has certain inherent characteristics that create CSR problems. The sweets are packaged in plastic shells that can be used as toys, which means that they are probably more harmful to the environment than if they were packaged in cardboard or in thinner plastic bags. The inclusion of a toy in the packaging might encourage children to consume more of the product than if they were just getting sweets.

All of these concerns could leave Black Company exposed and these possibilities should be planned for by management just in case there are problems in the future.

216   H COMPANY

(a)   (i)   A 'selling' company probably aims a generic product at a wide market segment and so as almost a 'commodity' i.e. cannot differentiate the product. This means that a high-volume/low price strategy may be evolved and so the emphasis of the business is less on the innovation and creativity to create margin but on selling techniques to ensure its products are chosen over those of a competitor – such as clever merchandising, offers, competitors, goods distribution, etc.

A marketing company however uses the 'marketing concept' which aims to establish customer needs first and then design a strategy to meet them. This may well include 'commodity' products and competition on price, but this should be a deliberate trade-off with other products which can be differentiated in Porter's sense and so create margin which can be used not to reduce prices by internal efficiency but by market research to influence patterns of demand e.g. women's perfumes at Christmas are sold to male customers buying them as presents so the ads must be attractive not to women, paradoxically, but to men.

(ii)   H can adopt this by a change in culture (role to task) and philosophy – 'customer first'. This needs to be the subject of a wide change – management programme, perhaps using TQM as a vehicle. In this way the various parts of it's value chain can be linked, backwards, from the customer through sales and marketing through to purchasing. Clearly marketing must lead the way (in terms of research, etc) but other functions must be part of **Task Force** teams to reduce their resistance to change.

(b)   The marketing mix is often referred to as the 4Ps – Produce, Price, Promotion and Place, but nowadays authors have extended the number of factors – some up to seven items.

Product – though it depends ultimately on customers, H must be able to retail products at a reasonable price or, however chic, it may not sell in volume and so overhead costs would increase as a % – if for example its customers want 'designer labels'.

As it is a retailer, it is less constrained than a manufacturer with production facilities and design departments. It can alter its products to appeal to different segments and merchandise them accordingly – with differing point of sale advertising (e.g. larger and smaller sizes for ladies).

Price – It may decide not to put the price on items in the shop windows in order to tempt buyers in who like the basic product. However, this is a dangerous strategy as customers often do not have time to enquire about prices. H has high-street competition and so must match the prices of similar items, while also conforming to traditional sales times, offers, etc.

Promotion – If H has a marketing concept it must differentiate its above-the-line and if possible below-the-line advertising to meet the expectations and values of each of its segments. So, it may re-brand itself generally as The Youth Shop but target older people, the middle-aged, the young executives and children all separately.

Place – The high street is increasingly not the place to be – malls, franchises in-store, catalogues and increasingly the internet are becoming the prime channels of distribution. H must spend money on these.

(c)   Inclusion in this feature is likely to prove far more valuable than any formal advertising in the press. This is because the company's clothes will be presented and photographed in a manner that makes them appear to enhance and flatter the wearer. The underlying message of the feature would be that anyone wearing the items recommended to the subject of the makeover will be choosing wisely.

The nature of this type of feature tends to stress that the wrong clothes impair the wearer's appearance and that this can be remedied by switching to a better choice of wardrobe. This association would be beneficial to the company's image.

The newspaper will wish to make the feature interesting in order to capture readers' interest. It will, therefore, be likely to deal with problems that tend to interest significant numbers of potential customers (e.g. how to dress when overweight).

Makeover programmes are popular on television. That will generate additional interest in the newspaper article and might tend to generate further sales for particular lines offered by H Company.

If H Company does not take up this offer then it is likely to be offered to the company's competitors. That could put H Company even further behind.

217   LO-SPORT LTD

(a)   The 'classic' life cycle for a product has four phases:

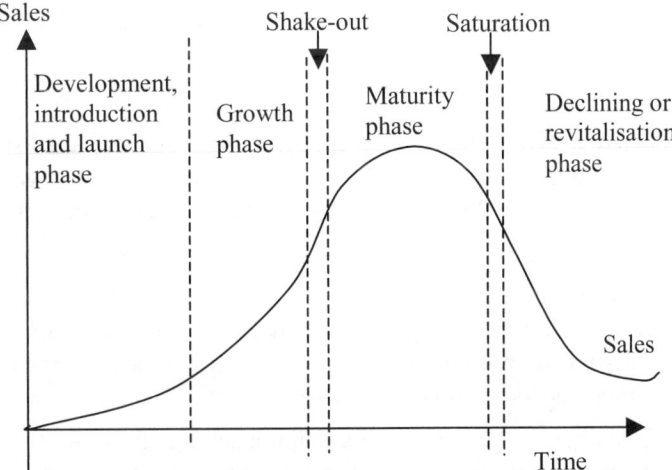

- An **introduction phase**, when the product or service is first developed and introduced to the market. Sales demand is low whilst potential customers learn about the item. There is a learning process for both customers and the producer, and the producer might have to vary the features of the product or service, in order to meet customer requirements more successfully.

- A **growth phase**, when the product or service becomes established, and there is a large growth in sales demand. The number of competitors in the market also increases, but customers are still willing to pay reasonably high prices. The product becomes profitable. Variety in the product or service increases, and customers are much more conscious of quality issues.

- A **maturity phase**, which might be the longest stage in the product life cycle. Demand stabilises, and producers compete on price.

- A **decline phase**, during which sales demand falls. Prices are reduced to sustain demand and to slow the decline in sales volume. Eventually the product becomes unprofitable, and eventually producers stop making it.

A large number of products have gone through this type of life cycle. For example, at the time of writing, it would appear that floppy disks for computers and video recorders are in the decline phase of their life cycle.

(b) **Rackets**

The manufacture of rackets for tennis, squash and badminton are all within a well-established industry which appears to be in the *maturity phase* of the life cycle model. This is characterised by market saturation and stiff competition. Market growth is thus low.

Implications

Consideration could be given to the continued viability of this product. However, thought also needs to be given to the continuing cash flow generation compared to any disposal price that could be attained.

There could also be wider considerations such as interdependencies between products. For example, the shoe product side of the business may be partly dependent in cash, marketing or operational terms on the continued existence of racket manufacturing.

In the absence of significant other factors, further investment in this product should be questioned.

Existing sports shoes

This industry appears to be in the decline phase of the life cycle model based on the information available – although this may merely be a temporary fall in industry sales.

This would suggest divestment, or at least no further substantial new investment to support the product.

The katex shoe

While there does not seem to be any current sales, there appears to be significant prospective sales and significant potential sales growth. The product can be classified as either still in product development or moving into market development.

Implications

The market is attractive but the lack of market share may need significant investment in order to grow by comparison with major competitors. This may include physical investment in larger scale production activities, but also in advertising to promote the brand in a fashion conscious industry.

There is therefore likely to be a need for a major cash injection. As there are no cash generators in the product portfolio, this may need to come from some form of joint development strategy. Alternatively, or additionally, new debt or equity capital could be raised.

(c) Penetration pricing would involve setting the price low in order to build market share for the new shoe. Ideally, this could lead to the shoe establishing a niche in the marketplace and building up a base of satisfied customers who might become repeat customers once their first pair of shoes reached the end of their lives.

Price skimming might have some benefits if the new shoe really does offer real benefits. The premium price might create the impression of high quality, thereby stimulating sales. The high price might create some interest amongst potential trend-setters (having a celebrity spotted wearing a pair of Katex shoes could be worth more than any advertising campaign).

The biggest drawback to price skimming is the risk that consumers might be sceptical of any claims made on behalf of the new shoe. If the materials are unproven then the public might be unwilling to risk paying too much for it.

Price skimming might also attract competition. If competitors see that Lo Sport Ltd can make significant volumes of sales at this price point, then they might develop their own use of new materials with similar properties. The fact that these would come to market later might create the impression that they offered improvements over the original.

218 SX SNACKS (NOV 05 EXAM)

(a)

Key answer tip:

Make sure you discuss the implications of the issues you have raised.

The main issues to include in the marketing action plan and their implications are as follows:

Product

The new preparation and packaging technology will save on direct labour but also gives SX an opportunity to consider restyling its products. The main emphasis is on high quality fresh products and the designs should reflect this.

The big danger of using packaging technology is that the sandwiches look the same as can be bought from any supermarket and lose their 'home-made' appeal.

Similarly, it is vital that the preparation equipment enhances or maintains quality rather than letting it suffer. For example, will coffee beans be freshly ground?

One implication of this is the need to train staff in the new equipment to ensure that quality standards are maintained.

Place

The plan at present is still to use SX staff to deliver the food and drinks. At some point they may consider outsourcing this activity but, until then, the key issue is to improve the reliability of the deliveries. This is vital, as a lack of reliability will compromise SX's brand name.

The suggestion put forward is to have more drivers, thus reducing workloads. With existing staff being redeployed, this will involve further training in food handling and the outbound logistics procedures (paperwork, scheduling, etc).

As the firm grows there will be a need to recruit further drivers who will also need training and inducting into the SX culture, with a particular emphasis on providing high quality products to customers.

Promotion

Presumably SX will continue to use local radio advertising but the main issue for promotion is the role of drivers. Drivers will be expected to market the products to both existing and potential customers so will need extensive training in sales techniques. SX's reputation will be seriously compromised if staff are heavy-handed in their enthusiasm to win more business.

SX should also consider the use of online and telephone ordering so customers can request further supplies if they run out. This would have resource implications in terms of building a website, assigning someone to deal with telephone orders and may require changes to the production system.

(b)

Key answer tip:

A relatively straightforward requirement – just use the standard contents of a job description and apply them to the scenario.

A job description for the revised post of driver should include the following aspects:

Job title

- Driver (*Note:* You could suggest a different title to reflect the new roles, for example, 'customer service operative')

The purpose of the job

- To improve customer satisfaction through quick, reliable delivery of products
- To boost sales of products
- To improve information about competitors

The position of the job in the organisation

- The driver will report directly to the marketing manager

Salary

- Presumably comparable with existing wages but slightly higher than normal driver wages
- Bonus of up to 10% of annual salary, depending on hitting delivery and sales growth targets

Principal duties to be performed

- Delivering products to customers, mainly petrol stations
- Getting feedback from customers
- Encouraging customers to take new product lines
- Getting information on competitors' products
- Marketing products to other potential customers such as railway stations and newspaper shops

The job environment

- Drivers will receive extensive training in the marketing aspects of the role and will be supported by the customer services team
- Most of the time the driver will work on their own visiting clients' premises

MANAGING HUMAN CAPITAL

219 TAXIS AND TYRES (PILOT PAPER)

Key answer tips:

To answer this question, you must understand what is a human resource plan. A typical human resources plan looks forward three to five years, and should consider:

- the objectives of the organisation in the planning period
- the demand for employees, and the skills of those employees
- the current numbers and skills of employees
- methods of closing the gap between current staffing and required staffing levels and skills.

(a) **Outline human resources plan**

Objectives of the organisation

The objectives of the organisation over the next few years are:

- To provide a taxi service at about the same level of sales volume as at present.

- To meet the growing demand for tyres.

- To provide a wheel alignment service to support the tyre replacement business.

Required staffing, current staffing and the 'gap'

	Immediate required staff levels	Current staff levels	The gap
Management (owner-manager)	1	1	0
Taxi drivers	10	8	2
Tyre fitters	2	1	1
Receptionist/taxi controller	2	1	1

Methods of closing the gap

- There is an urgent requirement to recruit two taxi drivers.

- Recruited staff will probably need training, for example in safety procedures, dealing with customers and learning the local 'street maps'.

- There is a need to recruit an additional tyre fitter. If the recruited individual is not an experienced tyre fitter, training must be provided.

- The existing tyre fitter and new tyre fitter should both be given training in wheel alignment.

- A new receptionist/taxi controller should be recruited. In the longer term, it might be worth considering developing one of the taxi controllers as a junior manager.

- A policy should also be devised for the regular recruitment and training of taxi drivers, since there appears to be a regular annual turnover of about two drivers each year.

The main elements of a human resources plan are:

- setting the objectives of the organisation or department, in order to establish the required numbers and skills of staff over the planning period

- carrying out an 'audit' of existing staff, to establish the current numbers and skills

- identifying the gap between staff requirements and current staff numbers and skills

- devising methods of 'closing the gap' to ensure that the required staff numbers and skills are obtained.

(b) To obtain maximum contribution from the workforce, attention must be paid to the following HR activities, in addition to recruitment and selection, and training and development.

- **Pay and conditions**. The pay and terms and conditions of working need to be established. They need to be sufficiently attractive to attract individuals of a suitable calibre. Staff pay might also include a bonus element, in order to motivate employees to achieve a high level of performance. For example, tyre fitters might be rewarded with a bonus for the number of tyres they have fitted or wheels they have aligned. Taxi drivers might get their 'bonus' from tips from customers, which might encourage them to provide a more customer-friendly service.

- **Health and safety.** It is essential to address health and safety issues at work. In the case of this entity, health and safety concerns apply not only to employees of the entity but also to customers.

- **Performance assessment.** Staff should be encouraged continually to improve their performance. A system of performance appraisal can help to achieve this. Each employee should be encouraged to discuss his strengths and weaknesses with his manager or supervisor, and to consider ways of improving on past performance.

220 T CITY POLICE

(a) The purpose of performance appraisal is to assess the performance of an individual in his or her job, in a process involving the employee (appraisee) and his or her manager or supervisor. There are several ways in which performance appraisal might be used.

- The appraisal should be used to assess current performance of the appraisee.

- The appraisal can also be used to discuss the progress the individual has made since the previous appraisal.

- There can be a motivational element to appraisal interviews, if the individual believes that the organisation is concerned about how he or she is performing, and management is willing to give time to this task.

- An appraisal should also be used to discuss training and personal development plans for the individual. It should therefore be seen as a tool to assist with career development.

- Finally, appraisal can also be used as a basis for deciding the remuneration for the individual for the next 12 months.

- For the T City police force, performance appraisal can be a valuable method of considering the training and personal development requirements of its employees. The individuals should be able to discuss the problems they have experienced in their work, due to lack of familiarity with new techniques and methods. They should also be able to discuss how they feel they can improve their performance by acquiring experience in other areas of policing. Feedback from appraisal interviews can be used both to plan the further training and development programme for each individual, but also to consider the training needs and development needs of the work force generally.

- The information provided in the question also states that the performance appraisal system will be used as a basis for performance-related pay. If the scheme is carefully planned and implemented, employees will be rewarded for achieving certain standards of performance in their work. This ought to motivate staff to achieve the performance levels necessary for obtaining the additional pay reward. As a result, the general standards of performance should improve.

(b) The potential problems of the performance-related pay system can be explained in terms of an expectancy model of motivation theory. Expectancy theory states that the motivation of an employee to put more effort into his work depends on three factors:

- the employee's perception of his own needs and wants

- the perception that putting in additional effort will succeed in achieving its objectives and result in rewards

- the perception that the rewards from achieving the objectives will satisfy the needs of the individual.

The comments from the staff association spokesman suggest there are two major difficulties.

- Although it is not yet established what levels of performance are required to earn rewards, the poor socio-economic conditions in the T City district will make it difficult for sustainable and significant improvements to occur. The additional effort put in by employees might therefore fail to have enough impact to earn a reward.

- Even if it is supposed that the employees would like more pay and that their efforts can succeed in meeting performance targets, the size of the rewards might be insufficient to satisfy employee needs enough. This is because there is limited government funding, which presumably means that there is not much money to put into a performance-related pay scheme.

The shortage of funds might also make it difficult to implement and administer the scheme successfully, since the scheme will undoubtedly cost money to operate (for example, it will use up the time of the officers carrying out the appraisals, and might therefore result in a requirement for more senior officers).

Although the spokesman did not mention the point, a further problem might arise because of the hierarchical nature of a police force, and the tendency for its management to be autocratic. A successful performance appraisal scheme, whether or not it is related to pay, requires openness between the appraisee and the officer conducting the appraisal interview. Appraisees might feel that they are unable to discuss their performance and problems openly and that the system is too dictatorial and unfair.

Given the shortage of funds for police work, appraisees might also want to argue that the reason they are unable to achieve performance targets is the lack of sufficient resources to do their work properly.

Another issue relating to fairness of the scheme will be the difficulties in identifying key performance targets, and rewarding on the basis of those targets alone. The question mentions that the audit identified crime prevention and convictions as key performance measures (presumably in all types of crime), whereas the general public appear more concerned with response times to emergency calls. Police work involves a wide variety of tasks, and handling many different types of crime and social behaviour. A fair performance appraisal scheme would need to recognise all the different types of police work, and the different measures by which all the different tasks should be appraised.

Another issue identified by the general public is racial harassment. If this is perceived to be a serious problem, for which performance improvement is necessary, it is arguable whether improvements in poor behaviour (a reduction in reports of racial harassment) should be a performance target on which to base rewards – given that the behaviour should not exist anyway.

Clearly there are potential problems with both the performance appraisal scheme and a PRP scheme. The scheme requires very careful planning before implementation if it s to have any chance of success.

221   RECRUITMENT

(a)   The standard procedure in the recruitment process is to first obtain an agreed vacancy: in some firms nowadays the first question after receiving a resignation is not 'where do we get a replacement from' but 'do we need to replace?' If there is a need, then the process should begin by reassessing the job and person description to see if it is current and, if not, altering the duties and/or the qualifications or skills in the person specification. This may be best done by the incumbent who has just resigned, with his or her supervisor.

From here, many firms create **internal job advertisements** first, which go up on notice-boards ahead of any external advertisement. Indeed in some cases, either from experience or from a formal development plan, there is no perceived need to advertise externally: internal candidates may even be identified straight away (such as the incumbent's deputy or assistant) and interviewed. In many cases there may be no competitive interview just an appointment.

Where time is of the essence, media such as agencies and 'head-hunters' may be used, perhaps to fill the position on a temporary basis. Simultaneously, depending on the level of the job and the expert of the perceived labour market, local newspapers and magazines, TV and radio and the Government Employment Agencies can be used to advertise. National jobs markets require advertisements in trade publications, quality daily papers and Sunday newspapers.

Attracting a good field of candidates is often seen as essential and a 'long list' of people who match the criteria can then be whittled down to a 'short-list' either by a paper-sift looking for the best-qualified, or by preliminary interviews. Where there is a national recruitment for a major expansion (e.g. in retail, hotel and catering, market research or sales) interviews can be held locally using hotels or conference centres.

Second or final interviews usually involve senior staff at a Head Office location and may be extended towards an assessment centre format where different skills of the applicant are tested and often an aptitude or personality test given.

(b)   At the stage of selection, the major problem is to find a way of ensuring the selected applicant will do a good job in the real world the firm operates in: this is called 'validity'. To make selection valid it should be as objective as possible, though this is reflected by how far the people the candidate has to work with actually **like** him or her. Thus 'fitting in' is subjective but should be considered an essential part of the process – introduction to colleagues and subordinates may pave the way for a more open relationship later.

Objectivity can be increased by involving several different interviewers (i.e. not one line manager), using the same job and person specification and a structured interview where more-or-less the same questions are asked. Interviewer bias should be circumvented by Panel Interviews and standardisation of questions. However, the use of an assessment centre approach brings in other skills, a group problem-solving exercise, a presentation, an in-tray exercise, a personality test. These are now marketed by major occupational psychologists and are becoming popular.

However, they are artificial. If a sales person has had several jobs with excellent results and does poorly on the selection process, does this mean that the process itself has not been pre-tested? This is the most common failing, the assumption that what you are testing really measures what it sets out to.

(c)   A clear understanding of the job that is to be filled will make it much easier to identify the type of candidate who is required. That, in turn, will enable the organisation to advertise in such as way as to encourage suitable applicants and discourage those who are likely to be unsuitable. For example, if a job requires specific qualifications and some prior experience in the industry this should be stated in the advert. It might also suggest that adverts should be placed in trade publications which will be read by those who are suitably qualified, rather than newspapers which will be read by a wider readership.

A clear job analysis will provide those responsible for selecting a shortlist and conducting interviews with a list of criteria that are necessary and those that are desirable. Candidates who do not possess each of the necessary attributes should not be interviewed. This will provide a more objective basis for rejecting unsuitable candidates and will also provide the company with a measure of protection in case of claims of bias or discrimination. A candidate who does not have a vital attribute, such as a relevant degree if that is deemed necessary, cannot complain if he or she is not interviewed for the post.

The process of conducting the job design might also alert the company to any problems with the post itself. If the criteria are too demanding, then it might be better to set lower entry requirements and then provide the successful candidate with either training or supervision until s/he has reached the required level of competence.

222 MANAGEMENT DEVELOPMENT

(a) **'Management development'** has been defined as 'the progress a person makes in learning how to manage effectively' (Weitrich). However, as a system, management development is aimed at improving management effectiveness in all areas by a planned process of evaluation, training, experience and performance improvement.

(Many reports in the past five years have shown that management in the UK lags behind our major competitors. It is calculated that Germany spends five times as much as the UK per head of management population.)

(b) The following steps could occur in a **typical management development programme**:

(i) The organisation's strategic plan will identify corporate objectives for the next three or five years. This plan should be analysed in terms of manpower needs. A key part of this manpower plan will be the definition of management positions over the coming years. For example, consider a company planning to establish a manufacturing unit in Eastern Europe; the necessary management positions can be defined and a specification of skills and experience levels stipulated. The strategic plan together with the proposed organisation structure provides the basis for this schedule of management positions over the short and medium term and an outline for the longer term.

(ii) Having defined the future needs, the next step could be to evaluate the existing management team. An analysis by skills, experience, age, promotability, past appraisals, career pattern etc, will provide categorisations which can be put alongside the future management schedule. It will be necessary to adjust the present management list for likely turnover for future years. Some turnover, such as retirements can be forecast accurately. Elsewhere, past statistics can be used to anticipate likely numbers leaving in main categories.

(iii) Any specialist skills necessary should be highlighted for separate consideration. Where such skills/experience are rare, the organisation may seek to head hunt selected individuals rather than issue a general advertisement.

(iv) By matching the adjusted basis of present management people against the expected management needs of the future, a gap will emerge. The organisation is now in a position to state the number of managers at particular levels of skill and experience that will need to be developed to fill these gaps. Some general principles will be established as guidelines e.g., younger understudying older, minimum three people identified as development for any management position.

(v) To close the gap, individual managers will need to be developed through training, selective experience, project work etc, whilst other positions will need to be filled through recruitment.

The training section will devise specific individual training programmes where necessary. These may overlap, or form part of, general training courses aimed at developing management effectiveness overall. Also selected periods of experience will be prescribed to develop and test potential of individuals. For example, any individual manager being considered for a senior position in an international company must have spent a successful period as a manager abroad. Appraisal of individual performance will form a key part of the development exercise and an accelerated appraisal scheme may be introduced for the management stream, whereby appraisals are undertaken frequently, not just annually. Such appraisals may be incorporated in a Management by Objectives approach where applicable within an organisation.

(vi) Recruitment of managers will be affected by the development programme. Shortage of time to fill a position, or disappointing appraisals, could lead an organisation to recruit to fill the gap. Some companies (e.g. Tesco, Marks and Spencer) have a policy of strong internal management development; such companies are infrequent recruiters of established managers.

(vii) The success of a management development scheme can be measured by the simple test of 'did the organisation get the right person in the right job at the right time'. This is the fundamental test of success. However, the organisation will need to know that this has been achieved at a reasonable cost. It is therefore important to develop a set of objectives for Management Development section that link achievement with budget stages and that performance should be audited by a senior manager.

Note: That the question requires 'the steps that an organisation should take'. Therefore detailed discussions of individual management responses has only marginal relevance.

(c) Succession planning should be an ongoing process so that staff requirements, particularly at the managerial levels, are anticipated and met.

An assessment of current staff resources should be maintained, analysed by departments, the types of jobs at each level and the number and quality of staff in those jobs.

A forecast of the staff requirements, by grades and skills, should then be assessed and agreed to highlight any shortages in terms of skills or numbers.

If there is a mismatch between job specification and existing employees, then staff development should be focused on resolving the problem.

Significant shortages might require recruitment programmes. Vacancies should be filled in sufficient time to have staff in place with the necessary skills and qualifications before a shortage actually arises. For example, airlines need to be conscious of the implications of losing pilots who are qualified to fly particular types of aircraft. This will often require the recruitment and training of replacements while existing pilots are still in post (and even before they have considered retiring or moving on).

Ideally, succession planning will aim to generate a throughput of staff so that promoted posts are filled from within. This will give staff the opportunity for career progression, which will be motivating. It may also make it possible for organisations to recruit largely in response to vacancies at the lower levels, where candidates will be more plentiful and potentially less expensive to recruit and train.

223 REWARD SYSTEMS

On the assumption that people are at the lower levels of Maslow's hierarchy of needs (basic/physiological) and need money to buy food, the employment relationship is usually characterised by an economic exchange. This means pay for work done. Although it must be emphasised that vast numbers of people work as volunteers, by definition they must be in higher levels of **Maslow's hierarchy**. Clearly in a modern society they or their family must have income – part of an economic exchange somewhere in the background.

To attract people to do work, therefore, employers must provide an attractive reward package. This is a complex amalgam of affordability, perceived internal statuses and the needs of a variety of applicants. Unskilled applicants living with their parents near to the place of work have fewer needs that those with children living some distance away. The cost of working for some is greater than those afforded by state benefits – the 'poverty trap'.

Local labour markets vary with age as well as skills, as older workers often will have paid off debts in raising a family such as mortgages and their dependants may well also have left home. Nevertheless, psychological factors make it unlikely that older applicants will accept lower wages – nor can internal structures and relativities cope with volunteers or age-related pay in most organisations.

What occurs therefore is a hierarchy of jobs, rated in a job-evaluation scheme or by collective bargaining, or by a management 'remuneration committee'. These jobs are often grouped into a number of levels requiring similar levels of skills – for the sake of simplicity if nothing else.

Pay is then attached based on market rates (especially local union rates for skilled workers or minimum wage legislation). Internal relativities are then set – in some firms, supervisors are automatically paid 10% more than those they supervise. For clerical and managerial jobs, skills develop in the job and are paid in a **progression of increments, rate-for-age scales** or **merit (performance-related) pay**. This usually involves a formal annual Appraisal of Performance.

Non-managerial jobs are very often hourly paid whereas managers receive an annual salary. In these cases, additional hours worked are voluntarily given and compensation at a higher rate is usually offered. This may be the hourly rate (time) plus 50% – time and a half – with double time – on days of rest, public holidays etc.

Further, some jobs attract bonuses or commission usually based on increased profitable sales, or production output. It is difficult to calculate the normal rates of performance above which bonuses are paid: **F.W.Taylor's scientific management** gave birth to a plethora of 'time and motion study' experts who measured effort and job difficulty to come to standard times. Sales managers are not fortunate and have to look into the future to estimate budgets and structure commission payments in excess of these. In Japan, profit-related-pay can account for up to one-third of earnings but in the UK it tends to be somewhat trivial, except in partnerships and professional firms (like solicitors).

Added to pay is a wide range of **non-incentive benefits from pensions**; through sick pay to expense allowances, even company cars, subsidised canteens and so on. The job of the 'compensation and benefits' manager becomes more complex daily.

224 DISMISSAL, RETIREMENT, REDUNDANCY

Planned leaving normally refers in the HR plan to retirements at the state retirement age. An age profile of current employees is easily built up and scheduled retirements each year can be filled in quite automatically so that future demand can be anticipated and recruitment planned for. Typical examples might be in manufacturing, where many employees joined 'en masse' when a factory opened, and were in their 20s. Thus, 40 to 45 years on they will be retiring 'en masse' over a period of five or so years. Mass recruitment may be needed at that time.

Unplanned leaving is of course more complex and disruptive, often called 'turnover' or 'labour turnover' and is **voluntary** i.e. employees leaving by resignation for better jobs elsewhere. Monitoring turnover can give indications of poor management or working conditions, stress, or low wages compared with the market-place. A reasonable level – 5% to 10% is healthy however as it enables the introduction of 'new blood' and the possibility of promotions. **Involuntary leaving** is not usually measured – this involves dismissal for various reasons under the contract of employment.

Capability often is given as a reason and may include long-term or frequent sickness absence. Early retirement on grounds of ill-health is an option for those in the pension plan and with sufficient service, while others must rely on state-provided benefits. Frequent absences however are difficult to handle as it is not easy to appear fair and reasonable: employees are usually counselled, then given targets to achieve well before dismissal, and this type of treatment spills over into an issue of 'conduct'. Poor job performance is similarly quite hard to prove definitively - there is always an element of judgement and comparison with other jobs/personnel. Issues of bad faith by employer's inept recruitment of people who prove unable to do the job can sometimes by circumvented by transfer to other work in a different department. Otherwise, dismissal is the only option.

Conduct, likewise, is a difficult area unless the firm has strict, written rules, which are made public to all employees (such as during induction training). Fighting, drunkenness, theft, refusal to follow a reasonable instruction, absenteeism and the like are more easy to handle than insubordination and rudeness to colleagues. The issue is whether dismissal is really necessary.

Redundancy is an acceptable reason and quite clear – but so long as criteria for selection are open and fair. Redundancy exists where the business ceases to be, where the job the employee is performing becomes outmoded or disappears, or when work is transferred to another location. This last category can be quite confusing especially in major cities where employees live near to main roads or railway lines which they habitually use to get to work. If the Head Office moves across town it might become extremely difficult for those employees to reach the new location in good time and so they may claim to have been made redundant. Employers also must consult staff, minimise the effect of the scale of the redundancy and its timing, giving advance notice, calling for volunteers, reducing overtime and part-time/temporary or contract work and so on. Following the redundancy the employer then has the problem of maintaining the morale of those left: not an easy proposition.

225 HUMAN RESOURCE PLAN

(a) Human resource planning (HR planning) was previously described as manpower planning, and has been defined as 'a strategy for the acquisition, utilisation, improvement and retention of an enterprise's human resources'. Manpower planning still provides a good starting point for the development of a human resource plan, but in recent years it has been recognised that there is more to people planning than quantitative estimates of the demand and supply of personnel.

Four main phases are involved in manpower planning:

(i) an analysis of existing staffing resources – its strengths and weaknesses, age spreads, experience and training levels, etc

(ii) an estimation of likely changes in resources – flows into, within, and out of, the organisation, and the ability of relevant labour markets to supply existing or future demands

(iii) an estimation of the organisation's future manpower needs in terms of numbers, type, quality and skill composition, and

(iv) the identification of gaps between supply and demand and the development of policies and plans to close these.

The HR planning process goes beyond this simple quantitative exercise by taking into account the broader environmental factors, for example patterns of employment and developments in automation and uses qualitative techniques, such as scenario planning, for estimating future manpower requirements. The process is also linked to the development of the organisation as a whole, and should be related to corporate objectives and to an organisation structure capable of achieving those objectives. It is also concerned with developing people so that they have the skills to meet the future needs of the business and with improving the performance of all employees in the organisation by the use of appropriate motivation techniques.

(b)   Briefing paper: Development of a human resource plan for the finance department

The key considerations for developing the human resource plan for the department will focus on three main areas:

(i)   making the required reductions, in line with the downsizing strategy

(ii)   addressing the changes that are affecting the department; and

(iii)   identifying the future role, in playing a fuller part in the management of the business.

Reducing staff numbers from 24 to 17 over the next two years and to 12 by the target date (in five years' time) will be by using natural wastage and early retirement wherever possible. Hopefully, this will avoid (or at least reduce) the need for compulsory redundancies, and will avoid or reduce the adverse effects on staff morale and motivation.

There is a good chance of achieving the reductions over the time period set, provided that the necessary steps are taken. Three of the older members are within five years of retiring; two more will move into this category within the five years set by senior management. If those employees nearest retirement could be encouraged to leave by offering them a generous retirement package and an enhancement of their pension, it would be the least painful option.

One or two of the younger qualified members of staff are already looking for posts elsewhere, so they may be encouraged to leave earlier when the news that the organisation is looking to slim down the department has been communicated to the department. One of the trainees has applied for maternity leave. She will have the right to return to work, provided that she comes back within the period set out in legislation, so we have no room for manoeuvre there. Some of the trainees will qualify within the time period under consideration, and the reduction in costs will not allow me to increase salaries substantially, so I think that they will look elsewhere for work.

The age/experience of the existing people, spread over financial accounting, management accounting and the treasury function, is a mix of older, experienced specialist staff, a young to middle-aged group of qualified accountants (many of whom also possess MBA degrees), and a group of trainees with limited experience who have yet to qualify. I would like to keep a similar spread and one of the problems will be retaining the most able of my staff. This will mean planning a package of financial inducements and a clear career structure.

Reducing staff will be possible, but coping with the current workload with the reduced resources will be more difficult. There are several solutions to help me to deal with this problem:

•   The department's existing operations will be thoroughly reviewed to make sure that it matches the corporate objectives, and its structure is capable of achieving those objectives. It may be that, following the general downsizing, there may be a reduced need for some of its services.

•   There are many changes in technology and the department can make more use of IT and the latest developments in computer software. This could allow an increase in productivity and result in better quality output from the department. It will mean developing some of the staff, so that they have the skills to meet the future needs of the business. Although staff training is expensive, it will provide some motivation and reassurance to staff that the organisation is still prepared to invest in them and is ready to equip them with the latest IT skills.

- The department has been under increasing pressure to outsource transactions, and some of its other routine work, to one of the new service centres. Although I am not keen to do this, it may be the only way of coping with the existing volume of work.

For the **future plans**, the department will have to monitor its expenditure to keep in line with the budget. Early retirement and additional staff training will add considerably to costs, but perhaps outsourcing some of the routine work will allow us to offset some of these costs.

It is inevitable that some of the department members will have to become more flexible and be ready to take on a wider range of responsibilities. The younger staff will welcome this, as their education and training has already prepared them for wider management responsibilities, and those with MBA degrees are in a good position to accept more responsibilities. However, additional training and development to handle future demands will need to be planned for some members of the department.

226 APPRAISAL

(a) The objectives of a formal appraisal process are:

(i) To **highlight areas of good/above average performance** in order to assist in reward systems and/or career development opportunities.

(ii) To **highlight areas of poor performance** which can be rectified by a Training Needs Analysis.

(iii) To **de-brief on targets set and achieved** thus creating a mutual understanding and opportunity for creative criticism. Some firms operate 180° Appraisal where the subordinate also appraises the supervisor.

(iv) **As a control mechanism** e.g. as part of Management by Objectives ensuring the ongoing improvement in critical areas.

(b) Appraisal systems are fraught by their very nature of formality.

Having a certain time for feedback may ensure it is done, formally correct, logged and actioned but may result in managers 'saving-up' issues for the predetermined time rather than addressing them as they occur.

Many managers see the process as one enabling them to set additional 'projects' for staff rather than an attempt to measure them against what they are supposed to do. This is easier than trying to create objective measures, for example in a finance department where adherence to standards is far more important than individual creativity and where many employees are doing very similar, repetitive tasks.

Frequently, managers see the appraisal as an opportunity for criticism and to bring out all the faults of the employee in circumstances where this would otherwise not be possible. Employees whose everyday work is exemplary and who have no cause to be worried can face a very personal judgement about their personal characteristics within a formal, confidential, 1-to-1 appraisal.

They suffer from the 'halo and horns' effect in that human judgement is poor, often based on impressions, so it is easier for a manager to look for faults or success in an otherwise patchy performance and bias his/her judgement one way or the other – particularly when the appraisee is generally seen as having 'potential' and it is politically expedient to emphasise success (e.g. in graduates).

Finally, most managers are not trained in, nor are they comfortable with, the process. They may tend to do it passively, aim for a 'middle level' to avoid conflicts, and spend little time in preparation or execution of what can be an extremely resource-hungry activity.

Some of these problems can be alleviated by:

- education and training of managers and subordinates

- central direction of target-setting, scale and indices of performance

- 360° appraisal involving peers and a judgement of the managers

- increasing the frequency.

All this can be greatly assisted by slick software, eliminating the 'paper chase'.

(c) The appraisal interview is the vehicle for giving feedback to the employee where strengths and weaknesses can be identified and the possibilities of improvement discussed. It also provides employees with an opportunity to describe their perspective of such concerns. This two-way communication is so important that the interview is a crucial part of the appraisal process. If managed properly it can ensure that the feedback is positive and that the overall effect is motivating.

The interviewer must be willing to listen to the subordinate and be prepared to change an evaluation in the light of valid evidence presented in support of any claims made. The emphasis should be on the future rather than the past, with both sides stressing opportunities rather than apportioning blame. It is often helpful to focus on specific job behaviour rather than on more general issues of personality or attitude.

If conducted properly, the interview can create a sense of self-appraisal in the employee and that should encourage improvement and development in those areas where they are necessary.

One of the biggest problems to be overcome is that the subject of the interview will have a natural desire to push for the best possible evaluation and that might make it difficult to be frank about weaknesses or areas where improvement is required.

227   S SOFTWARE COMPANY

(a) These concerns are typical of those expressed in many organisations, and could partially be due to the competing goals, objectives and consequent perceptions and attitudes of the employees who are conditioned by them.

Andy is a pragmatic, hands-on, production manager – with a strict schedule to complete. His down-to-earth style is suited to the solving of considerable numbers of relatively trivial production problems on a daily basis, but the thought of his people living a life of total luxury runs against his core values. To add injury to that insult, production may have to be rescheduled; some may be lost forever; some may be recouped naturally or overtime may have to be worked, pushing up his costs.

Colin has an external orientation as a marketer and is constantly worried about the activities of competitors. He may also have had considerable experience of the negative effect of training – where suitable opportunities are not available afterwards, trained staff often leave, not only will they take their labour and skills to competitors but in S's case, technical and proprietary sensitive information may be actually drained from S into T, U or V.

Maurice is only a 'bean counter' and without any objective way of evaluating training, the lack of faith school will serve no purpose in his area. Compared especially with other investments for which a rate of return of some kind is calculated, training runs counter to the norms and values inculcated in Maurice over the years.

(b) Jean needs highly trained, loyal, flexible and yet focused people to create any competitive advantage. This area of the labour market is very difficult indeed to compete in and indeed she may need to bear in mind the possibility of using agency staff or sub-contracting some areas out.

Her basic strategy is to determine the needs of the line functions and using a TNA determine the match of existing skills to those needed. The subsequent 'gap analysis' provides her with two major options: upgrading the skills of current employees, or external recruitment. There are costs (very high) and benefits of internal development of staff. If the opportunities are there for subsequent promotion, and if the key skills are fairly specific to S, then labour turnover may not prove such a problem as in other firms in IT because loyalty will be built up and transferability limited. On the other hand such training will be very costly compared with the 'quick fix' of recruitment.

Her recruitment option is limited by the compensation and benefits policies of S versus its competitors – and also its reputation in the industry for creative innovation, which attracts 'techies'. Advertising may not be enough and costly head-hunters or agency staff may have to be used, or tasks sub-contracted.

In capital intensive industries labour is not as important as commodity prices and technology; in the knowledge economy these roles are reversed. S needs not just an HR plan but an HR strategy which incorporates career development and training (via appraisals), appropriate rewards, and, unfortunately also a disciplinary policy whose standards weed out those 'creatives' who make continual mistakes in coding.

(c) Poaching staff from competing companies is a relatively high-risk strategy. While there is nothing wrong with competing against other businesses in the industry, these companies will do their utmost to retain their best staff. Those who are likely to be enticed away may be the second-best staff whose potential does not justify striving to retain their services.

Poaching staff is likely to require additional salaries or other benefits. That might lead to an increase in salaries offered by competitors, thereby pushing up employment costs for the whole industry. It would not be enough to offer these competitive rates to new recruits because existing programmers will be unhappy if their salaries are lower than those given to newly appointed colleagues at the same grade as themselves.

Filling more senior posts by recruiting from outside will do little for the morale of existing junior programming staff, particularly when they will not receive the training that would help them to develop themselves and seek promotion within the company.

Programming is very much a team-oriented activity. It will be easier to create a sense of cohesion if the company concentrates on retaining and developing staff, so that programmers have an opportunity to work together over a prolonged period.

228 R COMPANY

(a) An induction programme is a programme for introducing a new employee into an organisation. Ideally, it should be planned and structured, rather than a variety of ad hoc arrangements. An induction programme should enable a new employee to:

- learn what they need to know about the organisation, how it operates, what its rules are, and its way of doing things and culture

- understand the work that they will be doing, and their responsibilities

- meet the individuals in the organisation that they need to or ought to know.

- An induction programme should have a clear time frame. Typically, an induction programme might last three months, six months or as much as one year. At the end of the induction programme, the individual should be able to think of himself or herself as a fully-integrated member of the company's work force.

The key activities in a planned induction programme should be as follows.

Before the new employee's first day	The human resources department should write to the individual, with details of:
	• the job title and job description
	• conditions of employment, such as hours of work, holiday entitlement, sickness arrangements and so on
	• rate of pay, including any entitlement to overtime, bonuses, etc.
	There should also be a covering letter welcoming the new employee, and giving details of where to go on the first morning, who to meet and at what time.
On Day 1	The new employee should be met by a person in the HR department, who will welcome him/her, discuss 'personnel' matters such as the company's rule book and its pension scheme. The induction scheme should be explained, and then the new employee should be taken to meet his/her office manager.
	The office manager will either act as a mentor for the new employee throughout the induction period, or (more likely) will assign someone else to carry out the tasks of mentoring. The role of a mentor is to explain the work environment to the new employee and deal with any questions or problems he or she might have.
	The mentor will introduce the new employee to the work environment, for matters such as introducing work colleagues, touring the office building and facilities (canteen facilities, drinks machines and so on).
	The mentor will also introduce the new employee to the work that he or she will be doing, and the computer software that will be used.
Early in the programme	The HR department should contact the individual again, to provide 'regulatory' information, such as information about fire drill, health and safety, discipline procedures and grievance procedures.
At planned intervals	In a planned induction programme, the new employee might go through a rotation of duties, assisting with different elements of finance work in order to familiarise himself/herself with the organisation's systems, and to meet a variety of colleagues.
	The training needs of the individual might need to be reviewed. If there is a large enough number of new recruits each year, it might be possible to arrange an in-house course, where the employees are given a fuller introduction to the organisation and its operations, as well as a chance to meet each other.
At regular intervals	The new employee should have short, formal meetings with the mentor (in addition to any unofficial discussions they might have) to discuss how the employee is settling into the company and whether there are any problems. If problems arise, it might be possible to take action to deal with them, and remove the employee's concerns.

(b)   The problems that the finance department is experiencing are:

- the loss of several new employees within the first year

- under-performance by several of the staff.

It is by no means certain that the lack of a planned induction programme is to blame, nor that the introduction of such a programme will remove or even reduce the problem.

The process of recruitment might be inadequate. New employees might find that they are not entering the type of job that they had been led to expect. The HR department might also be failing to recruit people of the right calibre.

Alternatively, the problems could be due to poor management and/or low employee morale.

An induction programme might possibly help to reduce both problems.

Reducing staff turnover

An induction programme can help a new employee to become integrated more quickly into the organisation, by meeting work colleagues and learning how the organisation operates. If an individual feels 'at home' rather than an outsider, he or she will be less likely to resign.

Through introducing new employees to each other, it might be possible to create a 'self-help group' of individuals who are able to discuss their induction experiences and problems. Shared problems are generally more easily dealt with and resolved.

If an individual knows that there is a programme for induction, and can see a purpose to what he or she is doing, he or she might be prepared to be more patient in waiting for training, and to put up with mundane accountancy work in the short term.

Regular meetings with the mentor, if properly conducted, should provide an opportunity for the individual to discuss problems and concerns. To the extent that the mentor can help, the new employee will feel more valued and appreciated, and so might be less inclined to resign.

Improving performance

Lower-than-expected performance could be caused by a number of factors. These include:

- not understanding fully the tasks of the job and its responsibilities

- failing to appreciate the systems of the organisation and how they operate

- a lack of regular performance review after joining the organisation.

An induction programme could help to overcome these problems. The job responsibilities of the employee should be set out clearly in the job description, and the mentor should be able to give advice and guidance. An induction programme should also introduce the individual to the systems and the culture of the organisation, so that the individual appreciates more clearly how things operate and how his/her job fits into the 'general scheme of things'. By helping the individual to understand what is expected, he or she might perform better.

In addition, if the individual has regular meetings with the mentor, the mentor can give 'unofficial' guidance about the individual's performance, and discuss the difficulties the individual is experiencing.

229 CX BEERS (MAY 05 EXAM)

Examiner's comments

There was a real range of performance on this question from well-prepared candidates who successfully applied known theory to the scenario in a purposeful manner to those who merely reproduced their understanding of general HR issues.

Common errors

- A tendency to adopt an 'all I know about.....' approach.

(a) The main issues and stages involved in developing a human resource (HR) plan for the CX buy-out idea are as follows:

Issues

The HR plan must incorporate all three of the suggested initiatives:

- the museum
- bottled beers
- flexibility.

The HR plan must preserve the good reputation of the firm.

The company must be profitable in the longer term. Ultimately this is likely to be the main constraint on how many workers can be employed.

Stages

Four main phases are involved in HR planning:

1   Auditing the current labour force in the company, its strengths and weaknesses, age spreads, experience and training levels.

2   Forecasting the future labour demand in terms of number, type and quality of people the company should employ to meet planned requirements.

3   Forecasting the expected labour supply, looking at both existing workers, expected staff turnover and future training plans, and at the external labour market.

4   Developing a plan to ensure that supply equals demand in the future. If supply exceeds demand, then this could involve redundancies, relocating staff and/or reducing recruitment. If demand exceeds supply then the plan will involve recruitment, staff relocation, training programmes and so on.

These stages can be applied to CX beers as follows:

Stage 1: Auditing the current labour force

- Given that the factory has just shut, strictly speaking there is no current labour force to audit. However, unless they have already found alternative employment, most of the previous workers will want a job with the new firm if possible.

- The firm will want to identify and recruit the employees with higher levels of experience and skills. This will reduce the need for training and ensure a quicker start up for the new strategy. Previous HR records can be used here along with interviews.

Stage 2: Forecasting future demand

Since labour is a derived demand, the overall number of employees needed depends on the demand for each of the initiatives. The managers will thus have to estimate the number of likely visitors to the museum, the annual demand for bottled beer from supermarkets and future demand for current beers for the third initiative. Each of these demands will have to incorporate seasonal aspects and will be for both the immediate short-term and the longer-term future.

The precise nature of future demand for labour will depend on the three elements of the strategy:

- The museum option would require the minimum workforce to operate the older plant together with the most experienced workers to give authority to presentations, to be able to answer queries from tourists and maybe act as guides. This would also suggest that older ex-workers are likely to be preferred.

- The bottled beer for supermarkets plan may require new technology and methods. The type of machinery used will have a major impact on how many employees are needed and what skills they will need. The managers will have to decide whether to try to recruit workers with experience of the new techniques or ex-workers who will then need extensive training. If the latter plan is followed then it is important that workers who have shown an aptitude to learning new processes are specified in the recruitment plan.

- Employing a flexible but experienced workforce will involve specifying the type of flexibility required (see section (b) below) and the level of experience needed. There may be conflicts here as older workers may be more experienced but may want more stability due to having families. Younger workers may be more willing to accept seasonal work but have less experience.

Stage 3: Forecasting future supply

The immediate supply will be fairly easy to forecast, as most ex-employees will be available to work, given the area's high unemployment. Existing HR records will also detail their skills, experience, ages, etc. Whether they have the skills required depends on which of the three elements of the plan is being considered.

Future supply is harder to predict, as it will be affected by whether or not ex-workers manage to find alternative employment.

Stage 4: Developing a plan

The immediate plan would involve a mixture of recruitment and training. It is likely that any workers re-employed would be highly motivated, having been given a second chance.

The main training aspects will be for:

- conducting tours for the museum

- learning new skills for the bottled beers.

(b) **Numerical flexibility**

One of the main problems facing CX was the seasonal nature of its trade, with the winter being the busiest. With the new initiatives of the museum and bottled beers demand will be less seasonal but there will still be a seasonal element that the buyout team will have to deal with.

This will require the firm to have numerical flexibility – the firm can adjust the level of labour inputs to meet fluctuations in output.

The buyout team can achieve numerical flexibility by the following:

- temporary contracts

- part-time workers

- use of sub-contractors

- overtime

- outsourcing non-core activities.

Charles Handy suggested the idea of a 'shamrock' organisation, which would work well for CX. Such an organisation would have three inter-related 'leaves':

- a small managerial/technical core leaf

- an outsourced business-to-business relations leaf, and

- the contract and temporary contingency workforce leaf.

Functional flexibility

The new organisation would also benefit form functional flexibility – the ability to adjust and deploy the skills of its workforce to match the tasks required by changing workloads.

For CX this could mean museum staff being able to assist in production and vice-versa, or having brewers who can also carry our routine maintenance, for example.

This flexibility will be achieved by the following:

- training staff in a wider range of skills

- recruiting staff with a wider range of skills

- introducing a programme of job rotation.

230   COMPANY A AND B

(a)   **Staff concerns**

The staff of Company B will have a number of concerns, depending on their age, position in their career and personality.

Benefits

Most staff will be concerned that the overall benefits package they receive in Company A is not inferior to their existing terms. As well as the obvious issue of pay, this will incorporate:

- pensions

- holidays

- study leave.

Legislation may ensure that the new employment conditions of Company B staff are no worse than they enjoyed in Company B before it was taken over, depending on the country concerned.

Status

Senior managers in Company B will be concerned with whether or not they will enjoy a similar status in the new organisation.

Promotion

Junior managers in Company B will be concerned about opportunities for progression in Company A.

Cultural differences

Most employees moving to the Company A headquarters will be concerned about the different policies, practices and procedures of Company A. This could include:

- the quantity and quality of the work

- the technology and systems they will be using

- whether or not they will be able to work with the new team in Company A.

Routine matters

Staff will be concerned about routine issues such as the best way to travel to the new work place and whether there will be parking space.

Induction programme

All of these issues can be addressed via an effective induction programme. A well-structured induction programme should achieve the following:

- a greater sense of belonging in the new firm

- a greater sense of Company A's commitment to them – they will feel more valued

- a greater commitment to organisational goals

- reduced staff turnover

- a quicker understanding of new technology and systems.

Staff will be more aware of company rules and procedures and will be less likely to break safety rules, for example.

Together these should result in better quality work, fewer disciplinary problems, better morale and cost savings.

(b)   **Induction programme**

An induction programme to assist finance staff from Company B to become quickly effective in Company A could take the following form:

Timing	Focus	Responsibility
Prior to move	• Send background information about Company A (history, mission, products, etc)	HR department
	• Send copies of terms and conditions of employment, covering pay, holidays, pensions, study leave, sickness policy, etc	
	• Send details of rules and procedures, for example, unauthorised use of company computers, Internet policy, procedures for smokers, etc	
	• Send practical details, including hours of work, map of location, parking arrangements, start time, dress code, what to bring and who to report to on the first day	
First day	• Introduce new staff to colleagues	Line Manager
	• Explain department culture, covering lunch arrangements, tea breaks and personal phone calls	
	• Communicate locations of canteen, telephones, drinks machines, etc	
	• Clarify job description and role	
First week	• Clarify performance appraisal systems and targets	Line manager
	• Training session covering health and safety regulations, fire training, discipline	HR department

First month	• Opportunity for feedback	Line Manager
	• Training session to understand the company's aims, objectives, strategies and plans	Senior management
First six months	• Full appraisal of performance to date and future plans	Line Manager

and grievance procedures and trades unions/staff associations

(c) There should be a clear system for voicing grievances so that perceived problems can be dealt with as quickly as possible. This situation is one in which misunderstandings and rumours might circulate very quickly and a great deal of resentment might arise on both sides.

All possible care should be taken to reassure staff who raise a grievance that they should not fear any form of reprisal or retribution. Cases should be handled confidentially and those raising grievances should be treated courteously throughout.

All staff, from whichever company, should know to whom to address any grievances. Ideally, this should be their immediate line manager for matters associated with day-to-day working arrangements or a designated member of the personnel department for matters that are more related to terms and conditions of employment. It may be that an informal discussion with the designated manager will resolve the issue. If not, then the member of staff should know exactly who to raise the matter with in order to make a formal complaint.

Formal grievances should be dealt with as quickly as possible, consistent with gathering all relevant information and giving the matter appropriate consideration. The person raising the grievance should be informed of the results of this in writing and as quickly as possible.

The results of the grievance process should remain confidential. If there is an outcome that arises from an individual's complaint (e.g. the decision to give Company B staff travelling costs to cover the additional journey to work), then this should be communicated without referring to the fact that there had originally been a complaint.

231   Z COMPANY

(a) (i) The neglect of training and development during a period of rapid change has the following problems for Z Company's staff:

- Finance staff will learn less efficiently and effectively than if they had a structured programme of training and development.

- Finance staff will thus learn more slowly and consequently may not be up-to-date regarding changes in accountancy, legislation and software upgrades.

- This will cause staff to feel deskilled as equivalent workers at other firms leave them behind.

- As a result some staff may become demotivated.

- Training and development are often seen as a sign of a firm's commitment to its workforce, so Z Company staff will increasingly feel undervalued by the firm.

- Professional staff in particular may feel that staying at Z Company is harming their long-term career aspirations and so might look for other jobs.

(ii)   The implications for Z Company are directly related to the impact of staff, in particular:

- Z Company's competitive advantage will be eroded due to the lack of up-to-date knowledge, skills and competences.

- Z Company finance staff will be less able to provide senior management with the financial information needed to plan, co-ordinate and control the Company's operations.

- Even worse, staff may make mistakes, exposing the firm to the risk of failing to comply with current legislation and/or accounting standards.

- The lack of motivation will result in higher staff turnover, causing Z Company increased staff costs and problems with continuity and quality.

- The HRM process of selection, training and development, appraisal and rewards will be compromised, leading to reduced performance generally.

(b)   To provide a set of effective training and development programmes for Z Company's finance staff the following activities must be undertaken:

- Firstly the firm must distinguish between training and development because the activities necessary for development can vary from those of training.

- Training is a learning process whereby individuals acquire knowledge and/or skills to assist them perform their current jobs. Essentially training closes any skills gap present. This could involve the ability to use a word-processing package or the ability to speak a new language.

- Development is a longer-term continuing process of learning associated with a person's overall career. It is forward looking, anticipating the future movement of jobs (whether sideways as in a developmental assignment or upwards as a promotion). This can be organised internally by the organisation or externally by the individual undertaking self-development activities and/or applying for more demanding jobs.

Whatever form of training or development is used the overall process is the same:

1   defining training needs

2   deciding what training is required to satisfy these needs

3   using experienced trainers to plan and implement training

4   following up and evaluating training to ensure that it is effective.

Defining training needs

First it is necessary to consider the strategy of the Z Company and how it impacts on the finance department. For example, a strategy of rapid expansion will require new accounting systems and better information.

Once the objectives of the finance department have been decided upon, H will be in a position to consider the particular mix of knowledge and skills she requires of her staff. For example, a strategy of overseas expansion will require finance staff to have expertise in international accounting standards.

Given that H is new to the department and staff training has been neglected, H will need to perform a detailed analysis of the training needs of her staff. This will involve an audit of existing staff skills and competences and a comparison of these with the skills necessary to fulfil the finance department's obligations.

In doing this, H will need to consider future retirements and other leavers. She should also find out what the career plans of the staff are.

The results of existing performance appraisals may be a useful source of information on career aspirations and training needs but, given the circumstances, H will probably have to start from scratch. New information can be gleaned by interviewing staff and by careful observation and monitoring of staff in their current jobs.

Deciding what training is required to satisfy these needs

The next step is to establish training and development objectives for each member of the finance department. It is vital here that learning objectives cover the following:

- what the training and development will achieve

- a measurable objective expressed as what the employee will be able to do after the training/development.

The training will be more effective if the recipient participates in the training and development plan and in choosing the method by which the training/development is to be provided.

Using experienced trainers to plan and implement training

When organising training and development courses and activities H should bring in training experts and discuss where, when, and over what period the training/development can take place, the method of training/development and who can offer the most relevant course content.

H will need to consider the range of possible training/development methods, possible providers inside or outside the organisation, likely costs and their record of success.

Following up and evaluating training to ensure that it is effective

After the training has taken place it will be necessary to conduct an evaluation of the training programmes and the development activities to ensure that the training objectives have been achieved.

This will be made easier if learning objectives have been clearly stated as outlined above.

232 JANE SMITH

(a)   The concept of symptoms and problems is a useful way of viewing the 'people' situation at the Casterbridge office. In other words what may be perceived as problems – such as high staff turnover, sickness, deteriorating quality and increased mistakes – are quite likely to be symptoms of an underlying problem which, if removed, would then lead to an improvement in staff performance. The symptoms can be viewed as indicators. In fact organisations can track these indicators as part of their non-financial performance measurement so as to identify to management areas of concern. Experience suggests that a deterioration in the human resource indicators such as sickness and staff turnover are generally linked to a deterioration in staff morale which is itself a condition of the level of employee motivation. Given no other differences between Casterbridge and the other practice offices, then the incidences of high staff turnover, high sickness and poor work quality are classic outcomes associated with low staff morale.

It follows therefore that an understanding of what motivates and de-motivates employees is crucial to identifying the cause of the lack of motivation at the Casterbridge office. Motivation conditions behaviour, that is, motivation drives people to take certain actions. For example, if you are cold then you may put on warmer clothes - the objective thus being to feel warm which if you are feeling cold drives you to seek ways to change this state. Such objectives can be described as needs, and theory *(Maslow)* suggests that people have levels of, or a hierarchy of, needs ranging from basic physiological needs (such as keeping warm) through higher level needs such as social needs (friendship), ego needs (self-esteem) to self-actualisation. The work environment at the office must thus be satisfactory (clean, warm, spacious, etc) but staff need to feel self esteem, which can be achieved through management encouragement and the recognition of good quality work - an occasional 'well done' or 'thank you for that'.

Once basic needs are fulfilled then people will seek to satisfy the needs at the next highest level. Motivation theory (and common sense) also suggest that people themselves are different and that at the higher level differences arise (McClelland) in the way that different individuals are driven by achievement, power and affiliation objectives. For example some people are ruthless and others not, some people need close friendships at work and others less so. Managers themselves differ in their management style toward employees which is in part a reflection on how they themselves view peoples' relationship to work. Some managers, (McGregor) described as Theory X managers, are driven by the view that people basically do not like work and therefore need to be pushed to perform, be constantly watched and closely controlled. However Theory Y managers hold the view that people do not inherently dislike work but, given self-direction, recognition and self-esteem, will respond through improved work performance. The Theory X view appears to fit the attitude of the senior partner and would account for the probable lack of encouragement and recognition.

Other theories (Hertzberg) suggest that the satisfaction of some needs will help to remedy de-motivation but will not in themselves motivate behaviour while the satisfaction of other needs will actually motivate towards the type of behaviour we are seeking. Examples of the first category which are sometimes described as hygiene factors include salary and physical working conditions, while examples of the second category described as motivators includes recognition and opportunity for advancement. In other words the partners in Jane's firm cannot assume that paying a good salary will automatically result in motivated staff.

Taken together the theories allow us to make some observations about the likely motivational problem at the Casterbridge office:

- the senior partner appears to have a Theory X view of the problem – 'a case of far too slack management control and supervision'

- paying staff 'above market rates' and providing good working conditions will remove staff dissatisfaction but these are simply hygiene factors and will not in themselves provide motivation

- the unavoidable but frequent changes in the staff partner responsible for the Casterbridge office will have resulted in instability, uncertainty and probably little recognition of individual staff achievement.

(b)   If understanding motivation theories helps to identify problems then it also gives us a guide as to how to remedy the poor staff morale which is giving rise to low levels of motivation with the subsequent performance problems. In a sense Jane starts with an advantage in that the hygiene factors in the Casterbridge office are in place in that working conditions and pay are to standard and inherently there is no reason why the type of work activity carried out in a practice office cannot be made stimulating.

Jane's strategy should focus on confirming the probable cause of the poor performance through discussing with individual staff their thoughts about their job, the office itself, their aspirations and ways for improvement. Jane should spend more time listening than talking and should use a combination of open and closed questions to identify problem areas.

Theory suggests that, if Jane follows up her talks by removing any obvious remaining dissatisfiers and then adopts a management style which involves two-way communication about work issues, encouragement and praise for tasks well done, and delegates responsibility where possible, then her staff will respond through improved behaviour, underpinned by improved motivation, commitment and team spirit.

The firm should bear in mind that each of its offices is a work group of professional people. They are likely to be ambitious and keen to develop themselves and to progress. The firm has to take care to avoid giving signals that suggest the staff might be better off elsewhere. For example, the frequent replacement of the partners in charge of Casterbridge might have been perceived as indicative of a problem. Either partners see the office as a 'hardship posting' and wish to leave or the firm does not care about the disruption and uncertainty caused by constantly changing the management of that office. Either way, professional staff are less likely to be motivated. If changes are necessary then it might help to ensure that staff are told why.

Recruitment may also play a part. If staff are recruited locally then care should be taken to ensure that those selected are team players. If the culture in the Casterbridge office has been lacking in that area in the past, then local decision makers might not attach a great deal of value to that attribute in assessing potential staff.

It might help to provide greater opportunity for staff from Casterbridge to interact with colleagues from other offices in order to generate a greater sense of loyalty to the firm as a whole. Joint training programmes, or the use of staff from a variety of offices in any firm-wide committees or working parties might help.

233   NS INSURANCE COMPANY (NOV 05 EXAM)

(a)   The role of the HR division

Key answer tip:

With this requirement it is difficult to understand what the examiner is looking for as the term 'role' could be interpreted in many different ways.

Michael Armstrong sees the role of HRM as:

'A strategic and coherent approach to the management of an organisation's most valued assets: the people working there who individually and collectively contribute to the achievement of its objectives for sustainable competitive advantage.'

The role of HRM, as defined by Armstrong, can thus be viewed as follows:

Suggesting a strategic approach to the personnel function

The previous 'personnel' function probably had a more operational role than strategic. The new HRM division should have a more pivotal role within the firm's strategic planning. This will involve:

- using the value chain to see how human resources can contribute to the firm's competitive advantage

- increasing the weight given to human resource aspects within the firm's SWOT analysis

- viewing staff as contributing to the firm's core competences

- changing attitudes so staff are viewed as assets to be developed rather than costs to be controlled

- encouraging all line managers to see HRM as their responsibility.

Serving the interests of management

Management wants staff to make and implement decisions and to become more customer focused. The HR division will be instrumental in the training aspects of this (see part (b) below).

Dealing with gaining employees' commitment to the values and goals laid down by the strategic management

Management is keen to encourage staff to become more creative and innovative. This will require a change of culture within the firm and, again, the HR division will be central to facilitating that change.

Development of the human resources would help the organisation add value to **their products or services**

Traditional 'personnel' departments tend to focus on training, i.e. filling an identified skills gap, rather than on long-term development. The HR division should see development as a priority looking to enhance the competences of individuals and, in so doing, enhancing the competences of the firm.

(b)   The following aspects of HR strategy will change significantly:

Recruitment and selection

To help change the culture of the firm the HR division should seek to recruit people who have experience of the new culture. Ronald Corwin argues that an organisation can be changed more easily if it is invaded by creative and unconventional outsiders with fresh ideas.

Training

The training strategy will be key to encouraging the changes wanted by management. This could include:

- training in the new culture – especially the values involved as part of continuous improvement

- training in customer service – for example, telephone answering techniques, selling, etc

- training in decision-making techniques.

Development

The firm must initiate development programmes to incorporate:

- career planning

- long-term education in general skills as well as specific job-related ones.

Target setting and performance appraisal

Senior management wants a new system of performance measures. The HR team can interview managers and staff to help agree new performance targets and how they should be linked into remuneration.

Remuneration

To encourage innovation the firm may wish to offer some form of bonus system for good ideas – for example, offering staff a bonus equal to 5% of any cost savings or profit gains that result from staff suggestions.

Job descriptions

The changes in expectations of staff should be reflected in revised job descriptions.

234 NYO.COM

(a) Any disciplinary procedure must take account of local legislation. In the case of NYO there are a number of steps that should be followed:

- The company should write the procedures down to avoid misunderstandings and provide all members of staff with a copy.

- It should be very clear which sections apply to which staff (for example, some parts may only be relevant to senior executives).

- The procedures should state very clearly the forms of disciplinary action which can occur, for example verbal warnings and written warnings.

- The procedures should also state which levels of management are able to use certain kinds of action (for example, only senior executives being able to issue written warnings).

- Detail the steps that will be taken to investigate complaints that might lead to action being taken.

- Detail the procedures of how the employee will be notified of any complaint and of any action being taken against them.

- Detail the appeal procedures for workers who feel that the action taken is unmerited.

(b) At its most fundamental level, the existence of a written disciplinary procedure is designed to protect both the employer and the employee.

Benefits to employer

The employer should be protected from facing future actions (for example, for unfair dismissal). If the company has clearly set out what it views as unacceptable behaviour and the actions that will be taken if this behaviour is undertaken, then it becomes very hard for the employee to claim they have been mistreated.

If an employee does undertake some action that is deemed unacceptable, the sliding scale of various different punishments should mean that the employee is less likely to repeat the action.

Looking at the big picture, the point of a disciplinary scheme is to deter employees from breaking the rules, in other words, to make sure that the scheme never has to be used.

Benefits to the employee

The employee of an organisation benefits from having a formal disciplinary procedure since it reduces the risk that they will be arbitrarily accused and punished for their actions.

This is becoming more important as more individuals are left to their own devices at work rather than being given detailed rules and procedures (as organisations move from a mechanistic to an organic approach). This is likely to be particularly important in a company like NYO, which is growing and changing rapidly.

(c) Employers are under a statutory duty to demonstrate that any dismissal is fair, otherwise the dismissed employee would have a vairiety of rights and responses.

An employee might be dismissed on the grounds of a lack of capability or qualifications. This arises when the employee is effectively incapable of doing the job properly, for example because ill health has had an impact on his or her performance. In this case the employee must be given the opportunity to improve the position or, in the case of ill health, be considered for alternative employment.

An employee can be dismissed for misconduct if he or she is guilty of refusing to obey lawful and reasonable instructions, absenteeism, and insubordination over a period of time. Criminal actions relating directly to the job might also constitute grounds for dismissal.

An employee could be dismissed if he or she was unable to pursue normal duties without breaking the law. For example, if one of the company's sales staff was banned from driving and was unable to visit clients then that would probably consitute grounds for dismissal.

Any other good work-related reasons for dismissal might be treated as valid grounds, for example, if the business needed to change and the employee refused unreasonably to adapt to the change.

Section 7

MAY 2006
EXAM QUESTIONS

SECTION A – 50 MARKS

[The indicative time for answering this section is 90 minutes]

Answer ALL twenty sub-questions.

QUESTION ONE

1.1 **Charles Handy's vision of a 'shamrock' organisation suggests a workforce that comprises three different type of worker, namely:**

    A   strategic, operational and support

    B   qualified, trainee and unskilled

    C   'white collar', 'blue collar' and e-worker

    D   core, contractual and flexible labour.   **(2 marks)**

1.2 **Activities associated with Organisational Development:**

    A   require universal agreement that change must take place

    B   require 'interventions' into the social processes of an organisation

    C   naturally occur through a shared sense of purpose and a strong organisational culture

    D   result from the effect of Greiner's life cycle model.   **(2 marks)**

1.3 **Job family structures are examples of:**

    A   motivational tools

    B   similar levels of responsibility reflected across several distinct functions or disciplines

    C   Japanese employment practice

    D   pay structures for jobs within distinct functions or disciplines.   **(2 marks)**

1.4 **Abraham Maslow's theory of motivation is often represented as:**

    A   a hierarchy of needs

    B   individual behaviour labelled X or Y

    C   a scientific relationship between work and reward

    D   a series of negative and a series of positive factors.   **(2 marks)**

1.5 **Effective product promotion is centred on:**

A   production processes

B   customers and communication

C   bonuses for sales staff and product quality

D   effective systems of monitoring and control.   **(2 marks)**

1.6 **Conventional marketing wisdom suggests that, for successful segmentation of markets, segments must be:**

A   relatively unsophisticated in their needs

B   economic, efficient and effective

C   measurable, accessible and substantial

D   currently lacking in providers.   **(2 marks)**

1.7 **The technique of force field analysis depicts**

A   change as occurring through a series of restraining and driving forces

B   growth of organisations through evolution and revolution

C   an organisation's environment as a series of opportunistic and threatening factors

D   aggressive management styles used to drive change.   **(2 marks)**

1.8 **The 5-S model refers to:**

A   internal analysis involving structure, sub-structure, systems, sub-systems and strategy

B   internal analysis involving style, shared values, skills, staffing and 'soft' information

C   operations management practices of structurise, systematise, sanitise, standardise and self-discipline

D   the Japanese six-sigma model adapted to Western practice.   **(2 marks)**

1.9 **Distribution channels, transport, warehouse and sales outlet locations are all examples of:**

A   'place', one component of the marketing mix

B   'promotion', one component of the marketing mix

C   'physical evidence', one component of the marketing mix

D   the management of operations for a service organisation.   **(2 marks)**

1.10 **Gaining International Standards (ISO) in quality is mainly dependent upon:**

A   effective processes for documentation and control

B   a shared quality philosophy

C   commitment from middle managers

D   benchmarking customer-related performance against competitors.   **(2 marks)**

1.11   The set of activities designed to familiarise a new employee with an organisation is called:

 A job analysis

 B induction

 C selection

 D manipulation and co-optation.   **(2 marks)**

1.12   According to Kurt Lewin, the final stage of his three-stage model of change is called:

 A unfreezing

 B refreezing

 C unbundling

 D support and facilitation.   **(2 marks)**

1.13   Recruitment involves:

 A advertising a vacancy and interviewing

 B conducting interviews and tests

 C advertising a vacancy and initial screening of candidates

 D ensuring that contract negotiation complies with organisational policy. **(2 marks)**

1.14   Three hundred and sixty degree (360°) feedback is normally associated with:

 A exit interviews

 B quality circle activity

 C appraisal processes

 D reflection as part of a cycle of learning.   **(2 marks)**

1.15   Kaizen is a quality improvement technique that involves:

 A continuous improvement by small incremental steps.

 B a complete revision of all organisational processes and structures.

 C immediate, often radical 'right first time' changes to practice.

 D a problem solving fishbone technique to identify cause and effect. **(2 marks)**

             (Total for sub-questions 1.1 to 1.15: 30 marks)

Each of the sub-questions numbered **1.16** to **1.20** below requires a brief written response. Each sub-question is worth 4 marks.

These responses should be in note form and should not exceed **50** words per sub-question.

1.16   Describe the relationship between operations management and (using Mintzberg's terminology) the organisational technostructure.   **(4 marks)**

1.17   Explain how continuous inventory systems might work against an organisation's Just-in-Time (JIT) philosophy.   **(4 marks)**

1.18 Identify examples of external failure costs, and explain their significance for an organisation with a reputation for quality. **(4 marks)**

1.19 Distinguish between push and pull marketing policies and their impact on the promotion of goods. **(4 marks)**

1.20 Identify the main stages involved in developing human resource plans and programmes following the production of a corporate plan. **(4 marks)**

(Total for 1.16 to 1.20 sub-questions: 20 marks)

(Total for Section A: 50 marks)

SECTION B – 30 MARKS

[The indicative time for answering this section is 54 minutes]

Answer ALL parts of this question.

QUESTION TWO

S & C is a medium-sized firm that is experiencing rapid growth as evidenced by increased turnover. It has been able to develop a range of new consultancy and specialist business advisory services that it offers to its growing customer base. To cope with these developments, several organisation-wide initiatives have been launched over the past two years.

The existing financial systems are struggling to cope with these developments, but replacement software is due to be installed within the next six months. The new system was justified partly because it could reduce costs, although precise details have not been given. The application software does not fit existing business processes exactly. However, it has the clear advantage of giving S & C access to an industry best practice system and is identical to that used by all its main competitors and some of its clients.

A three-person project steering group has recommended that a phased approach to introduction should be used and has undertaken most of the project planning. A programme of events for implementing the system has been agreed but is not yet fully operational. This group has not met for a while because the designated project manager has been absent from work through illness.

You are Head of S & C's Central Support Unit. You also serve on the project steering group.

A partners' meeting is due to take place soon. The firm's senior partner has asked you to prepare a PowerPoint presentation to other partners on implementation issues. You understand that the partners are conscious that system implementation represents a form of further organisational change. They are asking questions about the approach that will be taken to the introduction of the new system, likely changes to practices, critical areas for success, system testing, support after implementation, system effectiveness, etc.

Required:

Produce **outline notes** that will support your eventual PowerPoint presentation. These notes should:

(a) discuss the options to overcome the fact that the software does not fit existing business processes exactly **(5 marks)**

(b) explain why a phased approach to introducing the system is, in this case, more suitable than a direct 'big bang' approach **(5 marks)**

(c) discuss the ways in which particular individuals and groups within S & C are important for implementation to succeed **(5 marks)**

(d)   explain how users should be involved in the implementation phase of the project   **(5 marks)**

(e)   describe the training that should be given to targeted groups within S & C   **(5 marks)**

(f)   explain the aims of a post-implementation review.   **(5 marks)**

(Total: 30 marks)

(Total for Section B: 30 marks)

SECTION C – 20 MARKS

[The indicative time for answering this section is 36 minutes]

Answer ONE question only.

QUESTION THREE

Banking services within the country of Everland are provided exclusively by a few well-established banks, all offering broadly similar 'traditional' banking services. Overall, the industry performance is viewed from within as satisfactory and historically all banks have maintained stable profits and employment levels. Marketeers would describe the industry as being classically 'product oriented'. The profile of senior Everland bank officials and managers is of well-qualified professionals, possessing long banking industry experience and considerable financial skills. Within the combined workforce other business skills (in, for instance, HR or marketing) are noticeably lacking.

In the external environment, the government will soon pass new legislation that will effectively break the oligopoly-type position of banks and open the market up to other providers. Senior bank officials, however, are unconcerned, feeling that banks are in 'reasonable shape' to face any new challenge.

You work for the Everland Banking Advisory Group (EBAG), an independent body, and have been asked to analyse the banking industry in the country of Utopia to identify lessons that might be learnt. Your investigation reveals that, since the sector opened up to more competition, a much wider range of financial institutions offer banking services. Despite this, banks in Utopia have all prospered over the past few years. This is thanks to wide-ranging changes in how they operate, the products and services they offer and their organisational structures. You identify some significant trends within the banking industry of Utopia, including:

- the use of marketing techniques

- a clearer focus on customers (who have become increasingly more demanding)

- a new generation of bank employees, many with commercial backgrounds

- banks now exhibiting a strong sense of ethical and social responsibilities towards customers.

Required:

(a)   Discuss the dangers to Everland banks if they do not change.   **(8 marks)**

(b)   Discuss the types of change that Everland banks could be making in order to survive and prosper.   **(12 marks)**

(Total: 20 marks)

QUESTION FOUR

CQ4 is a leading European industrial gas production company. CQ4's directors are each responsible for a geographical region containing several small strategic business units (SBUs). SBU managers report in monthly review meetings in great detail to their directors. CQ4 is showing signs of declining profitability and a new chief executive has been appointed and wishes to address the situation. She has complete freedom to identify organisational problems, solutions and strategies.

At their annual conference she tells SBU managers that they hold the key to improved company performance. She has a vision of CQ4 achieving longer term strategic goals of increases in profitability, risk taking and innovation. Under the slogan 'support not report' directors will in future support and provide assistance to their managers to a greater degree, and the frequency and detail of reporting by managers will be reduced.

She announces two new initiatives 'to address the lost years when managers were prevented from delivering truly excellent CQ4 performance':

- Revision of the existing performance appraisal system. Bonuses paid on turnover will be replaced by performance-related pay for achievement of individual 'performance target contracts'. Individual SBU managers will sign contracts to deliver these targets. Performance will now be reviewed at yearly rather than monthly meetings with directors. The remuneration and reward package will be adjusted appropriately with the current emphasis on increasing turnover shifting to profitability and innovation.

- A structural review to focus the resources and efforts of SBUs on improving net profit. Part of the restructuring will involve SBUs no longer providing their own 'enabling' services such as finance, information technology, and health and safety. These 'distractions from doing the real job' will in future be organised centrally. SBUs will be given far greater responsibility, autonomy and influence over their own profitability.

She tells managers that she is stripping away the things that stop them doing their job properly. In return they must manage their SBU in the way they see most appropriate. They will be better rewarded and 'star achievers' will be fast tracked to senior positions. SBU managers are informed that the HR department has already been tasked with redesigning the remuneration and reward package.

Informal discussions amongst managers afterwards confirm that the new chief executive's message has been well received. Comments such as 'work might be more enjoyable without central interference' and 'for the first time I can do my job properly' were overheard.

Required:

(a) Explain the thinking behind the two initiatives announced by the new chief executive using Herzberg's motivation-hygiene (dual factor) theory as a framework. **(10 marks)**

(b) Discuss the factors that should be taken into account by the HR department when redesigning the remuneration and reward package for SBU managers. **(10 marks)**

(Total: 20 marks)

(Total marks for Section C: 20 marks)

Section 8

ANSWERS TO MAY 2006 EXAM QUESTIONS

SECTION A

Note: From May 2007 onwards, Section A will be worth 40 marks.

QUESTION ONE

1.1   D

Handy's concept has it that each of the three leaves of the shamrock is symbolic of a different group of people within the organisation: the professional core of employees; the contractual fringe where all work that could be done by someone else is contracted out; and the flexible labour force all those part-time workers and temporary workers.

1.2   B

Organisational development solves problems using the diagnostic and problem-solving skills of an external consultant in collaboration with the organisation's management. Typical problems that are the focus of such interventions include lack of co-operation, excessive decentralisation and poor communication.

1.3   D

These are similar in concept to job classifications.

1.4   A

Maslow proposed a hierarchy of needs that can be used to explain human motivation. His work is used primarily in relation to work, but can be applied to customer motivation.

1.5   B

Attention to customer needs lies at the heart of all successful marketing strategies.

1.6   C

There is very little point in segmenting the market if segments cannot be identified and targeted.

1.7   A

Lewin developed force field theory to explain how interactions between human beings are driven by both the people involved and their environment. He was particularly interested in the forces that came into conflict around planned changes.

1.8   C

By definition.

1.9   A

By definition.

1.10   A

Much of the current emphasis on 'quality' is focused on the processes of documentation and control rather than on the outputs themselves.

1.11   B

Job analysis and selection occur before the person becomes an employee. Only a rather cynical organisation would aim to manipulate a new employee.

1.12   B

The three stages are: unfreezing, then change, then refreezing.

1.13   C

Interviewing is part of selection rather than recruitment, and contract negotiation follow these.

1.14   C

360° degree feedback involves the rating of an individual's performance by people who know something about that person's work. Those involved can include direct subordinates, peers, managers, customers or clients.

1.15   A

By definition.

1.16   Operations management involves transforming inputs (factors of production such as inventory and labour) into outputs (products and/or services) through a series of operations (manufacturing, assembly, etc).

The technostructure supports effective operations through functions such as Strategic Planning, Personnel Training, Operations Research, Systems Analysis and Design.

1.17   Continuous inventory systems have a different conception of 'efficiency'. The objective is to ensure that total inventory costs are minimised by ordering and manufacturing the economic quantity and by keeping a safety stock in order to avoid shortages.

JIT aims to have zero inventory, or close to zero.

1.18   Whenever substandard goods are sold the organisation is likely to incur the cost of replacing or rectifying the items. This will involve additional collection and delivery charges and manufacturing costs.

Selling defective goods may lead to customer dissatisfaction and loss of reputation.

1.19 A push policy provides the distribution channel with incentives to promote and market goods, e.g. a manufacturer might give its distributors discounts if they achieve high sales volumes.

A pull strategy involves creating demand, e.g. by a manufacturer advertising heavily so that consumer demand forces distributors to stock the product.

1.20 Analyse objectives – what shape and size should the organisation be?

Forecast demand – what are future staffing requirements?

Forecast supply – what resources are likely to be available?

Develop programmes to deal with any forecast shortages and surpluses.

SECTION B

QUESTION TWO

Requirement (a)

The two main options are to change the software (i.e. have it adapted to give a better fit to S & C's business processes) or to change the business processes themselves so that they fit with the software.

It may be possible to revise the software, although the vendor will have to agree to this because access to the underlying source code will have copyright implications. The actual revision to the software could be quite an involved and expensive undertaking. The changes might lead to problems later on. If there are bugs then the vendor might blame the company for making changes. Any future revisions and upgrades might also be more difficult to install.

S & C's staff might be unhappy about changing their systems in order to meet the requirements of a software package. However, it will generally be much easier to adapt the manual processes involved in a computerised system than to rewrite the software. In addition, it is unlikely that the software would have become an industry standard if it were significantly out of line with the processes and procedures of a typical user. It is, therefore, unlikely to require a great deal of change to create the fit.

Requirement (b)

A phased approach reduces the extent of the upheaval associated with the change, albeit at the cost of having this upheaval extended over a longer period. Seeing the new system come online in phases will be motivating because the partners and staff will see progress towards an end. The fact that the project manager is absent means that a series of small-scale changes might be easier to deliver and each step can be checked for integrity before moving on to the next.

The 'big bang' approach requires much greater confidence in the new system. If it works then it will allow for a clean change from the old to the new, but if there are problems then there is a danger that they will be difficult to rectify. The fact that this is a standard package reduces the risk of it going wrong, although there will always be risks associated with converting files to the new system and the interface with other parts of the organisation can go wrong.

Requirement (c)

The **partners** must demonstrate their commitment to the new system. If they are not clear in their enthusiasm for the change then their employees are unlikely to be keen.

The **project steering group** must set the pace for the change, particularly if it is to be implemented in phases. Deadlines should be set and a set of tasks and responsibilities assigned to users.

Middle management must ensure that their staff are trained in the new sub-systems as they come online and that any checks and balances that are used to ensure correct implementation are in place.

Users have to be keen to make the change work. If they are not willing to learn and adapt then the new system is likely to fail. Staff in the 'front line' are more likely to have a feel for things that are going wrong and they should ensure that any concerns are dealt with promptly and efficiently.

Requirement (d)

Users should have been consulted throughout the design stage of the project. Once it has reached the implementation phase then it should be clear to them what they need to do in terms of checking the output from different parts of the system and also in evaluating their own need for training and staff development.

Individual users might undertake specific responsibilities for testing the conversion of data and checking the output. It is generally too expensive to run the old system in parallel with the new for any length of time and so users should aim to test each phase as quickly and efficiently as possible.

Users who become proficient with the new system in the early phases might be able to mentor colleagues when it is their turn to make the change. Some users will have a greater affinity for IT than others and they might be selected for training in the initial stages.

Requirement (e)

Training needs to be pitched at an appropriate level of detail:

- Partners need to be aware of the strategic implications of the new system, such as its ability to provide information and contribute to control.

- Managers need more detailed training so that they can use the system to monitor their areas of responsibility and supervise those members of their staff who input data into the system.

- Users need detailed knowledge of operating procedures, menu structures, error correction and so on.

Training might be conducted in-house or it may be possible to buy training in from the software vendor or a third party training company.

Requirement (f)

The company needs to know whether the system meets its needs. Any shortcomings should be addressed as quickly as possible and remedied.

The cost and timing of the change needs to be reviewed to ensure that the project was completed on budget and on time. Any serious deviations from plan should be analysed to ensure that they are avoided in the future. It may also be possible to claim some compensation from the vendor or any consultant who was involved in the project.

The review will give the company a better idea of its strengths and weaknesses in managing projects of this type. This might affect the manner in which future projects are undertaken – perhaps future projects will be given to external consultants.

SECTION C

Note: From May 2007 onwards, section C will comprise two 30 mark questions.

QUESTION THREE

Requirement (a)

It is always dangerous for a business or even a whole industry to focus on the products that it wishes to provide rather than the needs of its customers. The banking industry may have enjoyed an artificial protection in the past because customers have been forced to take banking services from a limited number of providers who have tended not to differentiate themselves in terms of their products. If customers do not feel that their needs are being met then they will be willing to consider alternative offerings once the rules are relaxed to permit a wider range of business.

The prospect of a change should motivate the banks to re-examine their business models and make the effort to develop a deeper understanding of what their customers actually wish from a bank. It will take some time to develop new types of account, train staff in the provision of new services and recruit new employees with the necessary skills to fill any gaps in the present complement.

If banks do not change then experience from Utopia indicates that complacency could prove disastrous. The banking industry there had to adapt to the business methods used by new entrants to the industry. By implication, standing still was not an option. If they had left things as they were then they would have run the risk of losing significant custom to the new businesses and they would also have missed out on the new opportunities offered by the opportunity to sell new services.

The relaxation of banking law should be seen as an opportunity rather than a threat. The existing banks need not necessarily lose ground to newcomers provided they establish what services their customers need and plan to offer these as soon as it becomes possible to do so legally.

Requirement (b)

The banks should consider adopting a change in their overall strategy to emphasise marketing:

Strategic analysis

- The banks should identify their strengths and weaknesses, their core competences and the resources that they have available to them.

- The prospects for change in the external environment should be analysed. What sorts of banking will new institutions be permitted to offer? What additional services will be opened up to the banks?

- How are the banks currently perceived? Can perceptions for integrity and security be built on to retain customers while still offering room to innovate?

Strategic choice

- Can the market be segmented in any way?

- If so, which segments should the banks seek to retain?

- How should each target segment be approached? How will the banks compete with one another and with any new entrants?

Strategy implementation

- What resources need to be acquired? Does this require new staff with additional skills?

- How should the banks promote both existing and new services?

- What targets should be set and how will progress be monitored and controlled?

- How will the changes be managed without alienating those existing staff whose skills and enthusiasm will need to be harnessed?

QUESTION FOUR

Requirement (a)

Herzberg's theory of motivation is based on the idea that motivation is based on two needs:

- Hygiene factors are those to do with the context of the job rather than the job itself e.g. features such as the working environment (salary, the nature and extent of supervision, job security, etc). These factors are known as 'dissatisfiers' because a lack of attention to these areas can lead to dissatisfaction, but meeting these here will not necessarily lead to employee satisfaction.

- Motivational factors are concerned with the job itself. Generally satisfaction flows from the actual job – the recognition, any sense of achievement from doing it well and so on. Motivational factors meet employees' need for growth and self-achievement.

Focusing on motivating factors is usually more productive because employees will work harder and generally perform better if they are motivated.

The chief executive's proposals can be analysed as follows:

Motivating factors:

- Each manager has a personal 'performance target contract' and is to be left to achieve the required outcome.

- Managers are to be given greater recognition for their role in meeting the company's strategic targets.

- Individual achievement stands a chance of being noticed and rewarded with greater responsibility in the future.

Hygiene factors:

- Bonuses will be paid to reflect the anticipated boost in profits.

- The burden of monthly reports and monitoring has been lifted.

Requirement (b)

There may be constraints on the amount that the company can afford to spend on rewarding good performance. Even if the new system does turn out to give a worthwhile incentive, it may be more than the company can afford.

Some employees may feel disenfranchised and demotivated when they see their managers offered the opportunity to earn a performance-related salary enhancement that is not available to everyone.

Managers might be tempted to focus on the factors of their jobs that maximise their pay, even though that might not be in the very best interest of the company. It can be difficult to design such packages so that managers always have an incentive to do what is best for the company.

Linking pay to outcomes could make managers risk-averse. They might be inclined to adopt a 'safe' course that will guarantee a reasonable bonus rather than to take a better approach that could be more risky.

There has to be an objective mechanism for measuring performance for the purpose of settling the performance-related pay.

The balance between different elements of the remuneration package must be addressed. The relationship between salary and bonus elements is an important one.

The proposed system must be seen to be fair to all sides.

Section 9

NOVEMBER 2006 EXAM QUESTIONS

SECTION A – 50 MARKS

[The indicative time for answering this section is 90 minutes]

Answer ALL twenty sub-questions.

QUESTION ONE

1.1 **Frederick Herzberg's study of work and people is of significance to managers because it identifies:**

    A   a framework for HRM involving appraisal, training and motivation

    B   the need to assess the personality of job applicants

    C   factors associated with job satisfaction called motivators

    D   satisfaction from a participative, problem-solving environment.   **(2 marks)**

1.2 **Data redundancy arises as a result of:**

    A   viruses and computer misuse

    B   downsizing the organisation

    C   a lack of password controls

    D   duplication of data held.   **(2 marks)**

1.3 **Kurt Lewin's ideas on change are based on the view that change is:**

    A   capable of being planned

    B   emergent

    C   inevitable and uncontrollable

    D   transformational.   **(2 marks)**

1.4 **A network topology refers to:**

    A   the physical arrangement of a computer network

    B   the type of hardware used

    C   the hierarchy of access

    D   the range of software operated.   **(2 marks)**

1.5   Adding new tasks to a person's job, so increasing their responsibility, is called:

A   process re-engineering

B   job enrichment

C   HR development

D   career scoping.   **(2 marks)**

1.6   Data integrity refers to its:

A   accuracy

B   security of storage

C   adaptability for multiple use

D   ethical use of personal details.   **(2 marks)**

1.7   Entity relationship modelling is a technique used within:

A   an assessment centre test used in staff selection

B   market research and product testing

C   database analysis and design

D   business process re-engineering.   **(2 marks)**

1.8   The intervention of a consultant or change agent is a common feature of:

A   co-operation and negotiation strategies for change

B   an inclusive culture

C   high levels of management visibility

D   a programme of Organisational Development (OD).   **(2 marks)**

1.9   A local area network (LAN) normally contains:

A   a file, print and communications server(s)

B   distributed processing and local solutions

C   e-trading and e-marketing

D   internet access and firewall protection.   **(2 marks)**

1.10   Public relations activity can be used within marketing as part of:

A   marketing decision support activities

B   a promotional mix

C   customer feedback processes

D   segmentation practices.   **(2 marks)**

1.11   Remuneration is an example of:

A   self-actualisation reward

B   an intrinsic reward

C   an extrinsic reward

D   an individual's work/life balance.   **(2 marks)**

1.12 'Spot rates' normally refer to a specific pay rate determined by reference to:

A the marketplace

B incremental progression

C a negotiated point on a pay spine

D experience and qualifications of a newly recruited person. **(2 marks)**

1.13 Charging a very low price on one item in order to generate customer loyalty and increased sales of other items is called:

A market penetration

B loss leader pricing

C product penetration

D skim pricing. **(2 marks)**

1.14 'Corrective', 'perfective' and 'adaptive' are terms associated with:

A system maintenance

B change management approaches

C quality assurance

D HR disciplinary processes. **(2 marks)**

1.15 In the expectancy theory of motivation 'valence' refers to:

A a belief that an outcome will satisfy organisational tasks

B a person's own preference for achieving a particular outcome

C a belief that the outcome will be shared by others equally

D an understanding of the probability of an event happening. **(2 marks)**

(Total for sub-questions 1.1 to 1.15: 30 marks)

Each of the sub-questions numbered **1.16** to **1.20** below requires a brief written response. Each sub-question is worth 4 marks.

These responses should be in note form and should not exceed **50** words per sub-question.

1.16 Explain the concept of physical evidence when applied to the marketing mix. **(4 marks)**

1.17 Identify the potential benefits of a marketing database and the source data from which it might be constructed. **(4 marks)**

1.18 In HR planning how might an organisation match the projected 'supply' of human resources to future demand. **(4 marks)**

1.19 Identify the advantages and disadvantages of a policy of succession planning for a large organisation. **(4 marks)**

1.20 Identify both the advantages and disadvantages of a decentralised Human Resource provision for an organisation that has many business units and sites. **(4 marks)**

(Total for sub-questions 1.16 to 1.20: 20 marks)

(Total for Section A: 50 marks)

SECTION B – 30 MARKS

[The indicative time for answering this section is 54 minutes]

Answer ALL parts of this question.

QUESTION TWO

The country of Chapterland has a principle that healthcare should be free to its citizens at the point of access. Healthcare is funded from national taxation and organised through a series of large health units, one of which is known as 'Q2'. Q2 operates a huge, single site hospital and offers a variety of community services (such as health visiting) that are taken to the local population. Q2 has a management structure consisting of eight clinical and administrative directors who report to Q2's Chief Executive Officer (CEO). The Q2 CEO is directly accountable to the national government through regular returns of information and year-end reporting.

Published 'quality league tables' of hospital performance against government targets suggest that Q2 has one of the worst records in the country. (Targets are for cleanliness of hospital wards, treatment waiting times and staff employed per patient cases dealt with.) In addition, Q2 has in recent years been operating to a budget in excess of its funding, which is against government regulations. The current year budget again exceeds projected funding.

Last year, Q2's previous CEO decided that certain changes were necessary including:

- better cost control

- improved performance measurement; and

- benchmarking.

He revealed this thinking for the first time in a global email he sent to Q2's staff. Later, when conducting the annual performance appraisal of the Director of Human Resources (HR), he tasked her with implementing 'each and every form of benchmarking' within the next four months so that 'true' performance deficiencies could be addressed. However, the Director of HR left for a new job elsewhere within that period. The CEO then undertook to manage the changes himself but was surprised to find directors unenthusiastic and even uncooperative. Under pressure from the government the CEO resigned 'for personal reasons' and no progress was made with his initiatives.

A new CEO has just been appointed. Her immediate concern is to reduce expenditure and improve performance. On her first day as CEO she spoke of a need to re-establish a culture of 'care through quality' within Q2. She wishes to discuss a number of ideas and issues with her clinical and administrative directors at a special 'away day' meeting to be arranged soon. You work in the CEO's central policy team and she has informed you that some ideas for initiatives include outsourcing, improved supply management and new performance management measures.

Required:

You have been asked to provide the new CEO with briefing notes on a number of issues that will help prepare her for the 'away day' meeting. These notes should:

(a) explain why the changes attempted by the previous CEO were unsuccessful **(5 marks)**

(b) explain the role Human Resources could perform in supporting any new initiatives for change **(5 marks)**

(c) analyse the potential of outsourcing as a means of overcoming some of the problems facing Q2 (the CEO has identified two services initially – IT/IS and cleaning) **(5 marks)**

(d) discuss which forms of benchmarking Q2 should use in order to contribute to better performance management **(5 marks)**

(e)   discuss how a culture of 'care through quality' might be established within Q2   **(5 marks)**

(f)   describe the performance measures that will be needed in order to satisfy future management and strategic reporting requirements of Q2.   **(5 marks)**

(Total: 30 marks)

SECTION C – 20 MARKS

[The indicative time for answering this section is 36 minutes]

Answer ONE question only.

QUESTION THREE

B3 is a family-run personnel agency. It offers a range of services to both individuals and corporate clients (mainly local medium-sized organisations). The son of the managing director (MD) is currently studying for a specialist university business degree. His course includes a 'management consultancy' module where students are required to analyse an organisation and identify a range of development options for the business. The MD's son's investigations of B3 have led to a consultancy report being produced, extracts of which include:

"B3 should maximise the opportunities offered by information technology to a greater extent. In particular:

- *Opportunity 1.* B3 could develop its recent successful experiment in e-cruitment (the identification of employment opportunities through the world wide web and the emailing of clients). Currently details of vacancies are collected and matched to individual client's search criteria. When a match is identified clients are emailed and, if they are interested, interviews arranged. This service is not offered by any of B3's main competitors. There is a difficulty, however, in that many companies have barred access to personal emails at work and web access to recruitment sites such as B3's site from their offices. Market research suggests that significant opportunities for m-cruitment (jobs by mobile telephones) also exist. Making use of recent software developments, a text message containing a job title and some contact details could be sent out to individual clients instead of an email, so providing a more convenient and speedy service.

- *Opportunity 2.* Virtually all CVs are currently received in electronic form and a policy decision should be made to develop a paperless operating environment through the development of databases, so upgrading existing office technology.

Analysis of profit indicates that executive searches, corporate 'headhunting' and vacancy identification for individuals (traditional and especially e-cruitment) are all profitable activities.

Involvement in selection processes with corporate clients is unprofitable and should be discontinued. Instead B3 should identify clear guidelines for corporate clients to follow once the short-listing of candidates has occurred."

Required:

(a)   Evaluate the opportunities for B3 identified in the consultancy report.   **(12 marks)**

(b)   Produce guidelines for the selection process that should be adopted by an organisation presented with a short-list of candidates.   **(8 marks)**

(Total: 20 marks)

QUESTION FOUR

CM's founder first began producing breakfast food from a start-up unit on a small industrial estate. Now CM is the market leader in Europe and Oceania. Once established in Europe, the company made the breakthrough into Oceania thanks to demand from ex-pats and contacts with a family member who happened to be a director of a supermarket chain in Australia. The company's founder is very 'hands on' and has made all the major strategic decisions to date based on intuition.

CM spends heavily on promoting most of its 20 products on television, normally before and after children's programmes with high viewing figures. Research conducted ten years ago shows that children love small gifts contained within packs and the association of certain of the products to cartoon characters. CM also manufactures its most popular lines and packages them as 'own brand' alternatives for some large supermarket chains. These sell more cheaply than CM branded products, are less costly to produce (they contain inexpensive packaging and no gifts) but sales remain low.

CM is now facing a more uncertain environment with increasing competition (from a North American firm), sales levels that seem to have peaked and the prospect of the founder retiring very soon. Management consultants advising CM have identified a need to develop a structured marketing strategic plan for the organisation and for greater involvement of other staff in future strategic decisions. As a further complication, CM has recently received some adverse publicity from an international health 'watchdog' body that claims that CM's products contain potentially harmful levels of both sugar and salt.

Required:

(a)   Evaluate CM's situation making specific mention of marketing and ethical issues.

(10 marks)

(b)   Explain how CM might develop a marketing strategic plan.   **(10 marks)**

(Total: 20 marks)

Section 10

ANSWERS TO NOVEMBER 2006 EXAM QUESTIONS

SECTION A

Note: From May 2007 onwards, Section A will be worth 40 marks.

QUESTION ONE

1.1 C

Herzberg distinguished motivational factors, such as a sense of achievement associated with doing a job, from hygiene factors, which are more to do with the context of the job rather than the job itself. It is usually more productive to focus on motivational factors because employees will work harder and generally perform better if they are motivated.

1.2 D

Data redundancy arises when data is duplicated. This could be a sign of inefficiency if storage space is being wasted or it could be a deliberate act to make one or more copies available to speed up access to data or to provide backup (e.g. certain types of RAID mirror data).

1.3 A

Lewin argued that introducing a driving force toward change often produced an immediate counterforce to maintain the equilibrium. It is often easier to bring about change by removing the restraining forces since there are usually already driving forces in the system.

1.4 A

Network Topology is the study of the arrangement or mapping of the elements (links, nodes, etc) of a network, especially the physical and logical interconnections between nodes.

1.5 B

Job enrichment is a deliberate, planned process to improve the responsibility, challenge and creativity of a job.

1.6 B

Data integrity can be compromised by either malicious acts (such as hacking) or by accidental events (such as transmission errors).

1.7   **C**

An entity relationship model is a diagram showing the different entities (anything of significance about which data must be held) in a system and the relationships between them.

1.8   **D**

Organisational development is designed to solve problems that decrease operating efficiency at all levels. it uses the diagnostic and problem-solving skills of an external consultant in collaboration with the organisation's management.

1.9   **B**

This is a tricky question because all but one of the answers could claim to be correct. A LAN consists of a network that connects two or more computers together and permits them to communicate. With a LAN it is commonplace for data to be processed at the local level, with each PC undertaking its own share of the processing. This lends weight to the claim that a LAN offers distributed processing and local solutions. Answer A does have some merit because some LANs are structured around one or more servers, although others are peer-to-peer networks and no server is involved. Answer D has some merit because many LANs do offer users internet access. A and D must, however, be rejected because of the word 'normally' in the question. C is clearly incorrect because e-trading and e-marketing might be conducted on a LAN, but that is but one of many possible applications.

1.10   **B**

Public relations is part of the promotional mix. It involves the creation of positive attitudes regarding products, services or companies by various means, including unpaid media coverage and involvement with community activities.

1.11   **C**

An extrinsic reward is a reward that is external to the individual such as money, food or encouragement. An intrinsic reward is one that is internal within the person such as feeling good for a job well done.

1.12   **C**

Once an employee is given a spot rate then his or her salary is fixed (apart from cost of living increases).

1.13   **B**

Loss leaders are frequently used by supermarkets to attract customers into their stores.

1.14   **A**

Corrective maintenance involves eliminating faults and errors from a system. Perfective maintenance is carried out to improve the effectiveness and efficiency of the system. Adaptive maintenance is amending the system to adjust to changes in its environment.

1.15   **B**

Valence is the value of the perceived outcome: 'What's in it for me?'

1.16   Physical evidence is the material part of a service. There are no physical attributes to a service, so consumers tend to rely on material cues such as packaging, internet/web pages, paperwork (such as invoices, tickets and despatch notes), brochures, etc.

1.17 A database offers the ability to generate ad hoc reports quickly and efficiently. This could be of immense use in segmenting or investigating the buying behaviour of customers. For example, a supermarket loyalty card scheme makes it possible to generate reports very quickly on the buying habits of individual customers.

1.18 A deficiency may be met through internal transfers, promotion, training, external recruitment and reducing labour turnover (by reviewing possible causes). A surplus may be dealt with by running down staff levels by natural wastage, restricting recruitment or, as a last resort, redundancies.

1.19 Advantages:

- An ongoing supply of well trained, well-motivated people ready to fill posts.

- Defined career paths, helping to recruit and retain better people.

Disadvantages:

- Too long a wait for movement/promotion, potentially resulting in disillusionment.

- Selection of unqualified or unmotivated people for inclusion in the succession plan.

1.20 Decentralisation pushes responsibility for HR management closer to the point of delivery, in order to improve overall efficiency and to increase the accountability and responsiveness.

Decentralisation can also reduce control over important employment issues, with the potential for different standards in different parts of the organisation.

SECTION B

QUESTION TWO

Requirement (a)

'Better cost control' is likely to mean cutting budgets, which will never be a popular act in any organisation. Attempting such a change would require considerable finesse, but the CEO appears to have acted in a very clumsy manner and has not attempted to carry the other managers with him.

The CEO should not have been so dismissive of the external performance measures. While these are bound to be flawed, they have been adopted for use throughout the country and must have some value. Some attempt should have been made to perform well in these terms because the bad rankings mean that the unit is perceived as inefficient and ineffective, which will demotivate staff and harm their long-term career prospects.

Requirement (b)

Human Resources should ensure that progress in terms of the dimensions of any change is reflected in staff appraisal schemes. This will give an incentive to embrace the changes and work towards their implementation.

HR can also ensure that any new appointments are made with the needs created by the changes in mind. This might mean recruiting more experienced or better qualified staff, or ensuing that new recruits are willing and able to contribute to the process of change.

Requirement (c)

Outsourcing can reduce costs, sometimes through efficiencies and sometimes because service-providers are able to recruit staff at a lower rate of pay than was given by the client company for the same grades of staff. If outsourcing reduces costs then the budget deficit might be addressed to some extent.

If Q2 outsources its services then it will be able to pass some of the responsibility over to the outsourcing company. This might be particularly advantageous in the area of cleaning because Q2 does not appear to have a great deal of expertise in managing cleaning services. An expert third party should be able to improve matters.

Requirement (d)

Internal benchmarking might be used to identify good/best practice within Q2. For example, different clinical specialisms within the hospital might be very similar in terms of their staffing and administrative profiles. It should be possible to compare performance on areas such as cleanliness, staff absenteeism and so on.

Competitive benchmarking would be useful provided a suitable basis for comparison can be identified. Publicly-funded hospitals are not in competition with one another and so there should not be a major problem in finding another hospital or group of hospitals with which to share information.

Process benchmarking might be worth considering for areas such as patient catering in case it is possible to learn something useful from other types of organisation.

Requirement (e)

It should not be too difficult to create a caring culture within an organisation such as a hospital. Arguably, there will be a desire to work towards this type of change and this could be the basis for an action plan.

Lewin's planned change process might be a suitable model for this process.

- Existing practices and behaviour needs to be 'unfrozen'. The need for change needs to be communicated and understood.

- The change itself should aim to encourage participation by staff at all levels and support should be sought. The change process should be adequately resourced.

- Once the process has concluded, the new behaviour patterns need to be 'refrozen' in place. This might be accomplished in part by using the staff appraisal and reward system.

Requirement (f)

There are many ways in which performance might be measured. Given the complexity of the organisation, along with the fact that it does not have a single, measurable criterion, it would probably be useful to adopt a balanced scorecard approach. This would gather information on four main perspectives:

- Customer – including measures of clinical results, cleanliness, etc.

- Learning and growth – the extent to which staff are being developed and kept up to date, particularly in terms of new clinical matters.

- Business process – are there any ways in which the systems can be made more efficient?

- Financial – budgeted v actual income surpluses/deficits and expenditure.

SECTION C

Note: From May 2007 onwards, Section C will comprise two 30-mark questions.

QUESTION THREE

Requirement (a)

Opportunity 1. These new technologies might improve the quality of service by permitting B3 to contact potential recruits more quickly than by other means. It might not be possible to telephone applicants during normal working hours because they will not wish their present employers to be aware that they are in touch with a personnel agency. Many people have access to email at home and most carry mobile phones (some of which can access email as well as text messages), so electronic communication is likely to be faster and more efficient.

Email is probably better for communicating detailed information. Text messages are restricted in length. Texts could, however, be better for passing on relatively urgent information such as a change of time for an interview.

Some senior candidates for executive posts might find this form of communication too informal and would be slightly offended at the prospect of having career information passed on by means of email.

This would be a relatively inexpensive option. The computing requirements to send emails and text messages via the internet are modest and staff will not require any specific training because virtually all will be able to use this technology anyway.

Opportunity 2. Filing CVs electronically should make filing easier. Electronic documents should not go missing or get lost provided they are filed correctly when they are first received. B3 could create a database with basic details (name, type of post applied for, dates) and each database record could be linked to the associated CV.

Each recruitment consultant should have access to all current CVs without the problems that would be created if several people were working on the same group of files at once.

Electronic CVs could also be emailed to clients along with a short-list.

Requirement (b)

The first step should be to quickly review the members of the short-list to confirm that all candidates are suitable. This should have been done by B3, but there could be issues that might not be known by the personnel agency. For example, the shortlist could contain candidates who are known personally to the selection panel and could be deemed unsuitable for personality or other reasons. Candidates from some competitors might be regarded with slight suspicion because they might be using the interview process to gather information on behalf of their employers.

The short-listed candidates should be invited for an interview as quickly as possible. This is partly a matter of courtesy and of showing the candidates that their applications are being treated seriously and partly a matter of reducing the risk of them taking up posts with other employers.

The screening process offered by B3 should make it possible to proceed to the final interview. Candidates should have been briefed on the nature of the post, terms and conditions, etc before being short-listed.

The interview itself should be conducted by a small panel. Having more than one interviewer reduces the risk of personal bias. Sharing the responsibility for interviewing and selecting the best candidate should give more confidence. The interview should be planned in advance with a standard set of questions for each candidate, although there should be some opportunity to follow up points made. There should be a designated convener to chair the panel so that each interviewer has an opportunity to participate, but in a controlled and orderly manner.

QUESTION FOUR

Requirement (a)

Marketing issues. The involvement of the founder creates the risk that the company takes a production-oriented approach rather than a marketing orientation. If the focus is on selling existing products or the development of new products that are essentially the same as existing products, then the company might fail to spot changes in consumer taste and buying patterns until it is too late. Sales levels have already peaked and this trend is unlikely to reverse itself unless the company takes some active measures.

The company's products have a reputation for being unhealthy at a time when the health implications of diet are coming under increasing scrutiny.

Selling what are essentially the same products as supermarket 'own brands' is a dangerous strategy because of the risk that consumers might recognise the similarity (or be alerted to it by an article in a magazine) and buy the cheaper brands in preference to the branded.

Ethical issues. The company has enjoyed some success because of a family link to a major customer. That customer's board might be unhappy if it were to discover that it was buying heavily from a supplier who had been selected in this way. It might be better for CM to ensure that full disclosure of the relative's involvement is made and that the terms and conditions of the supply of goods have been on a normal arm's length basis.

The company actively sells to children via the packaging, use of gifts and advertising. This is a dubious ethical proposition at present. The fact that the products contain a heavy concentration of salt and sugar increases the risks because of concerns about childhood obesity.

Requirement (b)

The first step is for CM to conduct a strategic analysis of its strengths and weaknesses, its core competences and its resources. This should be drafted in the context of the company's external environment, emphasising issues such as brand recognition, the established distribution chain, etc. This analysis should be thorough and could involve commissioning detailed market research into the attitudes of various consumer groups. CM should not necessarily be thinking in terms of continuing with all of its existing product range at this stage, nor should it discount the possibility of using its expertise to diversify into complementary lines of business. The threat posed by the North American competitor must be analysed. If competing directly is likely to be uneconomic, then CM might have to face up to withdrawing from some of its traditional markets and make best use of its strengths in other areas.

Once the market has been analysed, CM should consider making a set of strategic choices as to which markets to compete in and how. This could leave the company faced with some difficult choices because of the involvement of the founder and the historical attachments to certain markets. The company may decide to carry on much as before, but only after carefully considering the economic merits of doing so. The market can be segmented geographically, by branded v own goods, by product line and so on. CM must decide where to focus its efforts in the future and then decide on an appropriate marketing mix (product, price, promotion and place) for each. One issue that must be decided quickly is the company's response to the health concerns associated with the product (should it reduce sugar and salt content?).

Finally, CM must decide how to implement its strategy. Detailed plans and budgets will have to be developed. Decisions should be taken about targets for sales, market share and brand recognition in different markets. These should be translated into advertising and production schedules. A set of benchmarks and a reporting system will have to be developed in order to monitor progress against the plan.